HISTORY, LITERATURE AND SOCIETY

S. N. MUKHERJEE

History, Literature and Society
Essays in Honour of
S. N. MUKHERJEE

Edited by

MABEL LEE
MICHAEL WILDING

SYDNEY STUDIES

MANOHAR
1997

History, Literature and Society:
Essays in Honour of S. N. Mukherjee

Sydney Studies in Society and Culture 15

Published by
The Sydney Association
for Studies in Society and Culture
PO Box 575, Leichhardt
NSW 2040 Australia
and
Manohar Publishers & Distributors
2/6 Ansari Road, Daryaganj
New Delhi 110 002

ISSN 0812-6402
ISBN 81-7304-201-2

Printed at
Rajkamal Electric Press
B-35/9 G.T. Karnal Road Indl. Area
Delhi 110 033

Contents

Preface

The essays collected here have been contributed in honour of Soumyen Mukherjee, for many years a member of the History Department and later the School of Asian Studies at the University of Sydney. In their range and variety they represent something of the range and variety of his interests.

Soumyen Mukherjee's vision is of the ideal coming together of the concerned intelligence, of the committed intellectual. It is a vision that will always attract institutional opposition, but it will always exist. This volume testifies to the endurance of that tradition. It is not an oppositional tradition at all. It is the true idea of the university, preserving its ground in the face of the ignorance of the entrenched establishment. This may seem a far cry from the blatant aberrance of today's university. But universities have always fallen into disrepute and discredit. That is their nature, today no less than in the last century or the centuries before.

Not every contributor shares Soumyen's political commitment. He has always been ready to work with and make alliances with a range of individuals, and has never been narrow in his sympathies. Nor has his work ever been confined within the arbitrary disciplinary boundaries. His interests have involved history, literature, economics and politics; and in those areas he has been equally involved in the European and what used to be called the Oriental. Soumyen's mission, which many of the contributors to this volume have supported, has been two-fold: to break down racial barriers, and at the same time to reveal class barriers, in order to break them down too. All these areas and concerns are represented in this collection. The contributions come from history, from literature, from economics; some pieces are scholarly, others are impressionist, even fictional. The sheer variety testifies to Soumyen's protean, or should we say kalian, prolificity of interest. This festschrift is just one more stage in the on-going argument, the promulgation of the case.

Michael Wilding

NOTES ON THE CONTRIBUTORS

Sekhar Bandyopadhyay
Senior Lecturer in History, Victoria University of Wellington

Debesh Bhattacharya
Associate Professor in Economics, University of Sydney

Suhash Chakravarty
Professor in History, University of Delhi

Bruce Fulton
Senior Lecturer in History, University of Sydney

Robert J. Hind
Formerly Senior Lecturer in History, University of Sydney

Stephen Knight
Professor in English, University of Wales

Mabel Lee
Associate Professor in Chinese Studies, University of Sydney

Marian Maddern
Lecturer in Children's Literature, Faculty of Education, University of Melbourne

M. N. Pearson
Professor in History, Southern Cross University

Maria Shevtsova
Professor in Theatre Studies, University of Lancaster

John O. Ward
Senior Lecturer in History, University of Sydney

Michael Wilding
Professor in English and Australian Literature, University of Sydney

Zdenko Zlatar
Senior Lecturer in History, University of Sydney

From Subjects to Citizens: Reactions to Colonial Rule and the Changing Political Culture of Calcutta in the Mid-Nineteenth Century

Sekhar Bandyopadhyay

1

Since the Battle of Plassey (1757) and the subsequent reconstruction of Calcutta, the city continually grew in size and splendour. 'It is difficult to describe', wrote the *Samachar Darpan* in April 1819, 'how Calcutta has developed in the last sixty-two years. Today's Calcutta makes it difficult to imagine how it looked before. The city where one could hardly find houses worth even six thousand rupees, now can boast of buildings worth more than three crores, not to speak of other forms of wealth.'[1] This development and extension of Calcutta were as much due to its being a port city as to its becoming the administrative centre of an expanding British empire in India. It prospered as a colonial metropolis, simultaneously with the decline of the older centres of trade and administration, such as Dacca, Murshidabad or Hugli.

The English victory at Buxar (1764) and the grant of Diwane (1765) completed the first phase of empire building in India, as already with decisive military strength in command, the revenue collecting authority made the British the supreme power in Bengal. The exertions of Lord Wellesley and the Marquess of Hastings pushed the imperial frontiers even further beyond Bengal, so that by 1818 the British empire stretched from the coast of Bengal to the river Sutlej. The process was finally rounded off by Lord Dalhousie, who incorporated by 1856 the whole of Punjab, an already truncated Oudh, Lower Burma, Jhansi, Satara and Nagpore. This territorial expansion was also accompanied by measures to evolve an administrative system that would consolidate

British power as well as legitimise the new role of the 'Company as an Indian ruler'.[2] So far as Bengal was concerned, Warren Hastings in 1772 directly took over the control and management of the diwane, and in 1790 the functions of the nizamat were taken over as well. This ending of the so-called dual administration and Cornwallis' later attempt to Europeanise the civil services put an unmistakable foreign stamp on the new regime, which now enjoyed an absolute control over the fiscal, judicial and police administration of Bengal. And Calcutta emerged as the chief administrative centre of this new empire, as the Regulating Act of 1773 subordinated the Bombay and Madras governments to the office of the Governor General of Bengal stationed in this city; by the Charter Act of 1833, the post was formally upgraded to that of Governor General of India.

The colonial character of the city of Calcutta also determined the way its human environment developed in the eighteenth century. 'The process', as an expert on urban settlement in Calcutta comments, 'worked in an overall setting of dualism, basically a feature of all colonial cities, between the white and the black town.'[3] This phenomenon of dualism reflected on the one hand the conquerors' concern for defence and security and on the other their racial pride and exclusivism. In the eighteenth century this spatial segregation along racial lines had been less sharply marked, as there was a White Town and a Black Town, intersected by a Grey Town or intermediate zone which was dominated by the Eurasians or East Indians but accessible to the 'natives' as well. Yet the oft-emphasised inter-racial social interaction and the army officers' attraction for Indian women in this period cannot obscure the fact that social life in the European quarters was being organised in such a way that to the 'natives' it appeared as a distant and inaccessible world. The spatial segregation also increased with the growth of the imperial élan, as the conquerors' impetuosity now surrounded them with an ambience befitting a master race. In the early nineteenth century, i.e. in the high noon of the British Indian empire, 'the social distance between the ruling race and the people' became an easily discernible reality in Calcutta's urban life.[4] As racism primarily is a function of power, this social distancing, which took various forms, was essentially a calculated political gesture to make the 'natives' feel their subordinate position in the new imperial power structure.[5] The Black Town or the 'natives'' quarter in Calcutta therefore developed under conditions of subordination and segregation, and was peopled by those who were dependent on subordinate collaboration with their new colonial masters. It was within this social context of urban Calcutta that the impact of colonial expansion was experienced. The reactions of the limited number of Europeans were understandably different from those of the indigenous people. In the initial stages of British territorial expansion, the European community anxiously watched the growth of British power and was jubilant at the news of the success of English soldiers against the French, the Marathas or against the forces of Mysore. Hicky's *Bengal Gazette* is full of such reactions.[6] About the Indian responses during this early period, precious little indeed can be gleaned from either the archival or the literary sources. The Persian-educated late eighteenth-century literati of Bengal, Ghulam Husain Tabatabai for example, felt alienated from British rule.[7] But he belonged to a class in decline which, because of its association with the previous regime, had reasons to be apprehensive. But in the meanwhile, new classes had emerged in Calcutta, whose interests were intimately linked with the British power. The Calcutta *pundits* of the early nineteenth century, associated either with the Srirampur missionaries or with Fort William College, felt an identity of interest with the forces of the new regime. Rajiblochan Mukhopadhyay in his *Maharaj Krishnachandra Rayasya Charitram* (1805) and Mrityunjay Vidyalankar in his *Rajabali* (1808) depicted the establishment of British rule as a welcome change that brought the oppressive Muslim rule to an end[8]—a stereotype that was later upheld by Rammohun Roy, shared by even the radical members of the Young Bengal like Dakshinaranjan Mukhopadhyay, and eventually subscribed to by almost every section of the Bengali intelligentsia.[9] Rammohun Roy, who had settled in Calcutta in 1814, 'accepted British rule as a regenerative force'[10]—a faith, which many of his contemporaries as well as immediate successors also gradually internalised.

In fact, the existing historical literature is full of evidence of the dependent attitudes of the Calcutta elites who equated westernisation with modernisation and progress. Unable to foresee the negative and alienating aspects of Western education, it is alleged, they welcomed it because of the scientific values it preached, and were delighted when in 1835 Bentinck and Macaulay decided in favour of introducing English education for the Indians. The free trade logic was accepted unquestioningly, with the expectation that there would be a bourgeois development in Bengal under the tutelage of the British. This failure to see that free trade could hardly benefit a predominantly agrarian economy, we are told, sprang from a pathetic ignorance of the already visible signs of reindustrialisation that had caused havoc in the countryside. They supported European colonisation of the interior, hoping that this would bring further agricultural development, although the plea itself had only been to help the Agency Houses to circumvent their problems of finance and investment. Rammohun and many others of his age lamented over the plight of the peasants, given over to unrestricted exploitation and oppression by the *zamindars*; but never was there any demand for the scrapping of the Permanent Settlement which had empowered the *zamindars*. Later, as the voluntary associations began to appear, this faith in the benevolence of British rule was expressed in the speeches delivered and resolutions passed at the meetings of the British India Society founded in 1843. The British Indian Association of 1851, which unlike its predecessor kept the Anglo-Indians out, proved to be no exception in accepting colonial rule and in operating within the parameters set by it.[11] The urban Bengali intelligentsia of the early nineteenth century, in other words, are usually stereotyped as the loyal subjects of the British empire, who looked at the establishment of colonial rule as an act of providence that was destined to deliver the Indian nation from medieval backwardness and set it in the path of modernisation and progress. And when this progress was seemingly threatened by the revolt of 1857, as the existing literature argues, this loyalty of the Calcutta literate society found an unabashed expression. It was not of course a 'slavish loyalty', writes a sympathetic critic, but a 'conditional' support of the British government.[12] 'Such men had material interests, and often a deep, ideological commitment to new ideas.' And hence they expressed loyalty and presented addresses of support to the government, instead of aligning with the rural rebels and disgruntled sepoys.[13]

But was this loyalty beyond question? Some recent historians have raised doubts. 'The boundary between "revolt" and "collaboration" was often very faint ...', writes one such sceptical historian. 'Many of those who apparently collaborated, the Calcutta intelligentsia for instance, regarded the British with contempt at some level....'[14] Such doubts become clearer from the writings of S. N. Mukherjee, who shows how the image of Calcutta in the Anglo-Indian literary imagination gradually changed during this period from one of excitement and harmony to that of gloom and doom. The imperial partnership with the Bengali *babu*, as he suspects, had come to an end by the middle of the nineteenth century and so the Anglo-Indians turned against Calcutta.[15] And by the end of the century, Calcutta was a city of rebels, loudly questioning the legitimacy of the Raj. So the question is, when and how did this metamorphosis happen? To answer this question, it is perhaps necessary to re-examine the political culture of Calcutta in the first half of the nineteenth century, usually stereotyped as the culture of loyalty. The most convenient method to do this would be to examine Calcutta's reactions to various rebellions against British rule that had become endemic during this period, culminating in the revolt of 1857. This re-examination would show that, despite overt expressions of loyalty, there was probably never a total acceptance of British rule in Calcutta society, and that certainly from the middle of the nineteenth century, since the troubled days of 1857 itself, a new consciousness began to emerge that completely turned the so-called 'loyal' subjects of the imperial city of Calcutta into articulate citizens.

2

The people who originally lived in the region that later developed into the Black Town of Calcutta, were mainly those who have been called the 'lower orders'—the artisans, labourers and the menials—who were gradually marginalised and driven out of the precincts of the city as urban development gained in momentum.[16] The rest of Calcutta society could be divided, *à la* Bhabanicharan Bandyopadhyay, into four categories.[17] To the first group belonged the most fortunate people who depended either on rental income of the *zamindaries* or on interests from other investments—the so-called *abhijat* or aristocratic elements, mainly the absentee landlords or the 'pure rentiers', created by the Permanent Settlement, 'who performed no economic functions towards the improvement of agriculture'.[18] The second category consisted of the *banians* and *dewans* (or agents) of the foreign commercial concerns or English private traders—the compradors in other words, who had made money through trade in collaboration with the foreigners and later had invested it in landed estates.[19] To the next two categories belonged the *grihasthas* or the upper and the lower middle classes, who did not have enough money to spend time in splendid idleness like those in the other two categories. In many cases their dwindling income from subordinate landed interests had forced them to migrate to Calcutta in search of alternative means of livelihood. It was from these two classes that there was the highest demand for English education. Around 1833, about three thousand young men were studying English in Calcutta[20] and most of them belonged to the middle classes. In 1842, out of 500 students of the Hindu College, only 20, according to the *Bengal Spectator* (July 1842), were in a position to live on their patrimony, while the rest had to look for subordinate government services or clerkships in merchant offices.[21] Despite Cornwallis' distrust of the Indians and the consequent Europeanisation of the civil services, the Company was hardly in a position to dispense with the services of the Indians, particularly in the subordinate positions. Such job opportunities for the Bengali middle classes increased further after the Act of 1833. In the course of the nineteenth century, the number of Indians employed by the Company's government, particularly in the uncovenanted lower grades of services, had increased phenomenally,[22] creating in the process a large group of intermediaries dependent on foreign rule for their subsistence. In Calcutta, therefore, people belonging to all the four categories of élite society were either the creation of, or at least dependent on, British rule—the people whose interests, as the *Hindoo Patriot* observed, were 'bound up with the interest of their rulers'.[23] These people could only be expected to be the Company's most loyal subjects. And the perceptions of the lower orders as regards colonial rule and protest against it, as we have been told, were also coloured largely by those of the elites.[24] There was also a sizeable population of Muslims in the city. But till the middle of the nineteenth century they do not appear to have been articulate enough and therefore remain outside the purview of our present discussion.

The early political culture of this Calcutta society, whose interests were so obviously tied to the fortunes of the new empire, can be very easily delineated from its reactions to various rebellions against British rule in the late eighteenth and the early nineteenth centuries. In contrast to the urban society, the rural society in India reacted much more vehemently to the imposition of colonial rule from the early days of its inception, since some of the colonialist administrative measures had seriously dislocated the existing social equilibrium in the countryside. The revenue experiments had created a class of *zamindars* whose only interest was in rent. Strengthened by the repressive powers conferred through Regulation VII of 1799, many of them took to rack renting and subinfeudation, thus shifting the burden of high revenue demand onto the shoulders of the unprotected *raiyats* (peasants). Many of these rentiers lived away in Calcutta, leaving the management of their estates in the hands of their tenure holders or their more rugged underlings. As a result, barring a few, the peasantry in general found their sufferings intensified by the beginning of the nineteenth century and this was at a time when pressure on agriculture was increasing due to the destruction of indigenous industries. Apart from this, the mystery that shrouded the new Supreme Court and the new district courts, with British judges and their unfamiliar linguistic and formal paraphernalia, only evoked terror. These institutions therefore came to be viewed as an 'unwelcome imposition by an alien authority'.[25] The Indians, it is true, were to be governed by their own traditional Hindu and Islamic laws. But the way the European judges interpreted, applied and later tried to codify these laws tended to change both their content and appearance.[26] Thousands of cases remained pending before the new courts, making judicial redress of the people's grievances an elusive proposition.[27] The new police system appeared to be another alien agent of oppression, as the *darogah* or the local police officer was often corrupt and tyrannical. And the gradually emerging *darogah-zamindar* nexus made life miserable for the poor peasants.[28]

The countryside therefore reacted violently to the imposition of colonial rule and the dislocations that it created in its social and economic life. During the hundred years that followed the Battle of Plassey, different parts of India were rocked by a series of revolts by traditional elements, like the dispossessed local chiefs, zamindars and religious leaders, with whom the disgruntled lower classes joined. In addition, there were peasant uprisings and tribal revolts that defiantly challenged the power of the new regime.[29] Bengal itself was rocked by a series of violent protests. Starting with the uprising in Midnapore by Chuars, and 'hill men' in Bishnupur and Birbhum, as well as the mountainous Chakmas in Chittagong, and the riots against high taxes in Rangpur in 1783 and repeated insurrections against revenue assessments in Birbhum in the 1780s, the disaffection of the Bengal peasantry found expression through the Sanyasi uprisings in northern and eastern Bengal through the second half of the eighteenth century, the Paik uprising among the Midnapore Chuars and Ghatwals (1798–99) and the Nayek revolt (1806–16) in Midnapore, the Pagalpanthi movement in Mymensingh (1802–33), Titu Mir's revolt in Barasat (1831), the Faraizi movement in eastern Bengal (1834–47), and the various minor uprisings in Sylhet, Chittagong, Bakarganj and Jessore-Khulna in the last few decades of the eighteenth century.[30]

Apart from these organised protests, there had been endemic violence and dacoities in the nominally pacified countryside. Even in Calcutta, as the *Samachar Darpan* reported in 1819, hardly a night passed without a dacoity.[31] Dispossession and consequent impoverishment of the people were certainly among the root causes of these violent acts that challenged the colonial state and its rule of law. As Lord Minto wrote in 1809, the bandits appeared to have 'established a terrorism as perfect as that which was the foundation of the French Republican power, and in truth the *sirdars*, or captains of the band, were esteemed and even called the *hakim*, or ruling power, while the real government did not possess either authority or influence enough to obtain from the people the smallest aid towards their own protection'.[32] This rising spirit of defiance and the accumulating grievances of the people all over India found an articulate expression in the great conflagration of 1857, that started from Barrackpore near Calcutta and then rapidly spread over large parts of northern India, but left Bengal more or less unaffected.

Calcutta during the early years of colonial rule remained apparently placid and impervious to, or even critical of, all these violent manifestations of protest. While various parts of India were being shaken by violent revolts, the Calcutta *babus* were enjoying their peace and, as Sibnath Shastri describes it, spending their time in afternoon naps, kite flying, watching bird fights, playing on musical instruments, patronising folk literature and spending nights in brothels.[33] While the rural folk or *gatha* literature of Bengal extolled the valour of the Sanyasi rebels and condemned the exploitation of the colonial rulers and their Indian agents,[34] the *Kabigan* of Calcutta remained immersed in the romantic love of the heavenly couple Radha and Krishna. And at the élite level, the urban Bengali literature, like Rajiblochan Mukhopadhyay's *Maharaja Krishnachandra Rayasya Charitram* (1805), adored the English for being as valiant as Arjuna and as benevolent as Yudhisthira—the epic archetypes of perfection—while stereotyping the Sanyasi rebels as criminals who indiscriminately attacked the wealthy households in the countryside.[35] It was not until 1886 that a novel, *Dewan Gangagobinda Singha,* by Chandicharan Sen appeared in Calcutta with the courage to condemn the atrocities perpetrated by Gangagobinda Singh, Debi Singh and their patron Warren Hastings, which caused the rebellion in north Bengal. Our educated men, the same author had written a year earlier, were painfully unaware of this history of their land. But he too appears to have shared with his contemporaries an intrinsic faith in the righteousness and sense of justice of the British, critiquing only what he considered to be an aberration.[36]

Thus in contrast to its rural counterpart, Calcutta society in the early nineteenth century seemed to be all praise for its new English masters. In January 1819, a few months after the death of Warren Hastings, the *Samachar Darpan* wrote in praise of his great achievements, like the extension and consolidation of British power in this country. A year later, notable Indians were contributing generously for the erection of his statue in Calcutta.[37] It was, therefore, not unnatural that the peasant rebels of Bengal—the Sanyasis, the Fakirs, the Chuars or the Pagalpanthis—would not find an advocate or sympathiser in this city of loyal subjects. The people in Calcutta believed that subduing these revolts would be 'child's play' for the mighty British army. And so they advocated—as Harachandra Ghose did with reference to the Chuars in a meeting of the Society for the Acquisition of General Knowledge, the forum of the Young Bengal—proper education for these people 'to elevate their character', otherwise they would 'ever remain in ignorance and would commit great mischief by their seditious disturbances which are constantly occurring'.[38]

The later rebels were even less fortunate, as their movements had an Islamic overtone. Titu Mir's revolt was thus portrayed in communal colours and condemned as senseless troublemaking. The *Samachar Darpan* condemned the revolt as 'seditious activity' of the Muslims under Titu Mir, who were oppressing the Hindus.[39] The *Jnanannesan* of the Young Bengal expressed the same condemnation, while the *Samachar Chandrika*, the mouthpiece of the orthodox Dharma Sabha, fanned further communal hatred on this occasion. The *Hurkaru* expressed relief as 'the government took such prompt measures in despatching an effective force against these marauders'. The *Samachar Chandrika* went even further to 'assert' that 'if ... the Moosoolmans who have been guilty are set at liberty, or no punishment be inflicted upon those who have not yet been apprehended, then a hundred of those Teetoos will again be seen'. To warn such future rebels, sixty-six years after the revolt, Beharilal Sarkar wrote a thoroughly critical biography of Titu Mir, portraying his protest as nothing but communal frenzy and sheer madness. Even some of his Muslim contemporaries in Calcutta —as a report in the *Reformer* (5 December 1831) indicates—were not sympathetic to Titu's defiance of British rule.[40] To many of them British India was *Dar-ul-Islam* and a *jehad* against the British government was therefore unjustified.[41] The Faraizi movement, taking place at a safe distance in eastern Bengal, attracted much less attention in Calcutta. But, whenever mentioned, it received the same communal portrayal and condemnation. A letter published in the *Samachar Darpan* in April 1837 described Shariatullah as a hundred times more harmful than Titu Mir. An appeal was made to the government for his subjugation which was deemed necessary for the protection of Hindu religion, properties and lives.[42]

It was really the Santhal rebellion that shocked Calcutta society more visibly and deeply, as its sense of security was now shaken by the apparent failure of the mighty British government to curb these primitive tribal rebels. 'The Sonthal revolt', lamented the *Hindu Intelligencer* (19 November 1855), 'has not yet been quelled with a large military and police force at the disposal of the authorities....' The *Hindoo Patriot* (26 July 1855) wondered how 'a few thousands of savages, armed with primitive clubs, bows and arrows, kept the British power at bay ...'![43] It was earlier expected, wrote the *Samachar Sudhabarshan*, that the Santhals would run away at the very sight of the British army. But this did not happen and the British, who subdued the mighty Marathas, Rajputs and the Sikhs, have been humbled by the savage tribals. So what looked like an impossible thing had now happened, it continued, as now the uncivilised Santhals would become the rulers.[44] The reports that appeared in the *Sambad Prabhakar* also depicted the Santhals as 'uncivilised hill people' who had unleashed a reign of terror in the countryside. The pillage and plunder, arson and murders had forced peace-loving people to leave their homeland, the government sadly failing to provide any protection for its loyal subjects.[45] Iswar Gupta's pen wore out while writing about the Santhals, yet this 'unholy trouble' did not stop—on the contrary it went on increasing day by day.[46]

But there was not condemnation alone, one must admit, for lurking behind the generally loyalist overtone there was also a plea for introspection. It was indeed the *Sambad Prabhakar* which raised the most important question: 'Is it true that those who were always loyal [i.e. the Santhals] have taken up arms against the king without any reason?' Since the railway officials exploited them and raped their women, it was quite expected, it wrote further, that a martial race like the Santhals would not take this dishonour lying down. But in the end, the same report expressed satisfaction as the British army made successful advances against the rebels.[47] The *Hindoo Patriot* (19 July 1855) also expected, perhaps with a sense of relief, that the insurrection 'will be quelled in a few days, we may almost say, hours'. But it also admitted that the rebels had a cause to fight for: 'Oppression is the cause, revenge the motive, and the object of the insurrection a vague undefined idea of freedom from sorely felt annoyances'. It, therefore, advocated a full and impartial enquiry into the grievances of the Santhals, objected to the promulgation of martial law in the disturbed districts and protested against revengeful treatment of captured rebels. But along with this, there was also an expressed concern for the Bengali peasants of the plains, who were harassed, tortured and dispossessed of their land by the unruly insurgents, and a statement of satisfaction at the return of 'peace and security'.[48] Similarly the *Sambad Prabhakar* published a letter which described in an uninhibited tone of condemnation the inhuman way the Santhal prisoners were treated in Birbhum. Yet the same journal also criticised the Lieutenant Governor for his earlier patronising attitude to the Santhals which, it suspected, had initially increased their courage and inspired them to take up arms to fight for freedom.[49] In other words, the Santhals had legitimate grievances, the Calcutta literati agreed. But they were condemned as they attacked the lives and property of the settled peasantry; and the condemnation grew bitter as British power, in which the *bhadralok* had reposited their faith for ensuring protection, failed to curb them.

This sense of insecurity and panic became far more manifest during the days of the revolt of 1857. As Sibnath Shastri tells us, the Calcutta streets wore a deserted look after sundown and there were rumours all around that the rebel sepoys were coming and they would kill all the Englishmen and plunder the city.[50] 'The inhabitants of Calcutta are reasonably in dread of a sepoy emeute', wrote the *Hindoo Patriot* (21 May 1857), as the 'sepoys in and near Calcutta have already evinced a not very loyal disposition'.[51] The news of the fall of Delhi and Kanpur, followed by that of the other parts of north-western India, spread like wild fire in the city and struck terror in the minds of those whom Kaliprasanna Sinha called in this context the 'unfortunate sheepish Bengalees'.[52] Their interests, observed the *Hindoo Patriot*, 'were bound up with the interest of their rulers'. They had, as they thought, 'a splendid future before them, but which ... [could] be realised only by the existence of the British rule'.[53] The Bengalees had benefited in a number of ways from the *pax Britannica*, said an editorial in the *Sambad Prabhakar* (17 Ashadh 1264 BS). They had received education, earned money and enjoyed the privileges of an improved communication system. 'Indeed, never before had the Bengalees enjoyed so much peace and happiness as they did under the tutelage of the British government....'[54]

The basis of this happiness was the security of life and property which British rule had provided, and this now seemed to have been threatened by the revolt. The 'Bengalees of Calcutta', wrote a panicky *Hindoo Patriot* (30 July 1857), 'would not have their heads particularly safe on their shoulders or their properties in their houses if a rising took place of the nature apprehended'.[55] 'India has become cheerless', exclaimed another *Sambad Prabhakar* editorial (15 Jaistha 1265 BS), 'due to loss of life, property, honour and everything.'[56] This sense of crisis was further exacerbated as some of the Englishmen, particularly the editors of the European-owned newspapers, held the entire Indian nation, the Bengalees included, guilty of disloyalty and treason, and therefore not trustworthy for appointment in government services.[57] The ever obedient Bengalee *babu*, 'who was never capable of holding the sword',[58] was now about to lose his means of livelihood due to the haughtiness of some headstrong sepoys. It was therefore essential to restate their loyalty as loudly as possible and condemn the rebels as bitterly as the literary capabilities of the educated Bengalees could.

In May 1857, a meeting was convened at the Hindu Metropolitan College, with Radhakanta Deb in the chair and many other notables of the city in attendance. It expressed unflinching loyalty to the British and assured them of all possible help for suppressing the sepoys who had risen in revolt against their masters and disturbed peace in the empire. Such demonstrations of loyalty took place all over the city and addresses were sent to Lord Canning to convince him that, whatever might have been his other difficulties, disaffection or disloyalty of the Bengalees was certainly not one of them. And in this ebullience the *Hindoo Patriot* saw only the manifestation of 'an unmistakable spirit of genuine patriotism and devotion'.[59] The motives are not difficult to imagine, as the same paper made it clear in an editorial on 4 June 1857:

> It has been insinuated that the Bengalees sympathise with the mutineers. That they are disaffected towards the Government. That they ought not to be trusted. And all manner of idle and malicious stories have been sent forth against men whose whole lives have been patterns of loyalty, zealous and devoted loyalty....[60]

This energetic effort to get away from the stigma of disloyalty was mainly, if not exclusively, to reassert their claims to government services; 'what we contend for', as another editorial in the *Hindoo Patriot* about a month later declared, 'is the employment of the fittest person in such offices without reference to their colour or creed ... we look upon the puny efforts ... to damage the character, reputation and prospects of our countrymen with sheer contempt....' To disarm such efforts and to set all suspicions at rest, 'signal chastisement' was advocated for the 'brutal and unprincipled ... body of ruffians' who had 'disgraced a uniform'.[61]

The *Sambad Prabhakar* also appealed to all its readers to pray to God for the victory of the government and the early restoration of peace. The rebel soldiers were criticised as an ungrateful and ill-advised lot who had been fighting a hopeless battle against the mighty British. The cacophony of condemnation of the rebels often crossed limits of civility, as the sepoys were described as dwarfs trying to reach the moon, or as foxes fighting the mighty lion, as frogs trembling at the sight of the snake or as ants who had developed wings to face an imminent death.[62] And Iswar Gupta's satirical portrayal of some of the leaders of the revolt, as it is well-known, often lapsed into vulgarity. This hysteria also seems to have affected the lower orders of Calcutta society. Although a few Kalighat *pats* (paintings) depicted Rani Lakshmibai as a valiant heroine riding a horse, popular songs in Calcutta sang of the glory of the highlander army which, it was expected, would curb the pride of Tantia Topi, catch Nana Sahib and recapture Delhi with ease.[63]

All these expectations and tensions of the Calcuttans ultimately came to an end with the final crushing of the revolt. On the afternoon of 1 November 1858, when in front of a mammoth gathering in central Calcutta Cecil Beadon read out the Queen's Proclamation extending the Crown's rule over the Indian empire, the whole city was immersed in celebrations and merrymaking that started from the evening and continued through the whole night.[64] To cash in on the popular euphoria, Praney Moira, an enterprising confectioner of north Calcutta, introduced a new sweetmeat, which is still popularly known as *Ledi-keni*, named after Lady Canning, the wife of the victor of the last pacificatory war in British India.[65]

3

However, the year 1857 also stands as a turning point in Calcutta's response to colonial rule. The profession of loyalty by the Calcutta intelligentsia during this troubled year was not without dilemma, as behind this loyalism there was also a growing awareness of the ignominy involved in their state of subordination. This emotional crisis of the Calcutta élite is writ large on the pages of the *Hindoo Patriot*. An editorial (21 May 1857)[66] in the early phase of the revolt started with a critique of foreign rule and a glorification of the rebels in unequivocal language:

> How slight is the hold the British government has acquired upon the affections of its Indian subjects has been made painfully evident by the events of the last few weeks.... It is no longer a mutiny, but a rebellion ... [which has] from the beginning drawn the sympathy of the country.... They [the sepoys] have rebelled against the authority ... and their countrymen view them as martyrs to a holy cause ... there is not a single native of India who does not feel the full weight of the grievances imposed upon him by the very existence of the British rule in India—grievances inseparable from subjection to a foreign rule. There is not one among the educated classes who does not feel his

> prospects circumscribed and his ambition restricted by the supremacy of the power....

But soon on a much more cautious note the same editorial hastened to conclude:

> Yet the grievances felt and the delusion believed in have not neutralised in the mass of the Indian population the feeling of loyalty which the substantial benefits of the British rule has engendered. We believe the prevailing feeling is that any great disaster befalling the British rule would be a disastrous check to national prosperity. We do not deny, that [there is] a pettish desire to see the high handed proceedings of its officials rebuked and the insolence ... of the Anglo-Indian community checked.... But, on the whole, the country is sound. The sympathy which the mutineers have found from the people extends no further than to a wish to see the British government humiliated to a certain extent.

Within a week the paper backtracked further and began to support the 'spontaneous bursts of fervid loyalty' by the Calcutta elites.[67] About six months later, when the revolt was coming to an end, it declared unabashedly: 'The Hindoo is essentially Tory in his politics. He cannot conceive of a sovereign who can do wrong.... As they [the people of Bengal] have gained the most by British rule, they have sympathised the most with British power in its day of trouble'.[68]

There in the above statements of the *Hindoo Patriot* was also perhaps concealed a pathetic sense of helplessness and self-rebuke, that haunted all right-thinking, educated people in the city of Calcutta around this time. A self-styled spokesman of the Young Bengal, who boasted that the majority of the educated natives did not entertain any 'cordiality of attachment to the British government', had to admit that there might have been '*an interested attachment to the government*', as 'under existing circumstances', he confessed, 'we know of no better government'.[69] The dilemma was indeed most aptly summed up by the *Hindoo Patriot* itself: 'The most enlightened self-interest ... prompts the "educated natives" to be loyal. *This loyalty, it may be true, springs nearer from the head than from the heart*'.[70]

Indeed, signs of this agonising of the Calcutta intelligentsia could be traced back to the early nineteenth century. Dwarkanath Tagore and his generation, bred in the atmosphere of eighteenth-century rationalism and nineteenth-century liberalism, had visualised an empire based on inter-racial collaboration.[71] But this precocious image began to fade out as the reality of an exploitative economy unfolded itself. Calcutta being the seat of this empire, the exploitative process was most visibly at work in this city, leading to a selective criticism of the various objectionable aspects of the new administration. It was Rammohun Roy who could legitimately claim the credit for beginning in a modest way a constitutional agitation for demands like separation of powers, freedom of the press, trial by jury, Indianisation of the services or modification of the Act of 1833.[72] Many of these issues were later taken up by the more radical members of the Young Bengal, who were also critical of various other aspects of colonial governance. Rasikkrishna Mullick, Dakshinaranjan Mukhopadhyay and Pyarichand Mitra criticised in no uncertain words the Act of 1833 and the Company's police, judicial and fiscal administration. The importance of these protests—like Rasikkrishna's condemnation of 'a body of merchants ... placed over us as our sovereigns', Dakshinaranjan's description of the courts as 'shamelessly corrupt', serving only the interests of the rich, Ramgopal Ghosh's spirited defence of the so-called 'Black Acts', Krishnamohan Banerjee's critique of the absolute monarchy and Kailashchandra Dutta's apocalyptic vision of an armed revolt against the foreigners in 1945—need not be unduly minimised, even though many of the protesters in their later lives made compromises with the same foreign rule.[73]

At the same time there was also a growing awareness of the economic ruin that colonial rule had brought to Bengal, and by contrast even the preceding Muslim rule, which had been a subject of general condemnation, began to receive admiration. Previously under Muslim rule, wrote the *Jnanannesan*, the people of this country had the freedom to engage in any business or to do anything they liked for a living. But now, having lost this freedom of choice, they had been reduced to a group of clerks and agents. The 'natives of British India still continue to think', it wrote further by way of condemning the conquest of Punjab, 'that the people of the West have come to rob them of all that they possess....'[74] The *Bengal Spectator* (15 September 1842) also wrote eloquently of this drainage of national wealth as a result of colonial exploitation and pointed out (15 October 1842) that the amount of revenue assessed under the decennial settlement had been four times greater than that which prevailed under Muslim rule, the Permanent Settlement being even more oppressive.[75] The *Tattabodhini Patrika* (Sraban 1778 Saka) therefore concluded that the outward glitter of development that dazzled the eyes of many in British Bengal only concealed the boundless sufferings of the people. When every family in every village had been so distressed, and when this was due only to the continued exploitation by the foreigners, only a deaf and blind person could call Bengal fully developed![76] Such realisation certainly stemmed from a consciousness of dependent status, as the *Tattabodhini Patrika* wrote again: 'we are under foreign rule, we are being educated in a foreign language and we are tolerating a foreign tyranny....'[77] That this was the root of all sufferings was also quite explicitly stated in October 1841 by the Derozian, Saradaprasad Ghosh, in the inaugural meeting of the short-lived Deshahitaishini Sabha [Society for the Welfare of the Country]: 'our deprivation of the enjoyment of political liberty is the cause of our misery and degradation'.[78]

As the revolt of 1857 gradually lost its intensity and the horror disappeared, this sense of disenchantment with foreign rule among the Calcutta intelligentsia was further reinforced. And this growing alienation was largely due to the unabashed display of racism that reflected the classic colonial dilemma of the colonisers professing certain principles which they themselves were unable to practise in order to maintain their monopoly of power. The debate over discriminatory state policies that reached its climax in the Black Acts controversy, had started with the passing of the Jury Act in 1826. The racial arrogance of the whites that had sought to deny the conquered race the right to equality now compelled the Calcutta elites to confront the stark reality of subordination. In the great Non-Exemption meeting (1857), the same Radhakanta Deb, who had earlier presided over a loyalist gathering at the Hindu Metropolitan College, now protested against justice taking a milder form for the conquering and a harsher one for the conquered race.[79] Even the *Sambad Prabhakar* wrote disapprovingly of the discriminatory attitude of the rulers: punishing white soldiers guilty of treason with only deportation, while sending to the gallows sepoys charged with the same offence. The harassing of innocent civilians by *gora* (white) soldiers now forced the local press to raise a voice of protest.[80] And often such protestations were couched in counter-racial language, as the *Hindoo Patriot*, writing about the white volunteers guarding the city, demanded that 'the town be not overrun with drunken *European anarchy*'.[81] The racial animus, as it thus appears, now had made the Bengali intelligentsia painfully aware of the inferior status that they had been relegated to in the new imperial power structure. The expressions of indignation against this state of existence also therefore became relatively more overt and uninhibited compared with those in the insecure days of the revolt.

The failure of the revolt also filled the Calcutta elites with a sense of frustration, or perhaps with an urge for fresh introspection. As Sibnath Shastri put it, 'The excitement of the revolt did a great benefit to Bengal and her society; a new society was born; a new desire was generated in national life'.[82] The Bengali *babu*, in spite of his loyalty during the troubled days of 1857, was gradually turning into a rebel and claiming his rights as a citizen. The European newspapers took up the cudgels against him and, as a result, official patronage after the revolt moved northwards to favour the so-called martial races, leaving the Bengalees in the lurch as objects of suspicion and contempt. They appealed to reason and complained against racism. But persuasion and prayers proved ineffective and loyalty remained unrewarded. It was this experience which articulated a latent consciousness, a proto-nationalism, that went ahead to proclaim that the 'Bengalee will not remain a slave. He is strong enough, if not in body, still in mind and knowledge to *assert his right of citizenship*....'[83] The new desire which Sibnath Shastri spoke of found a lyrical but candid expression in Rangalal Bandyopadhyay's *Padmini Upakhyan* (1858):

> Swadhinata heenatay   ke banchite chay he,
> Ke banchite chay?
> Dasatva-srinkhal balo   ke paribe pay he
> Ke paribe pay?
>
> Who wants to live without freedom?
> Who wants to wear on his feet the chains of slavery?

4

Within a few years after the suppression of the revolt of 1857, a sense of remorse for what they had done during this critical period began to haunt the Bengali literati. About four years later, Kali Prasanna Sinha in his inimitable satirical expression lashed out at the scandalous display of loyalty: 'Mother [Queen Victoria], we are your Bengali sheep; we have no desire to be Americans'.[84] These words of self-rebuke certainly evinced a new consciousness and an awareness of global political trends. By 1870, as the literary critic Gopal Haldar writes, the 'unmixed denouncement' of the 'mutiny'—though it was never unmixed as we have already noted—was 'definitely a thing of the past'.[85]

It was this new spirit which was partly responsible for the bold stand that the Calcutta elites were to take later in support of the indigo rebellion in 1861. Their faith in the benevolence of the British, weakened in the 1850s, was ultimately shattered by the undisguised display of racism in 1882–83 during the agitation against the Ilbert Bill, which even the Lieutenant Governor of Bengal, Rivers Thompson, is reported to have condemned for 'ignoring race distinctions' to 'establish equality' by 'a stroke of the pen'.[86] The vernacular press raised a hue and cry as the government ultimately succumbed to the pressure of the non-official Europeans. The political excitement which was thus generated in Calcutta finally transformed Her Majesty's loyal subjects into conscious citizens, preparing the ground for the emergence of the radical nationalists of the early twentieth century. At a lower level, the more plebeian culture of Calcutta in the nineteenth century also evinced an awareness of the basic contradiction between the rulers and the ruled, although it had not been able to develop as yet an idiom necessary to overthrow that oppressive order.[87] But that was the limitation from which, unlike their contemporary peasant patriots, the urban élite leaders of early nationalism suffered. Yet, despite this limitation, these leaders were also developing gradually an ideological critique of colonialism and starting to imagine a nation based on shared citizenship. If the suppression of the revolt of 1857 brought to an end the last phase of post-pacificatory resistance of traditional India to British imperialism, it also ushered in a new era of modern nationalism in India, Calcutta being at the heart of this new awakening.

Notes

1 Samachar Darpan, 13 Baisakh 1226 BS, in Haripada Bhaumik, *Sekaler Sambadpatre Kolkata* (Calcutta in old newspapers), Vol.1, Calcutta, 1987, p.55. Translation mine.

2 P. Spear, *A History of India,* Vol.2, Harmondsworth, 1970, p.93.

3 P. Sinha, *Calcutta in Urban History*, Calcutta, 1978, p.7.

4 K. Ballhatchet, *Race, Sex and Class under the Raj*, London, 1980, p.vii.

5 Some of these ideas on race relations in early Calcutta I derived from Basudeb Chattopadhyay, 'Changing Inter-Racial Relationship in Nineteenth Century Calcutta', unpublished paper presented at a seminar in the History Department, University of Calcutta in 1990.

6 T. K. Mukhopadhyay, *Hicky's Bengal Gazette*, Calcutta, 1988, pp.18–53.

7 For a discussion on Ghulam Husain's ideas, see A. Sen, *Iswar Chandra Vidyasagar and His Elusive Milestones*, Calcutta, 1977, pp.150–2.

8 S. K. De, *Bengali Literature in the Nineteenth Century (1757–1857)*, Calcutta, 1962, pp.180–1, 193.

9 S. Sarkar, 'Rammohun Roy and the Break with the Past' and 'The Complexities of Young Bengal', reprinted in his *A Critique of Colonial India*, Calcutta, 1985, pp.9, 28–9.

10 B. De, 'A Biographical Perspective on the Political and Economic Ideas of Rammohun Roy', in *Rammohun Roy and the Process of Modernisation in India*, ed. V. C. Joshi, Delhi, 1975, p.145.

11 For details, see S. Sarkar, 'The Complexities of Young Bengal' and 'The Radicalism of Intellectuals', in his *A Critique of Colonial India*, pp.1–36, 58–70; A. Sen, 'The Bengal Economy and Rammohun Roy', in *Rammohun Roy and the Process of Modernisation in India*, ed. Joshi, pp.103–35.

12 Benoy Ghose, 'The Bengali Intelligentsia and the Revolt', in *Rebellion 1857: A Symposium*, ed. P. C. Joshi, Calcutta and New Delhi, 1986, p.103.

13 Judith Brown, *Modern India: The Origins of An Asian Democracy*, New York, 1985, p.85.

14 C. A. Bayly, *The New Cambridge History of India: Indian Society and the Making of the British Empire*, Cambridge, 1987, p.170.

15 S. N. Mukherjee, *Calcutta: Essays in Urban History*, Calcutta, 1993, pp.57, 65.

16 S. Banerjee, *The Parlour and the Street: Elite and Popular Culture in Nineteenth Century Calcutta*, Calcutta, 1989, pp.59–60; also Sinha, *Calcutta in Urban History*, p.34.

17 Bhabanicharan Bandyopadhyay, *Kalikata Kamalalay*, Reprint, Chittagong, 1975, pp.35–6; for more details on the class composition of the Indian society in Calcutta, see S. N. Mukherjee, *Calcutta: Essays in Urban History*, pp.127–34.

18 A. Sen, 'The Bengal Economy and Rammohun Roy', p.115.

19 For details on these people, see Sinha, *Calcutta in Urban History*, Chapter 3.

20 R. Mitra, 'Unpublished Reports of the Calcutta School Society', *Bengal Past and Present* 96 (1977): 151.

21 Cited in N. Kabiraj, 'Bengal Spectator O Adhunik Chinta', in *Unish Sataker Banglar Jagaran: Tarka O Bitarka* (The Awakening in Nineteenth Century Bengal: The Debates), ed. N. Kabiraj, Calcutta, 1984, pp.41–2.

22 S. N. Mukherjee, *Calcutta: Essays in Urban History*, pp.121–2.

23 *Hindoo Patriot*, 26 November 1857, in *Selections from English Periodicals of*

19th Century Bengal (hereafter *SEP*), ed. Benoy Ghose, Calcutta, 1979, Vol.4, p.202.

24 Banerjee, *The Parlour and the Street*, p.67.

25 B. Chattopadhyay, 'The Initial Impact of the Introduction of the English Law in Bengal (1773–1792)', *The Calcutta Historical Journal* 5 (1981).

26 *Ibid*; also, P. J. Marshall, *Bengal the British Bridgehead*, Cambridge, 1987, p.126.

27 Marshall, *Bengal the British Bridgehead*, p.129.

28 B. Chattopadhyay, 'Crime and Control in Early Colonial Bengal, 1770–1860', unpublished Ph.D. thesis, Calcutta University, 1987.

29 From the long list, mention may be made of the tribal uprising at Rajmahal (1784), the Travancore revolt (1800–09), Khurdah rebellion (1804), Paik revolt in Orissa (1817–19), Bhil revolt (1818–31), Ho revolt (1820–21), Khasi revolt (1829–31), the Wahabi movement (1813–69), Kol revolt (1831–32) and the Santhal revolt (1855–56). Kathleen Gough gives a list of 77 violent peasant uprisings during this period. See her 'Indian Peasant Uprisings', in *Peasant Struggles in India*, ed. A. R. Desai, New Delhi, 1981.

30 We have by now a rich literature on these peasant movements, but still the most comprehensive account is Suprakash Roy, *Bharater Krishak Bidroha O Ganatantrik Sangram* (Peasant Rebellions and Democratic Movements in India), Calcutta, 1972.

31 Bhaumik, *Sekaler Sambadpatre Kolkata* 1: 64.

32 Quoted in Marshall, *Bengal the British Bridgehead*, p.98.

33 Sibnath Shastri, *Ramtanu Lahiri O Tatkalin Bangasamaj* (Ramtanu Lahiri and the Bengali Society of His Age), 2nd edn, Calcutta, 1368 BS, p.56.

34 R. K. Samaddar, *Bangla Sahitya O Sanskritite Sthaniya Bidroher Prabhab* (The Impact of Local Rebellions on Bengali Literature and Society), Calcutta, 1982, pp.44–73

35 De, *Bengali Literature in the Nineteenth Century*, pp.180–1, 273–349.

36 Samaddar, *Bangla Sahitya O Sanskritite Sthaniya Bidroher Prabhab*, pp.87–8, 94, 98–9.

37 *Samachar Darpan*, 23 January 1819 and 1 April 1820 in Bhaumik, *Sekaler Sambadpatre Kolkata* 1: 40, 110–11.

38 Quoted in Sarkar, 'The Complexities of Young Bengal', p.35.

39 Brojendranath Bandyopadhyay, *Sambadpatre Sekaler Katha* (Tales of the Olden Times in the Newspapers), Vol.2, 4th edn, Calcutta, 1384 BS, pp.379, 658.

40 For details, see Beharilal Sarkar, *Titu Mir ba Narkelberiar Larai* (Titu Mir or the War of Narkelberia), ed. S. Basu, 3rd edn, Calcutta, 1987, pp.1, 58–9, 61, 66, 80.

41 Abhijit Datta, *Muslim Society in Transition: Titu Mir's Revolt (1831)*, Calcutta, 1987, p.98.

42 Bandyopadhyay, *Sambadpatre Sekaler Katha*, pp.379–80.

43 *SEP* 2: 182–3.

44 'Haibe asabhya jati nripati santal', quoted in Samaddar, *Bangla Sahitya o Sanskritite Sthaniya Bidroher Prabhab*, pp.372–81.

45 Benoy Ghose, *Samayik Patre Banglar Samajchitra* (Social Portrait of Bengal as Reflected in the Periodicals; hereafter *SBS*), Calcutta, 1962, Vol.1, pp.197–205.

46 'Santhaliya samachar likhite likhite lekhaneer mukh kshay hoiya gelo tathacha e pap gol nibaran hoilona, barang din din briddhi paitechhe', quoted in Samaddar, *Bangla Sahitya O Sanskritite Sthaniya Bidroher Prabhab*, p.388.

47 *SBS* 1: 201–02.

48 *Hindoo Patriot*, 19 July, 9 August, 30 August 1855, *SEP* 3: 180, 186–90.

49 Samaddar, *Bangla Sahitya O Sanskritite Sthaniya Bidroher Prabhab*, p.386–7.

50 Shastri, *Ramtanu Lahiri O Tatkalin Bangasamaj*, pp.195–6.

51 *SEP* 4: 61.

52 'Hatabhaga myada Bangalee' is the term that Sinha had actually used; Kaliprasanna Sinha, *Hutom Pyanchar Naksha* (The Satires of the Owl called Hutom) ed. Brojendranath Bandyopadhyay and Sajanikanta Das, Calcutta, 1355 BS, p.54.

53 *Hindoo Patriot*, 11 June and 26 November 1857, *SEP* 4: 90, 202.

54 *SBS* 1: 217–18. Translation mine.

55 *SEP* 4: 137.

56 *SBS* 1: 229.

57 *Sambad Prabhakar*, 1 Baisakh 1265 BS, *SBS* 1: 229.

58 *Ibid*, 7 Ashadh 1264 BS, *SBS* 1: 219.

59 *Hindoo Patriot*, 20 May 1857, *SEP* 4: 70–2.

60 *SEP* 4: 80.

61 *Hindoo Patriot*, 4 June, 9 July 1857, *SEP* 4: 80, 116.

62 *Sambad Prabhakar*, 14 Jaishtha, 7 Ashadh, 9 Ashadh 1264 BS, 1 Baisakh 1265 BS, *SBS* 1: 213–28.

63 Banerjee, *The Parlour and the Street*, pp.145–6.

64 *Sambad Prabhakar*, 21.7.1265 BS, *SBS* 1: 235.

65 Banerjee, *The Parlour and the Street*, pp.228–9.

66 *SEP* 4: 63–6.

67 *Hindoo Patriot*, 28 May 1857, *SEP* 4: 70.

68 *Ibid*, 3 December 1857, *SEP* 4: 211–12.

69 Letter to the editor, by a 'A Loyal Bengali', *Hindoo Patriot*, 25 July 1857, *SEP*, 4: 129–31. Italics added.

70 *Hindoo Patriot*, 11 June 1857, *SEP* 4: 90. Italics added.

71 B. B. Kling, *Partner in Empire: Dwarkanath Tagore and the Age of Enterprise in Eastern India*, Calcutta, 1981, pp.1–2, 248–9.

72 Susobhan Sarkar, *Bengal Renaissance and Other Essays*, New Delhi, 1970, pp.12, 101–2.

73 For more details see S. N. Mukherjee, *Calcutta: Essays in Urban History*, pp.141–8; *Awakening in Bengal in Early Nineteenth Century*, ed. Gautam Chattopadhyay, Calcutta, 1965, pp.xvii–xviii, 21–2; Sarkar, 'The Complexities of Young Bengal', p.30; Susobhan Sarkar, *Bengal Renaissance*, pp.21, 23; R. Mukherjee, 'Radical Who Became a Raja', *The Statesman*, 23 October 1983.

74 S. C. Maitra, *Selections from Jnanannesan*, Calcutta, 1979, pp.83, 155–8.

75 Cited in Kabiraj, 'Bengal Spectator O Adhunik Chinta', pp.45–6.

76 Cited in N. Kabiraj, 'Tattobodhini Patrikar Bhumika', in *Unish Sataker Banglar Jagaran*, p.59.

77 Quoted in *ibid*, p.61.

78 Quoted in Sarkar, 'The Complexities of Young Bengal', p.31.

79 For details see N. S. Bose, *Racism, Equality and Indian Nationalism*, Calcutta, 1981, p.101 and *passim*.

80 *Sambad Prabhakar*, 15, 22, 27 Sraban 1265 BS, *SBS* 1: 232–4.

81 *Hindoo Patriot*, 18 June 1857, *SEP* 4: 97. Italics added.

82 'Sipahi bidroher uttejanar maddhey Bangladesher o samajer ek mahopokar sadhito hoilo; ek nabasaktir suchana hoilo; ek naba akanksha jatiya jibane dekha dilo....' Shastri, *Ramtanu Lahiri*, p.201.

83 *Hindoo Patriot*, 18 June 1857, *SEP* 4: 97. Italics added.

84 Quoted in Gopal Haldar, 'Bengali Literature Before and After 1857', in *Rebellion 1857: A Symposium*, ed. P. C. Joshi, p.267.

85 *Idem.*

86 Quoted in R. K. Ray, *Social Conflict and Political Unrest in Bengal 1875–1927*, Delhi, 1984, p.26.

87 Banerjee, *The Parlour and the Street*, p.201.

* I am indebted to Professor Barun De and Dr Basudeb Chattopadhyay for their comments on an earlier draft of this paper. The errors that remain are mine.

GATT and the Emergence of the World Trade Organisation

Debesh Bhattacharya

I met Soumyen Mukherjee in Sydney in 1971 for the first time during the Vietnam Moratorium days. I was impressed by his radical humanism, his concern for oppressed people everywhere particularly in India, and his search for the correct way of understanding historical materialism. I was very pleased to have a fellow Bengali to teach history at the University of Sydney. I talked to him a lot during the days he was the Director for the Centre for Indian Studies. I am convinced that here is a scholar who stands for non-racism, non-alignment and anti-imperialism. Soumyen has become a trusted friend who will never let his friends down and who is truly international in outlook. Narrow domestic and sectarian approaches to history outrage him and he is prepared to denounce them in the strongest possible manner. He does not listen to fools easily and is prepared to fight against the Bharatiya Janata Party. I sincerely hope that this paper will stimulate his approach towards international trade and development issues.

The central purpose of this paper is to present an overview of the General Agreement for Tariff and Trade (GATT) and its role in developing countries (DCG) during the last four decades. The results of earlier GATT rounds of agreements will be analysed in Section 1. The Uruguay Round of multilateral trade negotiation (MTN) which began in 1986 and concluded on 15 December 1993 will be critically examined in Section 2. The key agreements in Safeguards, Textile and Clothing, Agriculture, Anti-Dumping, Subsidies and trade-related investment will also be examined in this Section 2. Section 3 will examine the main features of the World Trade Organisation (WTO) whose main functions are expected to facilitate the implementation, administration and operation of the Uruguay Round of Agreements

(URA). The WTO aims at revising the rules of trade liberalisation of international economic relations so as to provide more equal opportunities to all countries. My policy recommendations and conclusions are also explained in Section 3.

1

Developing countries (DCG) have been arguing that the existing international order is an exploitative world order. It has resulted in the concentration of economic power in the hands of a few developed countries (DC), which lay down the rules of international trade, the monetary system, finance and decision-making arrangements. Consequently DCG are economically as dominated today as they were under direct colonial rule. It is not surprising, then, that the existing order of global capitalism has failed to solve the basic problems of developing countries—acute poverty, unemployment and underemployment, and low physical quality of life.

The first GATT MTN came from the meeting held in Geneva (1947), the second in Annecy (1949), the third in Torquay (1951), the fourth again in Geneva (1956), the Dillon Rounds of Agreement (1960–61), the Kennedy (1964–67) and the Tokyo Round in the 1970s. In each previous round of agreement, GATT was largely irrelevant to the problems of DGC in the 1990s and did not bring about any significant advantages to them.

DCG did not achieve much from the Tokyo round of trade negotiations. In the circumstances, most DGC have been continually suffering from their balance of payments crisis and hence they have not been able to achieve self-reliance. Self-reliance means that any country's requirements should be met from within to the maximum possible extent, since self-reliance and a persistent balance of payments gap cannot go together. From a favourable balance of trade position in 1950, the non-oil exporting (NOE) DCG now invariably suffer from deficits in the balance of payments on current account for all these countries during the years 1973–88. The aggregate current deficit of NOEDCG increased from \$11.6 billion in 1973 to \$109 billion in 1981 and to \$45 billion in 1985, and to \$15.3 billion in 1988. In the 1990s it has exploded again, increasing from \$47.2 billion in 1994 to \$65.7 billion in 1995 and finally projected to \$72.6 billion in 1996 (*World*

Economic Outlook, May 1995, p.156). For example, DCG exported $1231.2 billion in 1995 which is less than their import payment to the rest of the world, i.e $1274.9 billion.

There is a marked asymmetry between the relative shares of the different groups of countries in the total trade flows of each of them. International trade is primarily a North-North affair. Even the DCG trade more with the DC than among themselves. It reflects the persistence of colonial trade and finance relationships even though most DCG have achieved political independence. The relative absence of significant horizontal trade links between DCG (although growing very slowly over the last three decades) cannot be explained purely in terms of any economic theory. The comparative advantage trade theory cannot explain the limited participation of the Transition (formerly the Soviet Union) and of DCG in the international division of labour. Neither is there much evidence of the factor-price equalisation even after four centuries of trading between the DCG and DC . Table 1 shows the share of major groups of countries in World Exports before the beginning of the Uruguay Round of trade negotiations.

Table 1: Share of Major Groups of Countries in World Exports (Percentage)

	1950	1960	1970	1975	1978	1979	1980	1985
North	61.1	66.8	71.3	66.0	67.0	65.2	63.1	65.5
South	30.8	21.7	18.0	24.2	23.3	25.6	28.1	24.0
Non-oil South	23.6	14.2	11.3	10.1	11.0	11.1	11.2	14.0
Transition States	8.1	11.7	10.6	9.7	9.2	8.9	10.5	

Sources: *IMF Survey*, July 16, 1984, p. 221, July 28, 1986, p.238 and UNCTAD *Handbook of International Trade and Development Statistics*, 1981, p.25. 1986. *Handbook* gives us the 1985 figures as reported in the UNCTAD *Bulletin*, No. 230, March 1987, p.9. The North refers to all DC and the South refers to all DGC. Figures are from *IMF Survey*, July 27, 1987 and they represent all DCG.

Myrdal[1] provided his theory of cumulative causation to argue that advantages are cumulative, so that any initial competitive edge results in further increases in efficiency and hence to a cumulatively greater advantage. On the other hand, if countries start from an initial disadvantageous position, they tend to suffer cumulatively. Consequently if countries start from a position of inequality due to unequal bargaining strength, one can explain the present trade imbalances between DGC and DC. The colonial past is mainly responsible for the current international division of labour and international exchange relations. DGC mainly export primary commodities, raw materials, and minerals, which are processed in DC. The former are also markets for manufactured products and also places for the capital investments of the latter. DGC (importing goods which have been processed from their own raw materials) have to pay not only for the cost of processing but also for the profits earned and costs of transportation both ways.

The consequences of balance of payments crisis for most NOEDGC would require significant restraint in monetary, fiscal and exchange rate adjustments in these countries. As World Economic Outlook[2] points out, the median rate of monetary expansion in these countries declined substantially in the 1980s. Most governments have also started reducing their expenditures, with continued emphasis on reducing social wage (reducing subsidies on essential items like food, medicine, education, health and other welfare services). Poor people in most indebted countries like Mexico, Brazil, Peru, Ghana, Zambia and the Philippines were suffering extra hardships because of these reduced subsidies. Moreover, any consequent reduction in government activities in NOEDGC invariably aggravate the already acute un- and under-employment problems in these countries.

In my *Political Economy of Development*,[3] it was shown that the purchasing power of DGC's traditional export products—coffee, cocoa, tea, soya beans, cotton, jute, natural rubber, and copper—is only a third or a fourth of goods and services imported from DC during the last four decades. With declining real prices of the principal primary commodities exported by DGC during the last four decades, these countries were compelled to export greater quantities of their commodities in order to be able to import essentially needed industrial machinery and intermediate goods. As Castro[4] points out, in 1960 it took 200 tons of sugar to buy a 180-hp bulldozer, while in 1984 it took 800 tons of sugar at the world market price to buy a similar bulldozer. Similarly, in 1960, 37.3 tons of fertilisers could be bought for a ton of coffee. In 1982 only 15.8 tons of fertilisers could be bought for a ton of coffee.

It is a great pity that no previous GATT negotiation called for agreements towards a link between the prices of DGC's commodity exports and the prices they have to pay for essential imports from DC if they were to diversify their economies. Such a link would have stabilised the amounts of foreign exchange earnings of the NOEDGC and would also overcome the fundamental problems of persistent deficits in their balance of payments.

When DGC do manage to produce manufactured goods like textiles or shoes, their exports are usually confronted by quotas, tariff barriers and other restrictions. The protectionist policies of DC, plus the dumping and unfair competition with subsidised products which those same countries habitually employ in international trade, are the major obstacles to expansion and diversification of DGC. The case for preferential trade treatment in the form of a system of Preferences (GSP) is presented by Nowzad.[5] The object was to bind the preferential GSP tariff rates and to establish a 'built-in-differentiator' so that DGC may get compensation for any erosion of the GSP from general tariff reductions under the MTN. Imports from DGC were supposed to be totally exempt from 'safeguard action' (i.e., DC's authority to improve import restrictions to protect their domestic producers from injury) or at the least, much more stringent criteria be applied before 'safeguard' measures could be taken against such imports. DGC should have been able to keep both the GSP and MFN tariff preferential treatment.

Average MFN tariff rates in Table 2 on clothing in Canada, Austria and the USA ranged from 20 to 50 per cent, but they averaged 93 per cent in New Zealand. Tariffs on footwear stood at about 14 per cent in Japan. The MFN tariffs for these products were 40 per cent or more during the 1980s in Australia and New Zealand. On average, DC now impose tariffs on industrial imports from DGC from 2.1 per cent on raw materials, 5.4 per cent on semi-manufactures and 9.1 per cent on finished products. As Balassa[6] correctly points out, the existing tariff structure in effect discriminates against higher levels of processing and production, thus encouraging DGC to produce and export only primary products. For example, the applied tariff rate in Australia on raw sugar is 0.1 per cent while it increases to 16.4 per cent if it was imported in the form of refined sugar.

A reduction in tariffs alone is unlikely to have any great effect on the exports of manufactures of DGC so long as NTB and other forms of quantitative restrictions to trade remain. NTB have been

Table 2: Post-Tokyo MFN, Applied, and GSP Tariffs in Selected Developed Countries

Product Group	Australia	Austria	Canada	EEC	Finland	Japan	Norway	New Zealand	Sweden	Switzer-land	United States	All Developed Countries
Average MFN Tariff Rates												
All Food Items	4.9	8.0	6.2	3.7	8.9	9.7	2.8	9.7	1.6	10.0	4.1	6.4
Food and live animals	2.8	5.9	6.8	3.2	9.3	10.0	3.0	5.7	1.4	9.0	3.8	6.
Oilseeds and nuts	4.1	1.9	6.0	10.3	7.9	5.6	4.5	0.9	3.3	7.5	1.4	5.3
Animal and vegetable oils	2.0	0.8	0.0	0.1	0.8	0.3	0.0	0.0	0.0	0.2	0.9	0.1
Agricultural Raw Materials	5.1	2.3	0.6	3.4	1.1	0.7	0.6	1.0	1.7	1.9	0.3	0.8
Ores and Metals	10.2	5.6	2.1	2.8	1.9	2.5	1.5	6.0	2.5	1.4	1.9	2.3
Iron and steel	17.2	8.4	5.4	5.5	3.9	5.0	1.8	8.8	4.8	2.0	4.3	5.1
Nonferrous metals	3.9	6.1	2.2	3.2	1.2	5.5	1.9	4.0	1.0	1.2	0.7	2.3
Fuels	0.0	2.1	1.4	0.1	0.1	1.5	0.0	0.2	0.0	0.0	0.4	1.1
Chemicals	5.4	6.3	6.4	8.4	2.4	5.5	5.9	6.7	5.0	0.9	3.7	5.8
Manufactures excl. chemicals	17.7	14.1	7.0	8.1	8.2	5.7	6.1	22.6	5.4	3.3	5.6	7.0
Leather	17.8	5.3	3.8	10.2	11.8	11.9	4.7	20.9	4.1	1.8	4.2	5.1
Textile yarn and fabrics	15.3	18.2	9.4	17.3	22.7	8.6	12.8	16.2	10.6	6.0	10.6	11.7
Clothing	49.3	30.2	12.6	19.9	32.0	15.0	20.3	93.0	13.6	8.6	20.3	17.5
Footwear	43.9	25.9	11.9	22.5	16.0	14.2	11.2	40.3	14.3	9.6	11.7	13.4
Other Items			0.2	3.3	0.1	4.8	1.3	2.3	2.0	1.2	1. 8	0.4

Table 2 cont'd:

Product Group	Australia	Austria	Canada	EEC	Finland	Japan	Norway	New Zealand	Sweden	Switzer-land	United States	All Developed Countries
Average Applied Tariff Rates												
All Food Items items	3.1	6.8	3.0	4.4	5.2	9.4	1.4	7.8	0.8	9.1	3.5	5.3
Food and live animals	1.7	4.9	2.9	4.8	5.7	9.7	1.5	3.9	0.8	8.4	3.2	5.3
Oilseeds and nuts	2.0	1.5	4.6	4.9	5.5	4.8	4.3	0.7	2.2	7.4	1.0	4.0
Animals and vegetable oils	2.4	0.8	0.1	0.0	0.8	0.3	0.0	0.0	0.0	0.2	1.0	0.2
Agricultural Raw Materials	0.7	1.6	3.7	0.4	1.0	0.3	0.4	0.7	1.4	0.7	0.3	0.5
Ores and Metals	4.3	0.3	2.7	0.7	0.1	1.8	0.4	4.2	0.2	0.1	2.2	1.5
Iron and steel	7.3	0.5	5.6	2.3	0.1	2.9	0.7	6.4	0.4	0.1	5.0	3.4
Nonferrous metals	2.4	0.2	2.8	0.5	0.0	4.3	0.1	2.1	0.1	0.1	0.7	1.3
Fuels	0.0	1.5	0.2	0.3	0.0	1.2	0.0	0.0	0.0	0.0	0.4	0.6
Chemicals	4.0	0.5	3.0	3.4	0.1	4.8	0.4	4.9	0.4	0.1	3.9	3.1
Manufactures excl. chemicals	11.5	2.0	6.2	4.6	1.3	4.6	1.3	18.3	1.4	0.4	4.9	4.7
Leather	10.9	0.9	11.0	2.1	2.3	10.7	0.8	21.4	0.3	0.1	2.7	3.1
Textile yarn and fabric	11.3	2.0	18.3	5.3	1.0	7.1	1.6	10.9	1.7	0.6	12.1	7.9
Clothing	35.6	5.1	17.2	7.3	7.7	10.0	3.0	75.6	4.8	1.7	18.1	11.9
Footwear	27.9	1.2	23.4	6.5	3.8	12.5	2.4	28.4	2.8	0.6	9.5	9.0
Other Items	0.1	1.1	4.7	0.1	0.1	0.7	0.4	0.9	0.1	0.2	3.6	3.3
All Products	8.3	2.0	4.4	2.5	1.0	3.1	1.0	11.0	0.8	1.0	3.4	3.0

Table 2 cont'd:

Product Group	Australia	Austria	Canada	EEC	Finland	Japan	Norway	New Zealand	Sweden	Switzer-land	United States	All Developed Countries
Average Tariff for GSP Beneficiaries												
All Food Items items	1.3	9.0	1.5	5.0	7.0	11.1	0.3	6.2	0.4	6.3	3.6	5.5
Food and live animals	1.0	8.9	1.3	5.1	7.2	11.7	0.3	0.8	0.4	6.5	3.4	5.6
Oilseeds and nuts	0.7	0.1	5.6	6.2	8.8	5.0	3.2	0.0	1.7	9.0	0.3	4.5
Animals and vegetable oils	0.3	0.3	0.0	0.0	10.7	1.2	0.0	0.0	0.0	0.1	0.1	0.4
Agricultural Raw Materials	0.1	1.4	3.1	0.5	5.5	0.5	0.5	0.0	2.1	0.3	0.1	0.5
Ores and Metals	1.6	0.9	0.5	0.5	0.1	1.3	0.3	0.2	0.1	0.4	1.1	0.9
Iron and steel	4.9	2.9	4.0	3.3	0.4	2.0	0.4	2.3	1.0	0.4	3.5	3.0
Nonferrous metals	0.3	1.1	0.9	0.5	0.0	3.1	1.7	0.5	0.1	0.9	0.3	1.1
Fuels	0.0	1.5	0.0	0.2	0.0	1.3	0.0	0.0	0.0	0.0	0.3	0.6
Chemicals	4.2	4.0	6.1	4.1	0.1	5.1	0.2	1.1	0.6	0.4	1.0	3.7
Manufactures excl. chemicals	11.4	18.9	13.8	6.4	9.3	4.2	5.9	14.3	6.9	2.7	6.6	6.7
Leather	9.6	6.6	9.6	2.8	6.1	8.4	5.5	18.0	1.2	1.1	1.4	3.2
Textile yarn and fabric	6.3	17.5	19.8	7.6	6.0	6.1	11.0	8.5	6.8	2.7	9.0	8.4
Clothing	35.1	27.2	16.2	9.3	23.6	8.6	18.9	82.8	13.2	7.6	17.8	14.6
Footwear	25.6	24.4	23.3	9.1	14.8	7.9	11.6	22.1	13.4	4.4	9.4	10
Other Items	0.0	5.2	5.6	0.1	0.1	1.0	0.1	1.7	0.0	0.4	0.4	3.8
All Products	4.3	4.9	4.4	2.1	4.6	2.3	2.8	3.3	2.3	2.3	3.6	2.7

Source: Calculations on the basis of the GATT Tariff Study and UNCTAD Series D Trade Tapes. See Laird and Yeats (1987).

Table 3: Analysis of the Escalation in Post-Tokyo Round Applied Tariffs in Selected Developed Countries

Product Group	Australia	Austria	EEC	Finland	Japan	Norway	New Zealand	Sweden	Switzerland	United States
Meat products										
Fresh and frozen meat	0.0	0.2	6.6	0.0	10.1	8.3	4.3	0.0	4.2	1.6
Prepared meat	4.6	2.6	17.9	12.6	22.5	8.1	7.0	0.0	5.2	2.3
Fish										
Fresh and frozen fish	0.0	3.7	6.3	0.8	5.3	0.0	2.6	0.0	0.4	0.5
Fish preparations	0.9	7.2	12.4	1.2	10.7	1.6	1.2	0.1	1.4	1.1
Vegetables										
Fresh vegetables	3.4	2.1	6.7	14.0	9.0	3.4	0.1	5.1	4.9	7.6
Vegetable preparations	9.8	13.3	15.1	14.6	17.5	6.6	5.7	6.2	11.4	11.0
Fruit										
Fresh fruit	0.2	3.1	7.7	10.7	21.5	1.0	0.0	0.6	7.4	1.1
Prepared fruit	6.3	17.3	16.6	8.5	21.8	3.1	11.1	0.7	13.7	20.3
Coffee										
Green or roasted beans	0.0	14.3	3.8	3.5	0.0	0.1	0.0	0.0	8.5	0.0
Coffee extracts	0.5	3.5	13.8	0.0	17.4	0.2	31.1	0.0	6.0	0.0
Vegetable oils										
Vegetable oilseed	2.1	0.5	0.0	0.7	0.3	0.0	0.0	0.0	0.1	1.0
Vegetable oils	3.1	1.1	6.1	9.3	6.2	4.5	0.0	1.0	8.2	0.7

Table 3 cont'd:

Product Group	Australia	Austria	EEC	Finland	Japan	Norway	New Zealand	Sweden	Switzerland	United States
Sugar										
Raw sugar	0.1	0.0	0.0	0.0	3.3	3.6	0.0	0.0	42.3	0.6
Refined sugar	16.4	0.0	0.0	16.9	82.5	2.7	0.7	1.1	34.1	9.9
Chocolate										
Cocoa beans	0.0	5.0	1.9	0.0	0.0	0.0	0.0	0.0	0.0	0.0
Powder and butter	0.0	5.6	9.0	0.0	2.9	0.0	7.6	0.3	0.3	0.1
Chocolate	9.3	0.6	0.1	0.1	24.3	0.1	27.1	0.2	14.3	0.1
Tobacco										
Raw tobacco	9.1	9.7	0.0	0.0	0.0	0.0	9.6	0.0	0.0	8.8
Tobacco products	16.6	211.3	61.8	2.1	82.1	5.1	31.6	1.9	17.6	9.1
Rubber										
Natural rubber	0.0	0.0	0.0	0.0	0.0	0.0	0.0	0.0	0.0	0.0
Unvulcanized rubber	12.2	0.5	2.2	0.2	5.5	0.5	12.0	0.8	0.1	6.4
Rubber products	20.0	2.0	5.5	4.1	12.4	3.1	28.3	2.9	1.0	9.2
Wood										
Rough wood	0.0	3.0	0.0	0.0	0.0	0.0	0.0	0.0	0.0	0.0
Shaped wood	1.5	1.1	0.1	0.0	1.1	0.0	0.0	0.0	0.1	0.1
Wood manufactured	14.5	1.2	4.2	0.1	1.2	0.2	11.2	0.6	0.4	4.7

Table 3 cont'd:

Product Group	Australia	Austria	EEC	Finland	Japan	Norway	New Zealand	Sweden	Switzerland	United States
Paper										
Pulpwood	0.0	1.4	0.0	0.0	0.0	0.0	10.5	0.0	0.8	00
Paper and board	5.7	1.8	2.3	0.2	5.7	0.0	5.3	0.2	0.3	0.3
Paper manufactures	11.6	5.1	6.0	0.6	3.6	0.1	25.3	0.3	0.3	3.8
Wool										
Not carded or combed	0.0	0.0	0.0	0.0	0.0	0.0	0.0	0.0	0.1	5.2
Carded or combed	0.0	0.0	2.4	0.0	0.0	0.0	0.0	0.0	0.0	11.1
Wool yarn	3.4	0.0	1.4	0.0	3.9	0.1	19.7	0.0	0.0	12.9
Wool fabrics	25.6	0.1	2.7	0.0	11.0	0.2	33.4	0.2	0.0	37.3
Cotton										
Not carded or combed	0.0	0.0	0.0	0.0	0.0	0.0	0.0	0.0	0.1	0.5
Carded or combed	30.3	0.2	0.2	0.3	0.0	0.0	0.0	0.2	0.0	5.0
Cotton yarn	13.9	2.6	2.3	0.8	3.8	2.3	1.3	2.6	1.2	8.7
Cotton fabrics	2.4	3.2	5.6	1.4	5.9	4.0	1.3	3.6	0.7	10.4
Jute										
Raw jute	0.0	0.0	0.0	0.0	0.0	0.0	0.0	0.0	0.0	0.0
Jute yarn or cordage	8.9	0.8	2.0	0.7	5.5	0.0	0.0	0.0	1.4	1.3
Jute fabric	0.0	2.9	4.8	0.1	5.4	0.0	0.0	1.2	0.4	0.0
Jute bags	1.9	10.9	4.7	1.7	5.5	0.3	1.4	1.0	0.5	1.0

Table 3 cont'd:

Product Group	Australia	Austria	EEC	Finland	Japan	Norway	New Zealand	Sweden	Switzerland	United States
Sisal										
Sisal fibres	0.0	0.2	0.0	0.0	0.0	0.0	0.0	0.0	0.5	0.1
Cordage	8.3	1.0	4.3	2.1	3.4	0.9	17.4	0.8	0.2	0.3
Metal Ores	0.0	0.0	0.0	0.0	0.0	0.0	0.0	0.0	0.0	0.1
Iron										
Iron bars and ingots	0.0	0.1	2.3	0.1	3.7	0.0	0.0	0.0	0.1	0.8
Iron plates and shapes	7.4	0.6	2.2	0.1	2.3	0.2	6.5	0.5	0.1	5.3
Copper										
Unwrought copper	0.0	0.0	0.0	0.0	1.5	0.0	0.0	0.0	0.0	0.8
Refined copper	5.2	0.1	1.8	0.1	5.9	0.0	2.2	0.2	0.1	1.8
Aluminium										
Unwrought aluminium	2.0	0.3	0.8	0.0	6.6	0.0	0.2	0.0	0.2	0.6
Refined aluminium	4.3	0.2	2.1	0.0	9.0	0.3	7.0	0.4	0.1	3.2
Lead										
Unwrought lead	0.1	0.2	0.6	0.0	3.0	0.0	0.3	0.0	0.1	3.5
Refined lead	0.4	0.0	5.8	0.0	6.8	0.0	6.4	0.0	0.0	1.6
Zinc										
Unwrought zinc	4.1	0.1	0.9	0.0	3.0	0.0	0.0	0.0	0.0	1.7
Refined zinc	2.8	0.6	4.1	0.0	6.6	0.0	0.8	0.0	0.0	2.3

Table 3 cont'd:

Product Group	Australia	Austria	EEC	Finland	Japan	Norway	New Zealand	Sweden	Switzerland	United States
Phosphate										
Natural phosphates	0.0	6.9	0.0	0.0	0.0	0.0	0.0	0.0	0.1	0.0
Phosporic acid	19.0	0.0	6.1	0.0	5.2	0.0	0.0	0.2	0.1	1.7
Superphosphates	0.0	1.3	2.6	0.0	0.0	0.0	0.0	0.0	0.0	0.0
Petroleum										
Crude petroleum	0.0	1.4	0.0	0.0	1.4	0.0	0.0	0.0	0.0	0.3
Refined petroleum	0.0	1.6	1.0	0.0	2.2	0.0	0.0	0.0	0.0	1.1
Memo items										
Percentage of chains in which escalation occurs	88.0	88.0	96.0	68.0	96.0	68.0	88.0	76.0	68.0	96.0
Average tariff differeence from primary to processed stage	6.9	9.5	6.7	1.9	12.5	1.0	9.7	0.7	1.8	4.7

Source: Computed from data produced in the GATT tariff study.

used by DC as the most-effective instrument for the prevention of industrialisation in DGC and they include an infinite number of protectionist practices—UNCTAD has documented some 700 of such practices—which range from government subsidies, quantitative restrictions, health standards and technical standards to deliberately complex procedures. Morton[7] has stated that in 1969 DC imposed NTB measures on 28 per cent of all imports from DGC, as compared with 11 per cent on imports from other DC. In 1984, 21 per cent of imports from DGC were subject to NTB in DC, as compared with only 11 per cent of imports from other DC. In addition, some 29 per cent of the agricultural exports of DGC were subject to NTB in DC. Agricultural products still suffer NTB measures for 33 per cent of value from DGC, textiles 62 per cent and steel 46 per cent. Further NTB are high on food and agricultural product, cotton textile, iron and steel, while they are relatively low on raw materials and fuels and hence once again discriminate against the levels of processing in DGC.

Table 4: Fifteen DC NTB on imports from DC and DGC, 1984

	Percentage covered by NTB			
	Value of Imports from		Number of Categories from	
Product Categories	**DC**	**DGC**	**DC**	**DGC**
All	17	19	11	21
Agricultural	44	33	42	35
Fuels and ores	8	10	13	11
Industrial	14	21	7	18
Textiles	25	62	20	58
Steel	50	46	21	21
Footwear	2	4	14	14
Electrical	10	7	5	8
Vehicles	30	3	6	10

Source: Finger and Olechowski.

The European Union, Japan and the USA imposed NTB measures in the following Table 5 between 1988 and 1993.

Table 5: NTB Measures 1988 and 1993 (Per cents of imports covered)

	1988	1993
Core NTB	14.6	14.0
Quantitative restrictions	12.1	9.8
Export restraints	8.0	6.6
Anti-dumping, countervailing	2.4	3.7
Other price measures	1.6	1.6

Source: *IMF International Trade Policies, The Uruguay Round and Beyond,* Vol.1 *Principal Issues,* 1994, p.8.

The potential for an expansion of DGC exports to DC exists, and discriminating barriers against the exports from these countries should be reduced if that potential is to be realised. If DC were completely to dismantle their trade barriers against the manufactured goods of DGC, the latter could earn many billion dollars per year. If the Uruguay Round of Trade Negotiations leads to a tariff reduction of 50 per cent, this would add many billion dollars to DGC manufactured exports by 1995. The non-tariff trade barriers of developed countries could be partially relaxed. This could add many billion dollars per year to those earnings. The IMF recently estimated annual real income gains globally ranging from $212 to $274 billion (or about 1 per cent of world GDP) upon full implementation of the Uruguay Round, of which some $80 billion would accrue to poor countries.

2

The URA began in Uruguay in 1986. This time DGC wanted to negotiate meaningfully for trade liberalisation. They wanted to get rid of protectionism sanctioned by earlier rounds of GATT. GATT's Article XIX allowed members to escape their normal GATT obligations and erect trade barriers to safeguard any of their producers seriously injured by the liberalisation of trade. However, most governments tend to ignore other important clauses of this Article which provides that foreign suppliers may retaliate or be compensated for losses from the denial of market access. Tables 5 and 5(a) show coverage of Article XIX Action between 1950 and 1993 (situation as of 15 April 1993).

Discrimination against cotton textiles was incorporated into the short term Arrangement Regarding International Trade in Cotton-Textile in the early 1960s. This became in 1974 a long term Multi-Fibre Arrangement (MFA) was followed by MFA II (1978–81). MFA III (1982–86), and MFA IV (1986–1994); the current MFA now covers almost all textile and clothing products and has subjected nearly 40 poor countries to export restraints in most DC. This discrimination principle has been regularly extended in its product and country coverage against DGC. These measures in the forms of selective restraint arrangements reflect when the exporting country, voluntarily or not, undertakes not to ship more than a certain amount of goods to the importing DC. These are usually known as Voluntary Export Restraints (VER) or Orderly Marketing Agreements (OME). Currently, there are over 200 such measures and the most frequent users are the USA and the European Economic Union.

DC have increasingly used agricultural subsidies in recent years. Such subsidy programmes, originally motivated either by a desire for food security or to assist farmers needing support from their governments, have in many cases led to structural overcapacity. Indeed, many rich European countries which were previously major importers have now not only become self-sufficient in agriculture but have even become large-scale exporters of a number of products which they previously used to import from poor DGC. This has been the outcome of the European Community's Common Agricultural Policy (CAP) which was launched in 1962. Subsidies to the agricultural sector in DC have acted as barriers to the agricultural exports from DGC. Further the availability of cheap subsidised imports from rich countries inhibited domestic production of DGCs because of the lack of necessary incentives to cover the domestic cost and hence prevented the emergence of self-sufficiency for many food importing DGC.

Table 6 shows agricultural producer subsidy equivalents for the period between 1979 and 1993.

Table 6: Agricultural Producer Subsidy Equivalents

	1979-86	1990	1992	1993
Annual Average (In Billions of US Dollars)				
Australia	1.00	1.38	1.11	0.96
European Union	82.11	82.79	79.57	39.61
Japan	20.96	29.85	36.07	34.99
USA	22.73	27.70	25.41	28.35
Total OECD	167.44	168.29	163.12	97.88
(In Per cent of Farm Gate Prices)				
	1979-86	**1990**	**1992**	**1993**
Australia	10	12	10	9
European Union	46	47	48	37
Japan	64	65	71	70
USA	21	23	21	23
Total OECD	34	42	41	42

Source: IMF, *ibid.* p.9.

It is necessary here to point out that the monopolisation of control over the international monetary system and financial arrangements is a feature of the continuation of external control over the South. The IMF and World Bank still reflect the politico-financial balance of the 1940s and 1950s and they have not kept up with the changes that have taken place in the world. One of the founders of these institutions, Keynes[8] made the following statement: 'I conceive of the management and the effective voting power as being permanently Anglo-American.'

Developed countries, led by the USA and the IMF have shown an inadequate appreciation of the problems of a deteriorating world environment causing underdevelopment in DGC. Only 5.2 per cent of the current account deficits of DGC during the period 1976–82 were assigned by the IMF for compensating for these deficits. The IMF has attached strings in many cases that entail a high social, economic and political price that go against the interests of DGC. As the Brandt Report[9] has correctly observed:

> The IMF's insistence on drastic measures, often within the time framework of only one year, has tended to impose unnecessary and unacceptable political burden on the poorest, on occasion leading to 'IMF riots' and even the downfall of governments.

All three institutions, World Bank, IMF and GATT really looked after the interests of DC during the previous rounds of GATT. DGC were marginal players and their interests were never the primary focus of such MTN.

Table 7 shows the sector-wise UR tariff reduction together with DGC high export interest. It also shows that the biggest reductions, ranging from 69 to 60 per cent measured in terms of bound rates will be made in sectors (wood, paper, pulp, and furniture, metals, and non-electric machinery) where tariff level is already low. For textile, clothing, leather, and rubber, the reductions range from 22 to 18 per cent.

Table 7: DC: Uruguay round Tariff Reductions by Sector (in per cent)

Sector	Reductions	DGC with High-Export Interest
Wood, pulp, furniture, paper	69	Cameroon, Congo, Ghana, Indonesia, Paraguay
Metal	62	Bolivia, Cameroon, Sierra Leone, Zaire, Zimbabwe
Non-electric Machinery	60.	Mali, Singapore
Mineral products	52	Congo, S.Leone, Zaire, Zimbabwe
Electric Machinery	47	Malaysia, Singapore
Chemicals, photographic supplies	45	Jamaica, Namibia, Niger
Fish products	26	Belize, Cuba, Ecuador, Honduras
Transport equipment	23	
Textiles and clothing	22	Bangladesh, Egypt, China, India, Morocco, Pakistan, Sri Lanka, Tunisia
Leather, rubber	18	Kenya, Nigeria, Paraguay, Uruguay, Cambodia

Source: GATT (1994).

The post-URA tariff structure will still compel DGC to specialise in raw materials and discriminate against the levels of processing.

Table 8 shows Tariff Escalation on DC Imports from DGC. The URA would reduce all these tariff rates if they are implemented, but the then tariff structure will still discriminate against the higher levels of processing and value-added activities, 0.8 per cent on raw materials, 2.8 per cent on semi-manufactures, and 6.2 per cent on finished products.

Table 8: Tariff Escalation on DC Imports from DGC (in per cent)

	Share of each stage	Tariffs		
		Pre-URA	Post-URA	Percentage Reduction
All Industrial Products (ex.Oil)				
Raw materials	22.0	2.1	0.8	62.0
Semi-manufactures	21.0	5.3	2.8	47.0
Finished products	57.0	9.1	6.2	32.0
Total	100.0	6.8	4.3	37.0
All tropical industrial products				
Raw materials	35.0	0.1	0.0	100.0
Semi-manufactures	30.0	6.3	3.5	44.0
Finished products	34.0	6.6	2.6	61.0
Natural resource-based products				
Raw materials	11.0	3.1	2.0	35.0
Semi-manufactures	40.0	3.5	2.0	43.0
Finished products	17.0	7.9	5.9	25.0
Total	100.0	4.0	2.7	33.0

Source: GATT (1994 b).

Hence it is clear from the above table that following the URA, tariff bindings will actually increase; it will increase from 13 to 61 per cent of imports by DGC and from 74 to 96 per cent by transition economies. The URA is not reducing tariffs universally in the near future. Moreover all DGC are likely to lose their GSP. There is no trade-off for DGC for their inability to preserve preferential tariff margins.[10]

Two areas of world trade—intellectual property and services—are now within the fields of continuous MTN within the WTO. In the short run the enforcement of TRIP might create additional problems for DGC, especially in the fields of life-saving medicines. The services agreement in the UR provides a multilateral framework on the principles of non-discrimination and transparency. Foreign service suppliers will get market access and treatment no less favourable than that which applies to domestic supplies. Table 9 shows the extent of global tariff bindings agreed in the URA.

Textiles and Clothing were going to be gradually integrated into the WTO/GATT in 1994 in a four-stage phase-out over ten years, under the supervision of a Textiles Monitoring Body. Products accounting for not less than 16 per cent of total volume of imports in terms of the stated Harmonised System lines or categories in 1990 were to be integrated into GATT 1994 upon entry into force of WTO. After the third year of the first phase out period, at least another 17 per cent of total 1990 import volumes of the listed products to be integrated, followed by at least 18 per cent after the seventh year, and the remainder 49 per cent at the end of the ten-year period. Each phase out must encompass products chosen by the restricting country from four groups—tops and yarns, fabrics, made-up textiles, and clothing. Outstanding quota restrictions will be expanded by the prevailing (bilaterally negotiated) quota growth rate plus 16 per cent annually in the first three years, by 25 per cent in the subsequent four years, and by 27 per cent in the final three years. Safeguards may be maintained for a maximum of three years phased out over their duration.

The Uruguay Round on the Agreement on Safeguards has tried to confront the discriminatory use of Article XIX of GATT. It emphasises the importance of structural adjustment and the need to enhance rather than limit competition in international markets in 14 articles and an annex. Articles 1, 2, 3, 5, 6 and 10 establish basic principles, rules, conditions and scope for the application of the safeguard measures provided for in Article XIX. Article 4 defines the criteria of serious injury. Article 7 uses time-limits (initially for 4 years and the total life should not exceed 8 years for developed and 10 years for DGC) for the application of safeguard measures. Article 8 relates to the waiver on compensation requirements. Article 9 allows for preferential treatment for DGC. Article 11 prohibits and phases out these measures. Finally Articles 12, 13, and 14 state the procedures for monitoring and review of the operation of the Agreement and the requirements for notification,

Table 9: The Extent of Gloabl Tariff Bindings

	< Industrial Products >				< Agricultural Products >			
	Per cent of Pre-URA	Tariff Lines Post-URA	Per cent of Pre-URA	Imports Post-URA	Per cent of Pre-URA	Tariff Lines Post-URA	Per cent of Pre-URA	Imports Post-URA
By Major Country Group								
Industrial C	78	99	94	99	68	100	81	100
DGC	21	73	13	61	18	100	26	100
Asia	17	68	82	70	17	100	40	100
Central Europe	63	98	68	97	45	100	45	100
Western Europe	79	82	98	98	45	100	87	100
Latin America	38	100	57	100	36	100	74	100
North America	99	100	99	100	92	100	96	100
Transition Economy	73	98	74	96	51	100	54	100

Source: GATT (1994).

consultation and dispute settlement. Recently the USA has been championing the use of voluntary import expansions (VIE) as a form of export protectionism. Under VIE, countries like Japan are induced, by incentives or penalties, to import specific amounts from the USA. For semiconductor chips, the USA wanted the commitment from Japan that the USA would supply 20 per cent of the Japanese market by some target date. In April 1987 the USA imposed tariffs on $300 million worth of Japanese exports to punish Japan for nonfulfilment of its target. Further the USA has been pressing Japan to import more goods and services from the USA because of the latter's persistent surplus in balance of trade with Japan.

The following results of the Uruguay Round Agreements effectively place all member countries at broadly comparable levels of obligation:

(i) the strengthening of the existing rules to govern a variety of trade policy measures, particularly those areas which had consistently been sources of trade tensions and disputes;

(ii) the achievement of significant degree of tariff liberalisation;

(iii) the establishment of new rules to cover intellectual property and trade in services; and

(iv) the interlinkage of all these agreements within the institutional framework of the newly established World Trade Organisation (WTO), which aims to facilitate the implementation, administration and operation of the Uruguay Round agreements subject to an integrated dispute settlement mechanism.[11]

All TRIM inconsistent with Articles III and XI of GATT 1994 are to be notified within 90 days and eliminated within two years, five years, and seven years for DC, DGC and least DGC, respectively. There could be an extension of the transition period for both DGC and least DGC under certain circumstances.

Similarly TRIP demand that all patentable inventions on pharmaceuticals and agricultural chemical products made after entry into force of the WTO must be protected. DGC are permitted to delay implementation for a further four years, except for the national treatment and MFN commitments. Where patent protection is called for in areas of technology not currently protected in DGC, a grace period of an additional five years is provided in respect of the technologies in question.

3

The WTO Agreement consists of a preamble, 16 Articles and four Annexes. The preamble also recognises the 'need for positive efforts designed to ensure that DGC, and especially the least developed among them, secure a share in the growth in international trade commensurate with the needs of their economic development'.

DC do not expect reciprocity for commitments made by them in MTN to reduce or remove tariffs and other NTB to the trade of DGC. Developed contracting parties 'shall therefore not seek, neither shall less developed contracting parties be required to make, concessions that are inconsistent with the latters' development, financial and trade needs'. The Uruguay Declaration also stipulates that special attention shall be given to the particular situation, and problems of the least developed countries and to the need to encourage positive measures to facilitate the expansion of their trading opportunities.

At the Marrakesh Ministerial Meeting in 1994 a total of 111 countries out of 125 formal participants in the Uruguay Round signed the Final Act. The WTO was signed by 104 countries and seven countries (Australia, Botswana, Burundi, India, Japan, South Korea and the USA) are awaiting their respective national legislative procedures. The WTO organisational structure consists of a Ministerial Conference and a General Council, which will carry out the functions of a Dispute Settlement Body and a Trade Policy Review Body. A Committee on Budget, Finance and Administration, a Committee on Trade and Development, and a Committee on Balance-of-Payments Restrictions will be established by the Ministerial Conference. The Council for Trade in Goods, the Council for Trade in Services, and the Council for Trade Related Intellectual Property (TRIP) will establish their respective rules of procedure subject to the approval of the General Council. In general, decisions of the Ministerial Conference and the General Council that require a vote will be taken by the majority of the votes cast; however, in the case of an interpretation of the WTO Agreement or the MTA, the decision will be taken by a three fourths majority.

The Uruguay Round Agreements will address each country's trade, environment and sustainable development needs in a balanced and equitable way. The former Director-General of GATT, Sutherland, observes:

> All of these benefits are real and important. Every nation now needs an effective trading system, but especially so the small and poor. They have it. Everyone will also gain from the huge package of market access results even if they did not get every concession they were seeking from trading partners—it is the biggest market access deal ever negotiated.
>
> The importance of the Round can be seen in terms of the boost it gives to job creation; to development; to investment; to economic reform; to the rule of law.

On the other hand, Caldicott regards URA as the new global imperialism:

> The Uruguay Round was designed and planned by some of the world's most powerful transnational corporations (TNCs), 70 per cent of which are American based, in order to enhance their unimpeded access to global resources, cheap labour, and unrestricted markets. The TNCs have cleverly managed a new orchestration of the world economy, thus introducing a subtle and dangerous form of global imperialism. This new imperialism will provoke and legitimise rampant consumerism in developed and developing countries, and uncontrolled exploitation of the earth's natural resources. It will initiate destruction of trade unions, violate environmental laws, destabilise indigenous cultures and communities, increase the gap between the world's rich and poor, and possibly evoke national and international unrest in a world armed to the teeth with nuclear and conventional weapons.

The truth lies somewhere in between the fantastic optimism of Sutherland and emotional outbursts of Caldicott.

Serious injury was supposed to mean a significant overall impairment in the position of a domestic industry. Moreover the concept of 'market disruption' was introduced in GATT in 1960 as legitimising the use of discriminatory restrictions against imports from specific countries—DGC in particular. The acceptance of this concept opened the way for the establishment of a discriminatory regime of the MFA against DGC exports of textiles and clothing, which has never ceased to expand in product and country coverage since the 1960s. Hence the concept of 'market disruption', a denial of the growing competitiveness of DGC in international trade. Further, no compensation would be required for actions taken under this concept, unlike the concept of 'serious injury'. Article 4 of the Agreement on Safeguards now defines 'serious injury' to mean a significant overall impairment in the position of a domestic industry and the determination of the existence of a threat of serious injury shall be based on facts and not merely on allegation, conjecture or remote possibility. In considering questions of 'market disruption' account shall be taken of the interests of the exporting country, especially in regard to its stage of development.

My policy recommendations and conclusions are explained in this Section. The so-called 'free-market mechanism' of the existing world order of global capitalism does not reflect natural economic laws. These laws have been made, managed and manipulated by DC since the fifteenth century. Also they can be drastically changed without seriously affecting the development of global economic relations as a whole. The crucial accomplishment of the URA has been to tackle those areas where the absence of international consensus had frequently given rise to trade disputes and tensions. Hence the most important specifications are to be found in the Agreements, more honoured in the breach than in the observance, on Safeguards, Subsidies and Countervailing Measures, Anti-dumping, Agriculture, and Textiles and Clothing. Governments of the North felt no serious obligation to abide by the rules. Recent trends toward protectionism, discrimination, bilateral deals, regional arrangements, and cartel-like 'orderly marketing arrangements' were obvious and hence greatly damaged GATT's cornerstone, the most favoured nation (MFN) or non-discriminatory principle. This principle provided that each GATT member would grant automatically, unconditionally and without any compensation, any privileges or favour.

I am not going to argue about the rhetoric of these Agreements. But I still have significant doubts about the implementation of these Agreements. The most powerful North countries in North America and Western Europe will not choose to implement the proposed rules of URA in the interests of open, free and fair trade. From the historical experiences, even the benefit of the doubt cannot be given to these countries that they will abolish their protectionist regimes in the immediate future. Developing countries, on the other hand, did not want the MTN leading to rules and commitments that would inhibit the growth of their infant and still unborn service industries. They thought that most North countries would seek concessions and threaten retaliation on trade in goods to get their way on rules on trade in services or to force Japan to import more beef from the USA. The aggressive pursuit of Japanese markets in this fashion is causing damage to Australia; if trade had been liberalised under GATT, Australia would have outcompeted both Japan and the USA.

Ruggiero has been appointed as the Director-General of WTO. He secured the post by defeating two other candidates, South Korean trade minister, Chul Su Kim, supported by Asia and Australia; and the former Mexican president, Carlos Salinas de Gortari, supported by the USA and Canada and Latin America. But given the criticism the USA heaped on Ruggiero who was labelled as 'too protectionist' and 'too European', and given that good relations between the USA, the EU and Japan are important for the smooth functioning of WTO, the future does not look too promising. The global trade system could be facing more fragmentation if the major trading nations enter into bilateral or regional arrangements and hence fail subsequently to multilateralise the implementation of URA as required by the WTO's agreed norms. It will be interesting to follow the resolution of the disputation between the USA and Japan with respect to the unilateral sanctions imposed by the superpower by WTO in coming months.

The biggest losers of URA will be the least developed among the DGC, particularly in sub-Saharan Africa, who currently receive preferential treatment under schemes such as the Generalised System of Preferences (GSP). the Lome Convention, and the Mediterranean Agreements. They will have to pay more for their necessary (a) food imports which will be more expensive in the absence of subsidies to the agricultural sector, (b) medicines and services and (c) technology because of the proposed TRIP and TRIM. In the absence of substantial foreign aid to these countries, trade liberalisation may not be of much benefit to the least DGC. The erosion of preferential margins following the URA will reduce the standard of living of the least developed among the DGC. The abolition of all special and differential arrangement for DGC will not allow the necessary time for diversification of the export favours it granted to the products of any member country to like products from all other countries. Repeated violations of this principle by some North Countries lead many to believe that GATT cannot be depended on to do much good for DGC.

The URA will establish new MT rules in the fields of agriculture, intellectual property and trade in services. It will extend the scope of

MT rights and obligations to include such diverse aspects as professional qualifications and the movement of persons and electronic data across national frontiers, thus making them legitimate subject-matter for inclusion in MTA.

DGC must be prepared to tackle two issues which will be exploited by DC in the near future—first, better environment and second, labour standards—if they are to avoid future conflicts in trade negotiations. Although the GATT panel ruled that trade restrictions imposed by the USA against tuna imports from Mexico contravened GATT rules, the restrictions were defended on the ground that Mexican tuna fishing resulted in the killing of more dolphins than allowed under US domestic law. Last year trade ministers in Marrakesh agreed to establish a new Committee on Trade and the Environment under the WTO. Many supports of protectionism in North will keep on arguing that low environmental standards in DGC give an 'unfair' advantage in global trade—a case of eco-dumping. I am not sure whether the DGC replies, (a) that environmental standards could be achieved through raising income through more international trade liberalisation policies and (b) that if DC are really interested in maintaining their desired environmental standards, the rich countries must increase their aid to DGC to reduce the costs of implementing the accepted standards of proper environmentally sound policies. These replies are not necessarily accepted by DC.

Trade Unions in the North will be more convinced that low labour standards enable DGC to keep labour costs low, thereby conferring 'unfair' advantage on them in global trade. The GATT permitted trade restrictions on products made with prison labour, but WTO might extend these restrictions to cover the case of 'bonded and child labour' in the case of the carpet industry. Following the URA there is at present no agreement on the inclusion of labour standards in the future of activities of WTO on account of opposition from many DGC. WTO will get these complaints more and more from North. Consequently environment and labour standard safeguards issues cannot be ignored by either DGC or WTO.

Finally it is worth noticing that in principle URA introduced greater speed and automaticity into dispute settlement procedure under fully integrated arrangements. The normal practice of decision making in WTO by consensus will continue; with varying voting majorities where consensus cannot be reached. It will be interesting to see how WTO will settle the disputation between the remaining superpower, the USA, and Japan, with respect to the unilateral imposition of sanctions by the superpower when Japan refuses to enter into any bilateral managed trade. All the principles of multilateral trade negotiation are on trial by the USA and WTO could not start anything worse than the potential disaster it will be facing during the first year of its existence.

Notes

1 G. Myrdal, *Economic Theory and Under-developed Regions*, London, 1957.

2 *World Economic Outlook*, IMF Publication, April, 1984 and 1989.

3 Debesh Bhattacharya, *The Political Economy of Development*, Calcutta, 1993.

4 F. Castro, *Gramma*, 7 April, 1985.

5 B. Nowzad, 'Differential Trade Treatment for LDC', *Finance and Development*, March, 1978.

6 B. Balassa, 'Tariff Protection in Industrial Countries: An Evaluation', *Journal Of Political Economy*, Dec. 1965. Also see his paper, 'The Tokyo Round and the Developing Countries', *Journal of World Trade Law*, March 1980.

7 K. Morton, 'A Hand worth Playing: Stake of Developing Countries', *The International Trade and Monetary Negotiations*, Overseas Development Council, 1974.

8 See *The Collected Works of J. M. Keynes*, Vol.XXV, *Activities 1940–44, Shaping the Post-War World*, ed. D. Moggridge, Macmillan and Cambridge University Press, 1980.

9 *The Brandt Report—North-South : A Programme for Survival, Pan Asia*, MIT, 1980

10 J. Michael Finger and Andrzej Olechowski, eds, *The Uruguay Round: a Handbook for the Multilateral Trade Negotiations*, A World bank publication,1987.

11 UNCTAD, Trade and Development Reports, 1993 and 1994.

Architecture and Politics in the Construction of New Delhi

Suhash Chakravarty

Essential features of the political strategy that prompted the transfer of capital from Calcutta also influenced the style of architecture and town-planning for New Delhi. The re-unification of Bengal and the transfer of the capital to Delhi must be seen as parts of a larger imperial policy. The Government of India wanted to discover a more stable public opinion than was then available in Calcutta and to use it as the pillar for strengthening the crumbling psychological sensibilities and the ideological edifice of the Raj. Threatened by a runaway Bengali opposition, Hardinge[1] was in search of a fresh mandate. He sought the legitimacy of the Mughals and, accordingly, moved the metropolis of British India into close proximity to Shahjahanabad. Political considerations were reflected in the controversies and discussions around the problems of town-planning and architecture for New Delhi.

Proposals for the re-unification of Bengal became linked to the establishment of a new capital away from the 'pernicious influence of Calcutta's *baboodom*'.[2] The political atmosphere of Bengal was admittedly grave. In terms of organisation, mobilisation and self-awareness the anti-partition and *swadeshi* movements were unprecedented. The period following the partition saw a qualitative transformation of Bengali politics together with the rise of political terrorism and secret societies (*samiti*). The salient features of the agitation could easily remind one of the early phase of the Home Rule movement. It is small wonder, then, that Fleetwood Wilson found no 'little affinity between the Celtic and Bengali races'.[3] A strong impression was left with the administration that a little more provocation might produce an Ireland within the Indian Empire. The political temper of Bengal thus had already had a dampening impact on the administration. It was felt that Calcutta, being the seat of vice-regal authority, had become an object of special care and the pith of Bengali life preoccupied the Government of India to the exclusion of other areas of the country.[4] Carmichael[5] added, much to Hardinge's comfort, that no Bengali inspired him 'into as much confidence as certain Madrasis do'.[6]

Early in 1911, when the Government of India proceeded to make arrangements for the reception of the emperor in Calcutta, Valentine Chirol remonstrated with the viceroy. He was distressed to learn that the emperor was to sojourn in Calcutta. Probably, Madras deserved to be cold-shouldered, he argued, but this did not mean that Bombay ought to be ignored as well. 'Two wrongs don't make a right and it seems to me extremely unfortunate that the most disloyal city in India should be singled out for the king's entertainment.'[7] Before long Butler was prodded into suggesting that the Presidency College ought to be shifted from Calcutta to Ranchi so that the students could remain unexposed to the evil influence of the capital. Lucknow and Banaras, Hardinge exclaimed, offered 'a freer and wider atmosphere than Calcutta'.[8] In Lucknow he found himself assured of the future of the empire: 'I felt that I was in India, which one never feels in Calcutta, and that the people there have a far broader outlook than those *baboos* and *box-wallahs* who think that they are the masters of India.'[9]

Flamboyant Exhibition

Both Hardinge and Crewe[10] had decided to give a positive turn to British policy which might otherwise have dried up in an arid waste of recurring repression and immobility. They had decided to take the initiative. Neither thought of dropping India from the imperial charge. Both were aware of the irksome challenge of the nationalist movement. But they had faith in their ability to manipulate social forces in Indian life. They had coaxed a reluctant Minto[11] into admitting the favourable impact of the emperor, a 'semi-divine being', holding an impressive *durbar* in the Mughal capital. They thought that the King-Emperor, if he came with his retinue of princes and notables, would touch the credulous imagination of a traditional India.[12] Hence Hardinge and Crewe decided in favour of an amphitheatre as the venue of the crowning ceremony and not the *Diwan-e-am* so that there might be a large crowd of spectators[13] and it was they who resolved the lively controversy over the proposed procession, opting for a carriage instead of an elephant *yatra*, which they felt might 'appear unmanly, and so unkingly'.[14] Both felt exalted by the prospect of a flamboyant exhibition of the feudal grandeur of the empire.

The significant decision awaiting their approval was a definite scheme for offering some permanent benefit or a boon designed to fire the imagination and impressionability of the Indian people.[15] Various suggestions were advanced. What was essentially a political move had to be carefully considered. The king had determined to mollify the sentiments of those in India who regarded the partition of Bengal as a tactical blunder. Hardinge claimed that the extremists in India, Paris and London were discomfited by a rumour anticipating a dramatic announcement by the king at the *durbar* which might rally all shades of moderate opinion.[16] It was acknowledged that a recommendation for reverting to the *status quo* could no longer be considered or even entertained. The Congress, it was believed, was veering towards a compromise and might be satisfied if both Bengals could be placed under a lieutenant-governor and if chief commissionerships could be established for Assam, Bihar and Orissa.[17]

Crewe was nonplussed by the official request to institute a lieutenant-governorship for Bengal close to the viceroy's front door. From the unreal detachment of London he was apt to magnify the inconveniences. It would be equally troublesome, he argued, to send the Governor to the interior of the province to find a home for himself.[18] But the final decision, approved by all, was simple and direct. Some modification of the partition had become essential and the proposed scheme was to be camouflaged by an elaborate programme. It was decided that the administrative reorganisation must be accompanied by some adjustments of greater importance so as to overshadow the actual partition re-arrangement, that there must be no appearance of surrender to agitation and that the Muslim population must cordially acquiesce in any change which might be contemplated.[19]

The capital was, therefore, to be shifted to a more congenial site. It was maintained that the Government of India, when in Calcutta, was apt to look at things through binoculars, and when at Simla, the tendency was to reverse the glasses and look at things through the wrong end. In the former case the difficulties were unduly magnified; in the latter they were to some extent minimised. It was, therefore, necessary to insulate the seat of the Indian administration from the disproportionate impact of the most advanced outpost of Indian nationalism. In this context Delhi figured prominently in the official mind.

Delhi had been the capital of many Indian empires and it had been the focal point of the uprising of 1857. Was it not possible to construct the capital of India, it was argued, in the ruins of the earlier imperial citadels? As successors of the Mughals, the rulers fixed their eyes on Delhi. They did this in search of continuity and of escape from the seething movements of Bengal. Delhi would place them at a distance from the noisy Hindu pleaders of Calcutta and their more virulent literary exponents in the Bengali Press.[20] Surrounded by Mahmudabad, Rampur, Darbhanga, the Awadh Taluqdars, the Aligarh movement, the Benaras' orthodoxy and the native princes, the *Raj* would be more amenable to the needs and aspirations of its erstwhile friends, its present allies and its future defenders.

European Opposition

European opinion in Bengal, however, was critical. It saw in it a betrayal of trust, a surrender to 'unprincipled agitation', a breach of faith, a blatant step against the bureaucracy and, hence, an impolitic confession of weakness in the face of brute force.[21] *The Statesman* and *The Englishman* were the two principal spokesmen of the agitation. Their virulence was immoderate and they resorted to every form of opposition to administrative measures.[22] Initially, Hardinge had resolved to ignore it. But the opposition of the Islington Committee to the Delhi project and Ramsay MacDonald's public pronouncements gave the agitation fresh life.[23] In Minto and Curzon[24] it found faithful champions in Britain.

Hardinge was particularly incensed at the wily meddling of men who had little to do with India. Curzon had become, he scoffed, 'a Calcutta Gramophone'.[25] He was certain that Minto, fearful of accusations of running, had hesitated to transfer the capital, though he would have liked to. Hardinge had discerned in the agitation against the transfer of the capital the hands of the Bengal Chamber of Commerce. It was, he jibed, 'a question of *amour propre*'.[26] The Europeans in Calcutta disliked being reduced to the status of provincials.[27] The Chamber of Commerce sent a feeler to the effect that the headquarters of the government be shifted to Simla and the viceroy and his executive council should become what appeared to an irate Hardinge 'a peripatetic circus' perambulating between Calcutta, Bombay and Madras for six months every year.[28]

There was sneaking sympathy for the Calcutta agitation in official quarters who were inclined to offer some minor concession. Hardinge, for example, announced the appointment of an official of the commerce department in Calcutta to look after the interests of the chamber.[29] In June 1912 the chamber raised a hue and cry over the shortage of wagons in the Indian railways. The situation had been strained and the viceroy exasperated.[30] If the Bengal Chamber of Commerce continued its hostility he proposed to extend his patronage to other chambers to oversee the interests of Calcutta. Hardinge suspected that the object of the renewed movement was to induce the government to accept an enquiry by an outside expert who, in all probability, would advocate an abnormal and immediate outlay on railway construction, rendering it impossible for the government to divert adequate funds to New Delhi.[31] The viceroy, though pressurised, refused to yield.

Viceroy Vindicated

By March 1914 Hardinge was able to push Calcutta into an 'absolutely isolated position'.[32] He was also persuaded to give credence to the insinuation that their attitude was due to self-interest and a certain amount of spite. 'If I built a mean capital', Hardinge moaned, 'they would protest against my meanness, if I built a *godown* they would protest against my extravagence.'[33] The agitation crept and crawled to a premature death as Calcutta failed to gain the support of other chambers. The viceroy felt vindicated as he found that all the Indian members of his council 'played up in the Budget debate and insisted on the value of the transfer of capital to Delhi and on the new city being built upon a worthy' scale.[34] It was a significant and amicable performance. As the viceroy gleefully watched, 'the door was slammed in the face of Calcutta boxwallahs'.[35]

In 1914 Calcutta notables, encouraged by MacDonald and Islington, tried to work up an agitation against Delhi on financial grounds.[36] They maintained that money wasted on the construction of Delhi could have been fruitfully utilised for public services recommended by their committee.[37] Hardinge contested the merit of the point. Whatever their recommendations might have been, it was impossible to enlarge the public services immediately. In any case, he claimed, no final decision would be taken on the recommendations during the next three years. The viceroy was peeved by the manner in which the Islington Commission did everything 'to hamper the policy of the Government of India in order to grind their own axe'.[38] New Delhi, he was determined, would be built despite all vituperations.

The chamber of commerce, however, gradually came to recognise the significance of the new deal. In particular, the decision of the government with regard to the establishment of Dacca University and the appointment of Shamshul Huda to the viceroy's executive council were noted with satisfaction. It observed that the re-unification was a political move and that it involved no surrender of the basic imperial interests.[39] Thus emboldened, the government decided to disregard the carping of the two English papers of Calcutta, which were intent on criticising the Government of India no matter what it did. 'If the angel Gabriel came down from Heaven', wrote Butler in disgust, 'the Anglo-Indian press would see in him a Mephistopheles.'[40]

Hardinge concurred with Butler. He concluded that the policy of transferring the capital had been judicious. He was relieved to find his government placed in a 'more accessible and independent position than formerly'.[41] It was closely in touch with the commercial interests of the rest of the country. The viceroy's legislative council was no longer exposed to the baleful influences and propaganda of Calcutta and the government could at last acquire an appropriate perspective of the situation in Bengal.[42] Besides, the native princes had already begun to visit Delhi although they could never be induced to travel to Calcutta.

In this air of optimism, Hardinge pooh poohed Curzon's speech in the House of Lords defending the Calcutta agitation. 'I do not know what Curzon wants, and I doubt if he knows himself', he quipped, 'unless it is to create embarrassment and pander to the voice of the Bengal Chamber of Commerce, who now exercise no influence whatever, and are in reality an object of ridicule to the rest of India.'[43] From England Crewe extended his warm support. He assured Hardinge that he was not prepared 'to make squalid what ought to be splendid or to sacrifice the dignity which ought to belong to the seat of Imperial Government'.[44]

Oriental Splendour

When funds were short, Crewe advised, some economy might be effected by the reduction of the number of apartments, offices, stables, marble columns, mosaic works, etc., which could be erected subsequently but 'not in dimensions or general plan which is rigidly determined'.[45] Besides, the construction should permit growth every year so that the buildings, quite simple in decoration at first, ought to admit, as surplus accumulated from time to time, growth in grandeur for ever. The search for legitimacy appeared to have succeeded at last. New Delhi was to stand in all its oriental splendour as the heir of Shahjahanabad. 'As the buildings rise', the viceroy mused, 'enthusiasm will grow, and when once the Government of India is installed in the new city, the problem will be how to keep the city within proper limits and under suitable control.'[46]

The new city of Delhi was to be the heir of the grand Mughals. It was to reflect the majesty of an imperial metropolis, portray the confidence of matured authority. Above all, it was to possess an Indian air about it. Crewe and Hardinge were unanimous about the project. The architects fought intensely among themselves with regard to planning and design; Ramsay MacDonald[47] polemicised against it. But Hardinge surveyed the area across the ridge of the Raisina village overlooking the ruins of monuments of forgotten glories and decided the norms. These the architects, engineers and financiers adopted with a sense of participation in an imperial undertaking.[48]

Of crucial concern was the selection of the site. The committee[49] was not bound to a particular site and it was free to look in any direction. A fairly extensive study was made. This took many things into account: paramount needs of health; questions of sanitation; sentiments and costs; commercial, civil and military requirements; room for expansion; facilities for internal and external communications and adequate water supply. The Committee then submitted its report.[50]

The site across the Jamuna, despite its fine view of the fort and river frontage, was rejected because of its flat land which was subject to perpetual flooding and because of its unhealthiness and its featureless landscape. The western site, situated on the higher ground with a healthier climate, offered different problems. The new city at that site would have been entirely cut off from the view; the view it would offer would be that of factories, chimneys and railway lines. The minarets of the Jama Masjid and all the monuments of the Hindu and Muslim rulers would be hidden below the skyline. The committee was apprehensive that perhaps no-one would recognise it as Delhi.

Northern Site

The claim of the northern site was more convincing. Here, sentiments and associations alike combined to make it particularly the Delhi of the British. 'Fifty years ago', wrote an official correspondent, 'we consecrated this area with blood. In late years, in three successive durbars, we have identified it with all the colours and pageantry of royal magnificance.'[51] But the site did not meet the requirements of modern military strategy. Its position was not suitable for siege battery and it was not the model for a great city.

The historic ridge was the only picturesque feature in a monotonous landscape but it was believed to be far too sacred to be desecrated by the creation of modern buildings. The site was, however, rejected primarily on political considerations. 'It is that Indian public opinion, which rejoiced in the transfer of the capital', Hardinge expostulated, 'would have been alienated entirely if a city had been built which would have still further perpetrated and enhanced the memory of the events of the Mutiny, since all loyal Indians regard the episode with shame while disloyal Indians regard it as a defeat.'[52]

Towards the southern outskirts of the existing Delhi the committee found what Hardinge required: the site of seven cities of the earlier days, rich with crumbling ruins. The construction of the city would have meant a judicious incorporation of some historical relics and edifices into a modern town. Higher up on the slopes of the hills, lying to the right of the road to the Qutb, there was virgin soil. On one side of the ridge, the imperial capital ought to dominate the plains, and on the other side, the cantonment could muster the immediate military power by which that domination would be maintained.

Land, primarily agricultural, was fairly inexpensive, immense possibilities for expansion lay to the south and the south-east. The

Jama Masjid was close by and the approach from the old city would be magnificent. Open space between the two cities would provide ample room for all forms of sports and recreation. Talkatora was rejected on account of difficulties in alignment, and Malcha for being situated too far away from the Mughal Delhi. The Raisina Hill was selected by an impatient Hardinge and was forced on the town planners.

Originally, the axis of Government House was to face the Jama Masjid and the processional highway was to terminate at Shahjahanabad. Thereby the citadel would reflect the projected continuity of political authority from Mughal India to British India and underline the basis of unimpaired loyalty. But the celebrated Kali Masjid and the overcrowded Paharganj stood in the way of this design. The axis, accordingly, had to be altered slightly in order to acquire a fresh terminal point.[53] The whole panorama of Indian history, as reflected in the legendary Indraprastha and the Pathan-Mughal monuments of Purana Qila, was to provide, in the revised plan, a permanent view.

Thus would the representative of the emperor preside over the new Parthenon on the Raisina Ridge. Visions of imperial hegemony predominated. 'In India we must have space', Butler echoed Hardinge, 'we could not breathe with a Champs Élysées.'[54] With something like the Ring in Vienna and with a road down the centre flanked by graceful trees and room for large throngs, New Delhi was to be laid out for the future. Government House not only retained a good view of Jama Masjid, but also views of Indraprastha, Humayun's Tomb, the Lodi Tombs and Safdarjung's Mausoleum. It would hold a commanding position in the whole scheme. The imperial city was to draw legitimacy from the remnants of the empires of the past.

The Central Motif

Government House, the Council Chamber and the Secretariat were to be the central motif of the whole layout. In the first plan, Government House alone was to adorn the Raisina Hills. Owing to the intervention of Baker, the Secretariat buildings, in the final plan, climbed up the hill to be placed along with Government House on an even platform primarily to be viewed by the inhabitants as a spur of the hill itself. The Council Chamber reciprocated by climbing down the hill in keeping with the spirit of the Montagu-Chelmsford Act. Behind the hill a raised forum was to be built, flanked by the Secretariat buildings and terminated at its western end by the mass of Government House with its wide flight of steps, porticoes and dome, leading the imagination from the machinery of government to the moving vice-royalty itself.

The forum would be approached by the inclined ways on its north and south sides. The axis of the main avenue would centre on the gate of Indraprastha, the site of the oldest of all the Old Delhis. 'Right and left the roadways go', welding into an empire of today and merging with 'the empires of the past', and in the south into the Cathedral. At the intersection of this avenue with the main axis a place would be formed, around which would be gathered the buildings of the Oriental Institute, the Museum, the Library and the Imperial Record Office. To the south-east would be the park area in which stood the ancient monuments of Safdar Jang's Makhbara and the Lodi Tombs.

The axis running north-east from the Secretariat buildings to the station and towards the Jama Masjid would form the principal business approach to Old Delhi. At the railway station another place was to be laid out, around which would be grouped banks, shops and hotels with the post office in symmetrical relation to the station. The Connaught Place would faintly resemble the classic colonnade of Nash's Regent Crescent and the Royal Crescent of Bath. To the south-west of the station would lie the houses of the local bureaucrats and the residence of the European clerks.

For Indian Clerks

Between Talkatora Garden and Paharganj would be the area for Indian clerks, the press and other government establishments. From the baboo quarters it would be fairly convenient for ageing clerks to retire in the housing complex of Karol Bagh. In normal circumstances, with easy access to the North Block from Talkatora park area, provisions for market and temple and playing field, the Indian clerks would have a self-sufficient existence away from the European settlement and its shopping and recreation centre. To the south of the forum was to be placed the residence of the commander-in-chief. Round the vice-regal estate and the forum were to be grouped the residences of the members of council, the secretaries and other officials.

The principal avenues, in addition to the main avenues, enclosed the imperial centre and were the outer main sinews of the frame, thus giving the effect of a spider-web pattern. The commemorative column, situated on the axis, was the focal point of the roads and avenues on the parkway. The palaces of the princes around the focal point, the India Gate, would provide the outer periphery of 'fat Indians' settled as an important buffer between the white settlement and the distant old Delhi.

The Acropolis, the wide straight processional ways, the central vista connecting the Secretarial blocks, vice-regal palace and the Cathedral, the seclusion of the necessary undesirables of the city in the baboo quarters with adequate civic amenities, the vast squares of the official facades, the diagonal avenues, the places and squares with radiating roads, the strict proportion and ratio maintained between the height of the buildings and the width of the roads, the shadowy mystique of the bungalows of the white sahibs, the clever linkage between the Assembly, the Chamber of the Princes and the Federal Court hidden by the imperial colonnade almost encircling in strict privacy the potential hankerings of the natives for a parliament—all these provided the ceremonial furnitures of the imperial city which separated the rulers and the ruled.

A remote, awful and majestic pomp was to confront an admiring and applauding audience for ever. The *folie de grandeur* of the ruling class was impressive; the layout of the city, accordingly, was symmetrical and the desire for secluded existence in a closed society was ever increasing. Patrick Geddes' relentless plea for a generous dose of humility and reverence in dealing with human dwellings and social sentiments, his unfailing voice against the attempt to impose the Western cult of streets on the defenceless bank of Jamuna and his sharp polemics directed towards the 'death-dealing Haussmannism' of the 'callous, contemptuous city bureaucrats at Delhi' were irrelevant for the planners who wrote off Geddes as a 'crank who does not know his subject' but was 'apt to talk much "rot" in an insulting way'.[55]

Lanchester's reports on the Delhi project were discarded despite initial promise. The new imperial consciousness approved of another cantonment city submerged in a lush green garden. The importance of the roads and streets were foremost in the mind of Bordie despite the fact that Lutyens dismissed his strong provincial accent and his slow but steady mind whose rigidity could only match that of Lutyens himself. Captain George Swinton, a self-taught expert on town-planning, was the chairman of the committee. He was appointed because of his ability to appreciate the importance of military strategy, the problems connected with possible mob violence, and his remarkable skill in insulating the key zones, the axis and the principal poles of the city as well as its railway terminal, from a possible assault by an unruly public.

Lutyens, a domestic architect, understood little of it; he derided the pomposity of Swinton and his elaborate ornate style of expression. Swinton, however, continued to preside over the committee despite Lutyens' spitefulness and his intrigues. Swinton's paper on the military and security problems of the proposed city became the basis of the search for the site. Lutyens himself came to terms with a capital complex on an Acropolis in his own way.

Roman Colonial Establishment

True, no industrial revolution had created a suffocating cramped atmosphere in Delhi for a Haussmann to demolish the relics of the past and open up a congested community to fast moving vehicles and armed brigades, ready as ever to combat urban guerrillas behind intricate barricades. And yet, it was a repeat performance in modern terms of a Roman colonial establishment: a military bureaucratic order in a camp placed on a raised platform and insulated from the plebeians by a stratified city structure based on the coordinating principles of town-planning worked out by Baron Haussmann.

Peter the Great's Moscow was not expected to be a typical Russian city; it was more a European establishment and it offered a false promise. Washington was to provide an international image to the United States as different from the purely American city of New York. Rio de Janeiro was the Brazilian capital; Brasilia was meant to symbolise the nation's unfulfilled visions and hopes. Pretoria reflected the architectural endeavours of a closed community which sought to reinforce an arrogant racial aloofness by manipulating a Dutch tradition and the natural surroundings of a rugged surface and by invoking the spirit of the Roman Empire. Canberra, a safe colonial settlement of white people, was conceived as a simple spider-web pattern; considerations of hygiene, communications and security rather than those of tradition or cultural legacy occupied the imagination of its contemporary administrators and its architects.

New Delhi was to represent the determination of Britain, a European imperial power in Asia, to demonstrate the permanence of its rule in India. The poet in Lytton had dreamt of it way back in the 1870s. The grandiose imperial scheme of Curzon encompassed it. Hardinge sought to concretise that mission. In visual effect, sentimental importance and sheer magnitude the New Delhi of Lutyens was to surpass both Pretoria and Canberra.

Intense Controversy

There was intense controversy over the style of architecture to be adopted for New Delhi. The European experts wanted to apply Western forms. The problem, as Hardinge saw it, was whether or not it was possible to assimilate that style of Indian architecture which preceded the Mughals, i.e., the Pathan style.[56] It was essential, he urged, that the Secretariat and other government buildings should be of a broad and simple style of architecture within an 'oriental motif' that should blend itself with the Government House which ought to be a 'dignified and noble monument'.[57]

Hardinge emphasised that pure Eastern or pure Western architecture would be quite out of place. As he put it, 'we have to find a blend'—a broad style of architecture with Indian motifs throughout. Hardinge did not approve of the architects' opinion that such a style would clash with a Government House built in the Palladian manner.[58] It was with this in view that he insisted on the Government House in Lutyens' plan having a flat gilt dome, these being the 'oriental touches that should be appreciated in the country'.[59] The concept of a gilt dome on the Government House came from what Hardinge had seen on public buildings in Russia.[60] He seemed quite inflexible in his views. When seriously questioned on aesthetic grounds by the experts, a harassed Hardinge began to despise them and misprize their advice. He found Lutyens as 'obstinate as a mule' with fixed ideas; he would not touch the concepts of Eastern architecture 'with a pair of tongs'.[61]

Both Lutyens and Baker were slurred as absolute philistines with no regard for Indian sentiments and traditions.[62] Lutyens, according to Hardinge, was obsessed with Italian Renaissance architecture, having come to India with the utmost scorn for all Indian art forms, even calling the Taj 'rubbish'.[63] Brodie, Hardinge derided, had determined to construct a wider avenue than existed in any other city.[64] Swinton Jacob appeared to Hardinge to be a far more reasonable person than the two architects; he was amenable to Hardinge's ideas. Jacob's inclusion in the team of Lutyens and Baker would avert, Hardinge thought, the possible attempt at 'transplanting Whitehall on the banks of Jumna'. But Jacob was bullied and hectored by Lutyens and the retired engineer declined to join the team. Lutyens triumphed.

Hardinge recommended to the architects the ruins of Mandu near Indore, raised by the Pathans, as a model of solidity and breadth of treatment. A reproduction of St Paul's Cathedral or a glorified Apsley Home in the plains of Delhi would be, he contended, a 'magnificent monstrosity'.[65] Hardinge was confident of the popularity of the new imperial architecture of Delhi. 'I have no hesitation in saying that I have absolutely the whole of India at my back in wishing that the new city should be built in accordance with Indian sentiments. I do not by this mean that the town should be built of highly ornate or Hindu architecture; but my idea is that it should be a fine broad style with minimum of decoration, but that decoration should be of the purest and most ancient Hindu ornament. Opinion in this country is quite unanimous on the subject and after all who are we building for—the Indian or the British public?'[66]

He took keen interest in the minutest details of the work. He participated in the selection of the site; he approved the initial sketches; he suggested changes in style; argued with his architects; he saw to it that 'private and eccentric fancies' were not allowed to predominate;[67] he strove to make sure that New Delhi, 'the King's God-child,' should not be too cheaply provided for;[68] he arranged financial support for the construction and he even insisted on economy when required, approving the reduced proportions of the new rooms in the revised plan.[69] He was convinced that the structure of Government House ought to be a worthy residence of the king's representative. The internal decoration, though of the simplest kind, should be a prolonged effort and a succession of viceroys ought to take in hand each year the decoration of 'one piece of capital importance' so that the house would become something of which 'England and India can be proud'.[70]

The Imperial Idea

The government did not cavil about financing the construction of

New Delhi. The viceroy's council endorsed Butler's opinion on this score. They agreed that it was of imperial importance that things ought to be done on a big scale, 'something which will impress India with our determination to stay here and to govern the country on Imperial lines'.[71] One of the objects of the move to Delhi was to develop the imperial idea and this was the primary reason in favour of the selection of the site. In support of its gigantic proportions Butler urged Hardinge to overlook the various financial arguments advanced against it and insisted that the imperial idea could not be ignored. One could not lose sight of the greatness of the opportunity.[72]

Hence, departmental considerations were to be subordinated, Butler pleaded, to the imperial conception. 'What I am afraid of', he warned, 'is that the biggest thing in our time and one of the biggest things for centuries is going to be spoilt by being carried out in too small a spirit.'[73] New Delhi ought to be a big thing, he added, and he was sure that public opinion would veer round to support its expenditure. Nothing could be too high for it. 'It is so important in my mind to have these central buildings worthy of an imperial city that I would agree to this. We have to make New Delhi one of the world's wonders and topics of discussion.'[74] Crewe had already sanctioned the scheme. Nobody in London would suggest, he underlined, that the Board of Agriculture, for instance, must 'go on being housed in a variety of sunless dens because the Post Office wages were being raised'.[75]

It was assumed that the Government House of Calcutta would not be the best model for the viceroy's mansion. Despite its great suitability for entertaining, it was not enough of a residence to be an ideal palace.[76] Crewe wanted to see the atmosphere of Hampton Court and the Louvre reproduced.[77] Montagu pleaded for a fine chamber for the legislative council with the appearance of a parliament house. Of course, Montagu[78] did not desire to extend parliamentary powers to that body. But he felt that the council's growing importance would eventually demand such recognition.[79] Crewe demurred. He endorsed the view of Hardinge that names and forms contained subtle significance in politics of which Montagu seemed quite innocent. 'A number of your advanced politicians', wrote Crewe to Hardinge, 'who are the reverse of sedition (sic) regard a Parliament as the goal of their ambition; and ... no colour should be given to any notion that we favour their hopes.'

Thus, 'a good council chamber with a separate entrance to go with it' was officially prescribed. 'It is going to be the Viceroy's Council', Crewe decreed, 'and the circumstances and surroundings should emphasise the fact.'

Laboured Exercise

The planning was a laboured exercise involving constant shuffling of ideas, plans and blueprints and by the end of the initial phase of the programme Lutyens agreed to be persuaded. 'Of course, my idea is a compromise between the Eastern and Western architecture', Hardinge elucidated his views, 'and the purists who demand entirely Western architecture will call it a bastard style, and if I am forced between the two, I would reluctantly have to agree to a purely Eastern rather than a Western style of architecture.'[82] Hardinge was anxious to remind his audience that it was Indian public opinion that had to be considered.

Lutyens could not altogether comprehend the reverence with which the oriental style of architecture was mentioned. He had examined the wonderful architectural creations of India which 'were full of strange ideas' which 'shook his Western sense of truth'.[83] He was struck by the 'monotonous riot of nonsense' with an 'occasional lapse to really fine proportions and great simple conceptions'.[84] Amber failed him. Mandu disappointed him.[85] Agra and the Taj teased him.[86] 'The Mogul architecture', Lutyens was ready as ever to pass judgement, 'is cumbersome, ill-constructed building covered with a veneer of stone marbles and very tiresome to the Western intelligence.'[87] The whole country was full of shrines, mosques and temples. 'But nothing,' a vexed and disturbed Lutyens lambasted, 'was built to last, not even the Taj.'[88]

He conceded that some of the buildings including the Taj had inscrutable charm but the effect, he hastened to add, was ephemeral. 'When in ruins the buildings—especially the Mogul—are bad ... and have none of the dignity a ruin can have that has been the work of any great period.'[89] He was annoyed by the official 'tongue wagging' in defence of the Indian style.[90] He did not believe that there was any Indian architecture or any great tradition—'they are just the spurts of various mushroom-dynasties'.[91] The Indians, he argued, knew the Italian mouldings and used them. But they had no knowledge of anything other than two-dimensional work.[92] One could not do a portrait or a statue, he pontificated, in Mughal or Hindu style.[93] There was no scope for sculpture within the accepted line of Indian architectural conceptions. 'It is all tommy rot.'[94]

He found in them a fanciful use of stone and marble. But they had been used not for structural purposes but for decoration. 'When they built', he contemptuously dismissed the impressive specimens of Indian architecture, 'it is exactly like children's bricks.'[95] He was scornful of the suggestion that some Mughal structural forms and innovations ought to be applied in the buildings of New Delhi. Splendour of size, Lutyens claimed, of the Mughal architecture was offset by their sheer vulgarity.[96] 'Why should we throw away', he raised his voice, 'the lovely ... Greek columns for the uncouth, careless, unknowing and unseeing shape' of the Qutb Minar?

India had turned him 'very Tory and even pre-Tory feudal'.[97] Hardinge's attempts to separate architecture from the problems of town-planning was viewed by him with suspicion and concern.[98] The Indian bureaucracy, despite its acknowledged efficiency, shocked him by its remarkable 'tastelessness'.[99] The viceroy's desire to evolve an Anglo-Indian architecture seemed to him meaningless sentimentality.[100] If one wishes to be logical, Lutyens asserted, one cannot get anything that might be termed Indian 'for all that they have done is constructively illogical and its very essence is fairy tale elusiveness got by veneers'. If the desired effect was to be achieved, he derided, it ought to have been accompanied by 'Tom Tom music'.[101] 'I shall try and start an Indian school and Western traditions must be there for as Englishmen we cannot help it', wrote Lutyens, 'and then send the Indians straight to nature and let them invent and conventionalise to fit given space and teach them to think in three dimensions ... to build in stone for stone and wood for wood.'[102]

Universality of Beauty

Beauty, Lutyens claimed, was ageless, dignified and simple. It had, he expatiated, no nationality. It was universal in its application. The daffodil was, Lutyens pointed out, beautiful in itself; the rose had no nationality and a rainbow had no distinct sentimental idea.[103] He was not opposed to adaptations and adoptions in art: 'I adopt a pattern with a great tradition', but creation 'is not the easy method of a mean copyist'.[104] He was a stickler for perfection and perfection was rational.

It had to be worked out methodically. It ought to be self-contained and also functional.[105] It could not afford to live in peace with the superfluous excursions of an unrestrained mind. It had to be trained, tutored and measured.

A great work of art should not stand in need of the imagination of a poet or his well-framed sentences for expression.[106] It must speak for itself. 'Artistic endeavour', he developed the theme in one of his letters to Baker, 'means hard labour, hard thinking on every line in three dimensions and in every part; and no stone can be allowed to slide.... Every stone being mentally handled must become enveloped with such poetry and artistry as God has given you.'[107] Treatment of a particular style, he added, must be conducted with a sense of sympathy. It must always provide a 'new care and invention'.[108] Certainly, it was not a mean game and could not be dealt with light-heartedly.

Lutyens was adamant about using a chaotic architecture in the name of local style. Indeed, he did not mind being 'scolded for not being Yorkshire in Yorkshire'.[109] 'In modern work—unlike the old—the thinking machine is separated from the labour machine so that the modern architect cannot have the same absolutism as we gave the old man when the thought and labour came from the same individual.'[110] Designing and thinking, he emphasised, were specialised areas of work and he insisted that they ought to remain so.[111] As specialised 'super thought', modern architecture would remain distinctly 'beyond the conceptions of the architect's fellow man—the poet'.[112] An architect, he underlined, could only express himself in his buildings, as a painter could only express himself in his paintings, a sculptor through his clay and a poet through his words.[113]

Extreme Positions

As he had to drive his point home against the determined and aureate vocabulary of Baker, who had arrived in India with well-conceived notions of a modern Acropolis towering over the plebeians of the Raj,[114] Lutyens was often forced to adopt extreme positions. He was aware of the limitations of his own expression. The poet could inspire the artist, he wrote in haste, but 'once inspired, he should go to work, not dissipate his inspirations and emotions by absorbing more poetry'.[115] The formulation might not be neat, the point was made nevertheless.

He approved of Baker's flexibility and his adaptibility but not his irrational excursions into abstract theory. These often spoilt the natural light and shadows and disturbed the 'majesty of atmosphere on a perfectly geometrical shape'.[116]

Rationality involved a sense of order and priority, a mathematical discipline and simplicity of form. It operated against impulsive and accidental decisions. Every line and curve was, he reminded Baker, 'the result of force against impulse—through the centuries'.[117] Nothing substantial in art, he added forcefully, was done by accident. As an architect he would not shake off the responsibility that nature imposed on man. He would not avoid the demand made on his intelligence by the compulsions of topography and contours by saying, 'Why not build on another site?'.[118] He was in favour of incorporating the details of the environment and natural surroundings within his drawing board. He would recommend a plan only if it was 'well digested and worked-out'.[119] To make a good house in which people were happy would be a great thing; but to make a house which would satisfy the architect's own critical judgement was greater.[120] What was most rewarding, however, was to work for a near approximation to refinement.

Lutyen's treatment of the site was singularly interesting. He was eager to ensure that the roughness of the material did not destroy the texture and the articulation of the building, did not make it crude and bald.[121] He impressed on Baker that to make a desert bloom with roses 'would in the first place destroy the desert'.[122] He, therefore, wanted to put an oasis in the desert, an enclave bounded on all sides by walls forming a great room sharply contrasting the desert beyond. The room becomes, as a result, not a temporary camp but an eternal city.[123] He found the highest attainment of European art in the simple forms, mathematical restraint and noble ideals of Greek art.[124]

John Ruskin[125] was his ideal in conceptualising standards of arts and values. He was keen to execute in reality the staggering contrasts so vividly described by Ruskin. He was enamoured by the concept of a desert rolling up 'and stopped abruptly by walls—within them gorgeous culture in marbles, bricks, textiles and roses!'[126] Indeed, he had inherited in full measure the legacy of John Ruskin and William Morris.[127] They had sought to demolish the Benthamite criticism of the fine arts and architecture.[128] Every bit of interior decoration and every household article, however utilitarian, should possess a beauty of its own. Outside the home, the eye should be soothed and nourished by well-designed structures of every sort, their architecture being both functional and complementary to the natural features of the landscape. Lutyens followed their tradition.

There was, however, some confusion in Lutyens' conceptions; his ambivalence was that of his era. The factories, foundries, collieries and smoky cities and the encroachment of the ignorant multitude upon contemporary culture disturbed his devotion to the Ruskinian view of art which was inseparable from the artist's concern for society. William Morris had reinforced it. But the environmental ugliness unfortunately pushed Lutyens on to an élitist position claiming an uneasy autonomy of beauty.

Genius Tempered

By the time he arrived in India a 'Lutyens house' had begun to mean something. It was generally assumed that he was about to be recognised as the Pontifex Maximus and Architect Laureate of the British Empire. Following the tradition of Butterfield and Philip Webb, Lutyens believed that living architecture must have more in it than imitated style. The Central Square of the new Hampstead Suburb anticipated a large conception.[129] In India his genius was tempered and mellowed. In the vice-regal palace, Robert Byron wrote, 'The coloured and theatrical facade of Islam has been annexed to a more intellectual, three-dimensional tradition of solid form and exact proportions—the tradition of Europe'.[130]

The result was an impressive palace—large, arrogant and yet lovely. Its climax was the extraordinary dome rising suddenly from the middle of the house. The principles of lines, proportion and mass were fused with local traditions—the Buddhist railings of Sanchi and Pathan compositions of Mandu. Nevertheless, it remained distinct, imperial and 'a monumental affirmation of temporal power'.[131] It creates, all the same, the impression of the simple perspective of a Doric temple. There was no attempt to storm the heavens, no effort to defy the laws of gravity and matter. Instead, it reflected a sonorous Greek balance and a sense of harmony with the universe.[132] Lutyens had worked out the great fusion of the West and the East despite himself. The Parthenon of New Delhi's Acropolis echoed an Athenian tradition as it was judiciously placed to welcome the rising sun every morning.

Lutyens' collaborator, Herbert Baker, had developed a distinct individuality of style. In South Africa he had taken advantage of the existing Dutch tradition to produce a mature colonial architecture. He was successful in introducing in the governmental architecture in Pretoria a sense of dignified aloofness and stern grandeur, reflecting the racial arrogance of a small ruling community. His treatment of the rocky and uneven surface of Pretoria was original.[133] His model, the Athenian Acropolis, had particularly attracted him to the architectural possibilities of an imposing propylaeum along the slopes of a rising surface.[134] He lacked Lutyens' intensity and attachment to pure forms. He was also less rigid than his colleague in his devotion to precision, simplicity of lines and the beauty of the interplay of light and shadows in architectural creation. Theory came first.

Eclectic Mind

Architecture, Baker seemed to conceptualise, was to reflect that theoretical proposition.[135] It was not for him to concern himself with whether the work of art represented faithfully all the rules, conventions and aesthetic sensibilities of a true form. The political principle of the organic unity of a universal empire envisaged by Cecil Rhodes, Alfred Milner and Lionel Curtis had a lasting impact on his eclectic mind.[136] He drew strange and exotic parallels between Western and Indian or Eastern forms. He favoured primarily the ideas of the classic style of Jones and Wren and their followers in the eighteenth century, as being easily adaptable to the needs of a tropical climate.

Without losing its more 'eternal' qualities and their finer national characteristics, this style, he considered, should gain in freedom and power of expression by adaptation and expansion to the needs of a more southern climate. It might be asked, Baker argued, whether the employment of such styles ruled out any of the noble features of Indian architecture. 'There should exist, therefore', he contended, 'in the style which has been advocated, all the necessary elements ready to the hand of an architectural alchemist.' But to the artist's creative power must be added 'sanity of judgement'. He must avoid a Whitehall on the one hand, and a Palace of Delight which must come perilously near a 'White City' on the other.[137]

His architecture must have the spirit of life and growth, so that it may take root in the country and not prove 'sterile and unproductive in the generations to come'. He pleaded that there should be no conscious attempt to initiate originality.[138] A frank acceptance of modern methods and materials, he insisted, ought to be adopted. 'The controlling mind must heat and weld into his orderly conception all that India has to give him of subtlety and industry in craftsmanship.'[139] Finally, the architect must arouse imperial consciousness in artists and craftsmen of the empire to create an imperial hegemony in arts and leave a permanent record in the 'history, learning, and romance' of India.[140]

Baker had a marginal difference with Lord Curzon who believed that some form of the classical style was well-nigh inevitable. The form of this style, he maintained, had been most widely adopted by the English in India, and the best examples were to be found at Calcutta and Madras. It might be described, he added, as a colonial adaptation of the Palladian style. Referring to the Renaissance architecture of Spain, the visible legacies of the Moors, Curzon wondered if the architects of New Delhi could find in India models which would 'give a similar Indian flavour, a native aura to the forms of the West'.[141]

For Herbert Baker an imperial architecture, though derived from the classical tradition, encompassed other styles and other concerns as well. He wrote to Lutyens at the very outset of their collaboration: 'It must not be Indian, nor English, nor Roman, but it must be imperial. In 2,000 years there must be an imperial Lutyens tradition in Indian architecture, as there now clings a memory of Alexander.' In a letter to *The Times*, 3 October 1912, Baker spelled out what he conceived to be the proper style for the New Delhi. At its heart lay a political objective: that of capturing in stone the spirit of the British Indian Empire. 'The new capital', he wrote, 'must be the sculptural monument of the good government and unity which India, for the first time in its history, has enjoyed under British rule. British rule in India is not a mere veneer of government and culture. It is a new civilisation in growth, a blend of the best elements of East and West.... It is to this great fact that the architecture of Delhi should bear testimony.'

Arrogant Gesture

Baker believed that Indian sentiments could be satisfied by grafting onto classical architecture certain decorations expressing the myths, symbols and history of the Indian people. Thus, spacious colonnades, open verandahs, overhanging eaves or cornices, small high window openings, the *chajjas* or wide-projecting shade-giving stone cornices, the *jaalis* or pierced stone lattice screen to admit air and not sunshine and *chhatris* or free-standing pavilions breaking the long horizontal lines of the flat roof were incorporated in his scheme for the two Secretariat blocks.

The result was a patronising and arrogant gesture by a self-righteous political forum.

In common with Lutyens, Baker disparaged the Indo-Saracenic tradition. But his objection was guided by political considerations. This style, he argued, simply did not have 'the constructive and geometrical qualities necessary to embody the idea of law and order which has been produced out of chaos by the British Administration'.[142] Classical architecture, on the contrary, had 'eminently the qualities of law, order, and government'. European classicism, then, was to be offered a predominant place in New Delhi, primarily because of its political expressiveness. The architects wrote in their joint report: 'The old buildings that have most impressed the imagination of mankind are those raised upon an eminence, such as those of ancient Greek cities and the Capitol at Rome'. The whole capital complex, as they conceived it, stood from 'one high platform expressing the importance of the unity of the viceroy with his government', a unity which would grow in importance with the constitutional evolution of the future.[143]

For Baker, schooled as he was under Rhodes and Milner, architecture served always a political purpose. For Lutyens the Empire was incidental. And yet, while working within the context of an imperial architecture, he imbibed unconsciously Baker's political principles of imperial norms. Emotionally Baker belonged to the generation of empire-builders who found in the 'moots', 'eggs' and 'omelettes' of Lionel Curtis' Round Table a permanent solution to the complex political problem of the empire.[144] The viceroy's house represented the Parthenon on the Acropolis and reflected the divinity of Zillulah. It would be somewhat obscured by the dominant secretariats, themselves more ornate than the Government House; and they would represent the propylaeum of the Acropolis. The Athenian complex in its Indian setting offered Baker the architectural blueprint for the capital of a reinvigorated

British India. While Lutyens wanted to reject Indian elements as childish and ornate, superficial and ephemeral, Baker extended his moderating influence to soften Lutyens' austere and uncompromising standard.[145]

Eerie Uncertainty

The project was undertaken in an age of crisis in imperialism. The Raj was still full of life but the extravagant strides of Curzon had given way to the cautious steps of more circumspect and less spectacular administrators. The high noon of the empire was past. The prospect of a gloomy evening must have disturbed the minds of the rulers in their pensive moments.[146] The situation was dangerous but not desperate; it was explosive and capable of taking unpredictable turns but it was not threatened with extinction. The government was autocratic but it was conscious of the necessity of striking a new equilibrium of relationship between the ruler and the ruled. The Montagu-Chelmsford declaration was still to be announced and there was an element of eerie uncertainty in Whitehall and the Writer's Building. But there was no lack of eagerness to guide Indian policy along a more durable strategy and to impart to it a sense of purpose.

The arrangement of the buildings on the Raisina Hills betrayed the ideology of those diffident middle class imperialists and their endeavour to offer a programme of an organic development of the empire. As a poet and a painter, Baker, a close associate of the Round Table Group, loved words, worked out a political principle in theory and then turned to his drawing-board. Lutyens abhorred theory. He sniffed at Baker's continual preoccupation with the Round Table and sought beauty for its own sake. But the amateurs in charge of policy-making listened to Baker, who in his turn, eagerly lent his ears to the set of phoney theories and well-meaning phrases of an Oxford don. With an almost humourless sincerity he executed what appeared to Lutyens a well-hatched plot to overshadow the supreme achievement of his career by means of a pair of sentimental secretariat buildings commanding (as an oversized propylaeum) a gradient processional way.

Baker pleaded that a remote aloofness maintained by the Government House affirmed a desirable political idea. It invested the unapproachable and dignified vice-regal authority with an element of semi-divine mystique. But he could not meet Lutyens' trenchant architectural arguments. For two decades Lutyens grumbled, protested and petitioned. Experts sympathised with him but a succession of viceroys encouraged, backed and confirmed Baker. They sought to use architecture as a political front which was brought into line with economic and administrative activities of the government.

New Delhi was to be a subliminal advertisement of the might of the Raj; it was to embody the determination of the British to hold India. But the Acropolis on the Raisina Hills merely remained a reconnaissance flight sent to unknown territory and it brought back unexpected and unwelcome reports.[147] The viceroys desired to use art exclusively to implement Britain's so-called social mission in India. But official resolutions and leading articles in *The Times* offered a poor diet. New Delhi, which turned away from all social contents, tendencies and possibilities, ran the risk of dying of malnutrition. It became blind, deaf and mute.

Notes

1 Charles Hardinge of Penshurst, 1st Baron (1858–1914), British Diplomat and Viceroy of India (1910–16).

2 Hardinge to Butler, 3 February 1912, Hardinge Papers, Cambridge University Library.

3 Carmichael to Hardinge, 1 April 1912, Hardinge Papers.

4 See, for example, Craddock to Hardinge, 27 April 1913, Hardinge Papers.

5 Lord Carmichael of Sterling, the first Governor of Bengal (1912–16).

6 Note by Fleetwood Wilson, Fleetwood Wilson Papers, India Office Library, London.

7 Chirol to Hardinge, 9 June 1911, Hardinge Papers.

8 Hardinge to Sydenham Clarke, 26 February 1912, Hardinge Papers.

9 *Idem.*

10 Robert Offley Ashburton Crewe-Milnes, 1st Marquess of Crewe (1858–1945), British Statesman, Secretary of State for India (1910–15).

11 Gilbert John Eldiet-Murray-Kynynmound, 4th Earl of Minto (1848–1914), Viceroy of India (1905–10).

12 Secretary of State to the Viceroy, 16 December 1910, Hardinge Papers.

13 Secretary of State of the Viceroy, 27 January 1911, Hardinge Papers.

14 Secretary of state to the Viceroy, 23 December 1910, Hardinge Papers.

15 *Idem.*, also Hardinge to Crewe, 25 January 1911, Hardinge Papers.

16 *Idem.*

17 Hardinge to Crewe, 20 February 1911, Hardinge Papers.

18 Secretary of State to the Viceroy, 13 December 1910, Hardinge Papers.

19 Note, by Fleetwood Wilson, Fleetwood Wilson Papers.

20 Duke to Hardinge, 1 April 1912, Hardinge Papers.

21 Bayley to Hardinge, 12 February 1912, Hardinge Papers.

22 Butler to Hardinge, 16 February 1912, Hardinge Papers.

23 Sydenham Clarke to Hardinge, 6 March 1913, Hardinge Papers.

24 George Nathaniel Curzon of Kedlestone, 1st Marquess (1859–1925), Viceroy of India (1898–1905).

25 Hardinge to Sydenham Clarke, 26 February 1912, Hardinge Papers.

26 Hardinge to Crewe, 7 February 1912, Hardinge Papers.

27 *Idem.* 28 *Idem.*

29 Hardinge to Crewe, 9 May 1912, Hardinge Papers.

30 Hardinge to Crewe, 19 June 1912, Hardinge Papers. 31 *Idem.*

32 Hardinge to Crewe, 12 March 1914, Hardinge Papers. 33 *Idem.*

34 Hardinge to Crewe, 2 April 1914, Hardinge Papers. 35 *Idem.*

36 Hardinge to Crewe, 19 February 1914, Hardinge Papers.

37 *Idem.* 38 *Idem.*

39 *Idem.*, also Butler to Hardinge, 7 February 1912, Hardinge Papers.

40 Hardinge to Butler, 3 February 1912, Hardinge Papers.

41 Hardinge to Crewe, 2 April 1914, Hardinge Papers. 42 *Idem.*

43 Hardinge to Holderness, 13 May 1914, Hardinge Papers.

44 Crewe to Hardinge, 13 March 1914, Hardinge Papers. 45 *Idem.*

46 Hardinge to Crewe, 2 April 1914, Hardinge Papers.

47 James Ramsay MacDonald (1866–1937), British statesman, one of the founders of the British Labour Party.

48 Crewe to Hardinge, 13 March 1914, Hardinge Papers.

49 It included George S. C. Swinton (Chairman), John A. Brodie and Edwin L. Lutyens.

50 See the final report of the Delhi Town Planning Committee in Crewe Papers 1/9 at Cambridge University Library.

51 'The New Delhi' from a correspondent in India, undated 1912, Hardinge Papers.

52 Hardinge to Crewe, 24 April 1913, Hardinge Papers.

53 Hardinge to Crewe, 6 June 1912, Hardinge Papers.

54 Butler to Crewe, 1 August 1912, Hardinge Papers.

55 Lutyens to Baker, 10 August 1912, Lutyens Papers.

56 Hardinge to Crewe, 11 July 1912, Hardinge Papers.

57 Hardinge to Crewe, 16 July 1912, Hardinge Papers.

58 Hardinge to Crewe, 22 August 1912, Hardinge Papers. 59 *Idem.*

60 Hardinge to Crewe, 8 October 1912, Hardinge Papers. 61 *Idem.*

62 *Idem.* 63 *Idem.* 64 *Idem.*

65 Hardinge to Crewe, 22 August 1912, Hardinge Papers.

66 Hardinge to Crewe, 29 August 1912, Hardinge Papers.

67 Hardinge to Crewe, 2 April 1914, Hardinge Papers. 68 *Idem.*

69 Hardinge to Crewe, 22 August 1912, Hardinge Papers.

70 Hardinge to Crewe, 2 April 1914, Hardinge Papers.

71 Butler to Hardinge, 1 August 1912, Hardinge Papers.

72 *Idem.* 73 *Idem.* 74 *Idem.*

75 Crewe to Hardinge, 13 March 1914, Hardinge Papers.

76 Crewe to Hardinge, 5 June 1912, Hardinge Papers. 77 *Idem.*

78 Edwin Samuel Montagu (1879–1924), British politician, Parliamentary Under-Secretary to the India Office (1910–14), subsequently, Secretary of State for India (1917–21).

79 Crewe to Hardinge, 5 June 1912, Hardinge Papers. 80 *Idem.*

81 *Idem.*, also, Hardinge to Crewe, 24 July 1912, Hardinge Papers.

82 Hardinge to Crewe, 22 August 1912, Hardinge Papers.

83 Lutyens to Emily Lutyens, 16 February 1913, Lutyens Papers, Royal Institute of British Architects, London.

84 Lutyens to Emily Lutyens, 15 April 1912, Baker Papers.

85 Lutyens to Emily Lutyens, 16 December 1912, Lutyens Papers.

86 Lutyens to Emily Lutyens, 25 April 1912, Lutyens Papers.

87 Lutyens to Emily Lutyens, 7 June 1913, Lutyens Papers.

88 Lutyens to Emily Lutyens, 3 June 1912, Lutyens Papers. 89 *Idem.*

90 Lutyens to Emily Lutyens, 2 December 1913, Lutyens Papers.

91 Lutyens to Emily Lutyens, 3 June 1912, Lutyens Papers.

92 *Idem.* 93 *Idem.* 94 *Idem.* 95 *Idem.*

96 *Idem.*; Lutyens to Baker, 14 June 1913, Baker Papers.

97 Lutyens to Emily Lutyens, 14 April 1912, Lutyens Papers.

98 Lutyens to Emily Lutyens, 26 December 1912, Lutyens Papers.

99 Lutyens to Emily Lutyens, 26 May 1912, Lutyens Papers.

100 Lutyens to Emily Lutyens, 31 August 1912, Lutyens Papers.
Lutyens to Emily Lutyens, 29 August 1912, Lutyens Papers. 101 *Idem.*

102 Lutyens to Emily Lutyens, 14 April 1912, Lutyens Papers.

103 Lutyens to Baker, 23 December 1910, Baker Papers.

104 Lutyens to Baker, 29 January 1911, Baker Papers. 105 *Idem.*

106 Lutyens to Baker, 29 January 1911, Baker Papers. 107 *Idem.*

108 *Idem.* 109 *Idem.* 110 *Idem.* 111 *Idem.* 112 *Idem.* 113 *Idem.*

114 Baker to C. Hill, 18 March 1916, Baker Papers.

115 Lutyens to Baker, 29 January 1911, Baker Papers. 116 *Idem.* 117 *Idem.*

118 Lutyens to Baker, 23 June 1910, Baker Papers. 119 *Idem.*

120 Lutyens to Baker, 28 December 1910, Baker Papers.

121 Lutyens to Baker, 29 January 1911, Baker Papers.

122 Lutyens to Baker, 26 December 1904, Baker Papers. 123 *Idem.*

124 Lutyens to Emily Lutyens, 14 April 1912, Lutyens Papers.

125 John Ruskin (1819–1900), writer, critic and artist, who more than anyone else influenced the public taste of Victorian England.

126 Lutyens to Baker, 26 December 1904, Baker Papers.

127 William Morris (1834–1896), English poet, artist, manufacturer and socialist, whose decorative designs revolutionised Victorian taste.

128 Richard D. Altick, *Victorian People and Ideas*, London, 1974, pp.281–8.

129 Robert Lutyens, *Six Great Architects*, London, 1959, p.168.

130 Cf. *Country Life*, 6–27 June 1931. 131 *Idem.*

132 H. W. Janson, *History of Art*, New York, 1962, Part I, Ch. 5, pp.76–122.

133 Lutyens to Baker, 28 December 1910, Baker Papers.

134 H. Baker to C. Hill, 18 March 1916, Baker Papers. 135 *Idem.*

136 Lutyens to Emily Lutyens, 23 November 1913, Lutyens Papers. Lutyens to Emily Lutyens, 27 November 1913, Lutyens Papers.

137 H. Baker to C. Hill, 15 April 1916, Baker Papers.

138 *Idem.* 139 *Idem.* 140 *Idem.*

141 Note of New Delhi, 15 April 1913, Curzon Papers.

142 Baker to Lytton, 13 May 1913, Baker Papers.

143 Baker to Lutyens, 6 February 1912, Baker Papers.

144 Cf. Papers of the Round Table Group and those of Lionel Curtis, Bodleian Library, Oxford.

145 H. Baker to C. Hill, 18 March 1916, Baker Papers.

146 Sydenham Clarke to Hardinge, 2 December 1910, Hardinge Papers.

147 Cf. Ernst Fischer, *Art Against Ideology*, London, 1969, pp.56–62.

The Schooling of English Workers' Children, 1780s-1880s: Some Themes

Bruce Fulton and Robert J. Hind

> *I have no quarrel with the student of history who brings to his work a touchingly childish, innocent faith in the power of our minds and our methods to order reality; but first and foremost he must respect the incomprehensible truth, reality, and uniqueness of events.... To study history one must know in advance that one is attempting something fundamentally impossible, yet necessary and highly important. To study history means submitting to chaos and nevertheless retaining faith in order and meaning. It is a very serious task ... and possibly a tragic one.*
>
> Hermann Hesse, *The Glass Bead Game*

National Contexts

Any sketch of the educational experiences of English workers' children —which in this instance excludes those who attended workhouse, factory, industrial and ragged schools and those who had no schooling— must remain partial and tentative. Well before their postmodern demise, certainties were—or should have been—elusive. Workers' views about religion, politics, familial obligations, etc., contrasted sharply. Living and working conditions in specific trades, within and between urban districts, between town and country, between rural districts close to and distant from industrial or mining expansion, between a 'close' and open parish in geographical proximity, varied greatly. Economic expansion and innovation, which differed markedly in place, chronology and intensity, continued to alter these variations. Comparisons of regional studies demonstrate the dangers of general conclusions. Young wine was also stretching the old social skin: 49 per cent of the population was under the age of twenty in 1821. The growth of population (in millions) 7.5 (1781), 15.9 (1841), 26.0 (1881), its changing location and increasing urbanisation—about a third (1801), a half (1851) and three quarters (1901)—kept augmenting local diversities. Urbanisation obviously had many common characteristics. The 'multiplicity of urban systems and varieties of internal urban', which 'safeguarded capitalism by scattering rather than exposing it as a target', should nevertheless not be overlooked.[1]

Historiographical debate about English education remains too rudimentary and about English history too vigorous and too unresolved to address adequately in a short article. There is, however, a degree of consensus about such frameworks as the nature of economic expansion —and its indebtedness to women and children, a significant component of the first industrial proletariat, as much as to male artisans and factory workers. Simplistically, statistics support perceptions of declining real wages until the 1820s, with subsequent improvement. England's most rapid economic expansion, between the 1840s and 1870s, remained distinctly uneven. Amelioration of workers' circumstances then stemmed primarily from greater stability of employment. Late nineteenth-century declining food prices—30 per cent less in 1887 than a decade earlier—generated further improvement. These developments occurred notwithstanding the removal of most paternalistic legislation by the early nineteenth century. This removal intensified workers' hardships caused by trade-cycle fluctuations and, some would argue, by the later adoption of free-trade policies.[2]

Religious renewal was transforming English society with a dynamism almost equal to that of industrialisation and demographic growth. If middle-class charity flowed primarily from religious impulses, it was also an insurance premium for social stability that workers' progressive alienation from institutional Christianity accompanied. Many of them never entered a place of worship by the 1850s. 'Churches, both established and dissenting, have become either aristocratic or middle-class societies.' Pompous officials, fashionably-dressed congregations and ministers' partially comprehensible language made workers who attended feel uncomfortable. Too frequently they were made to feel that they were

> but poor men. The pastor visits the more wealthy ... members, but he crosses not the poor man's door. Weight and importance are attached to every suggestion of a rich member, but it is almost a piece of presumption

for a working man to express his opinions at a church meeting.[3]

Workers' belief that they had no right to belong to a congregation unless they could contribute to its incessant fund-raising solicitations 'was probably more fundamental than the "respectability" barrier' in keeping them away. Attitudes some workers expressed in *The Parson's Creed* probably lacked denominational precision.

> Money. O money thy praises I sing,
> Thou art my Saviour, my Lord and my King.
> It is for thee that I preach, for thee that I pray,
> And give praises to God three times in the day.

The menace of pauperism dogged workers throughout the transformations of lives effected by waves of industrial and demographic growth and religious renewal. Despite such substantial material benefits as a 60 per cent increase in real wages between the 1860s and late 1890s, poverty remained 'a regular feature of the life of almost all working families ... especially in old age or before young children started earning'. A mother might be indebted throughout her early married years and begin to repay her debts as soon as her children started to work. J. S. Rowntree showed (1899) that even with the most judicious expenditure every 'labourer who has as many as three children must pass through a time, probably lasting for about ten years, when he will be in a state of "primary" poverty; in other words when he and his family will be *underfed*'. 'Abhorred as it was because of the stigma that attached itself to the bereaved family, a fifth of the population could expect a pauper's burial as late as 1900.'[5]

If one became a 'burden to society', one ceased '*pro tanto*, to be a free' person and came under the jurisdiction of 'a special code of laws applicable' to one's social condition. Until 1865, laws of settlement and removal impeded the mobility of labour and made the 'parish of settlement a prison, and every other parish a hostile fortress'. The need to obtain a certificate to leave one's parish was an onerous provision, particularly when one or a few individuals owned a parish. In such cases parishioners 'may be said to be the property of the proprietor[s], and to be sold with the land. The labourer has but one chance of emancipation; to quit the country. But this chance is very small'. A measure of 1795 augmented the security of workers who had found employment where they lacked settlement rights but gave no protection from compulsory removal if they needed poor relief. This provision constituted a 'cruel and costly instrument of tyranny and arbitrary oppression' of working people.[6]

The manner in which parishes fulfilled their poor-law obligations before 1834 was local, expedient and unpredictable, ranging from the humane to the inhumane. From the late eighteenth century the Webbs maintained that parishes acted with greater clemency. Perhaps they did. Some young orphaned children were nevertheless transported in closed waggons from London to provincial centres where they were apprenticed, sometimes for fourteen years, to harsh manufacturers. Presumably to remain independent of poor-relief, lace-making families of *fin de siecle* Nottingham, for instance, enforced and endured the 'seasoning'—their terminology albeit more customarily applied to slaves' revitalisation after transhipment—of their children. Healthy breast-fed infants were drugged

> in order to prevent their cries interfering with the protracted labour by which they [parents] strive to obtain a miserable subsistence. The infants became pale, tremulous, and emaciated, the joints and head enlarge, they become listless, and death at length steps in to [great numbers of] their relief.

In this declining trade, wives' and children's labour had become indispensable. Children who survived until they were three or four began to recover once the laudanum, etc., was discontinued. They then had to work as soon as they could use the needle. 'Almost all the families employed' were 'supported, more or less, by the labour of their children.'[7]

The poor law amendment act of 1834, 'perhaps the most sustained attempt to impose an ideological dogma, in defiance of the evidence of human need, in English history' associated poor relief unequivocally with indignities and degradation in a way that had not generally been the case earlier. This brutal measure 'arguably made the deepest, most bitter, and widespread impression upon the labouring classes, rural and urban'. To avoid pauperism, workers at Bolton in the 1840s made 'all sorts of shifts and sacrifices to live above it, by pledging their furniture and even their clothing; their food is deficient, their physical strength greatly reduced, and the rate of mortality is rapidly increasing'. A suicide note affirmed: 'I can face poverty and degradation no longer, and would sooner die than go to the workhouse, whatever may be the awful [eternal] consequences.' One lad, placed in a workhouse in 1842, returned to his beloved Sunday school in his workhouse clothes. The other pupils, almost as poor as he, taunted him and drove him away. He was 'tainted with a social leprosy'. Half a century later, when poor-law administration had lost some of its severity, Charles Booth noted workers' 'absolutely universal' aversion to the workhouse and their acceptance of 'almost any amount of suffering and privation' to avoid it. At least 90 per cent of unemployed people, for instance, never approached the poor-law authorities.[8]

Workers, more particularly that proportion—between a tenth and a third—who lived in poverty, imposed onerous sacrifices upon themselves and their families to avoid pauperism. Far more 'physical deprivation and suffering ... [lay] buried in silence ... clothed in the garb of respectable poverty' than street beggars or statistics suggested. Concealment of 'the unrecognised destitution that preys, like a consuming ulcer' possibly outweighed savage social indictments in official documents and helped to mislead mid-nineteenth-century writers. They generally assumed that most workers had an income sufficient to provide adequate housing and food, and to cover life's vicissitudes. In 1858 Lord Shaftesbury claimed that there was 'no good reason whatever for pauperism'. The annual report of the Charity Organisation Society (1876) depicted good wages as the norm.[9]

Earlier assumptions that overlooked structural factors and perceived individual worker's behaviour as the cause of social ills persisted. The propensity to discriminate between the deserving and undeserving poor therefore remained constant. Middle-class charitable endeavour, frequently uncoordinated, acquired impressive dimensions. In the 1870s it probably gave more money to alleviate the rigours of the independent poor's lives than the poor-law authorities spent on paupers. Investigations of workers' circumstances, inspections of their homes and families, primarily by legions of middle-class women and town missionaries, preceded assistance usually given to those who struggled to survive without resort to poor-relief or begging. This approach, which provided opportunities for the surveillance of all the poor and for homilies to the allegedly undeserving, exploited the indomitable independence of many poor people and utilised it to subordinate them to the rich.[10]

The Schooling of English Workers' Children

The functioning of social forces amidst the complex interacting realities touched upon previously limited working people's capabilities in relation to their children's schooling. Working people were legally free to determine all matters relating to it until the enforcement of compulsory instruction in inspected schools after 1880. Poverty and employers' insatiable appetite for child labour, however, qualified this freedom. If parents did not educate children at home—and seven per cent did in part of Bristol in 1851—they could choose between two sets of schools. Voluntary day schools founded by some richer people for workers' children as a charitable endeavour gradually formed one network of schools. Their limitations, however, owed much to the limited financial support they received from other prosperous people. The principal recommendation of the monitorial system, for instance, was its alleged cheapness. Only 5 per cent of income tax payers subscribed to voluntary schools in 1863. Alternatively, there were schools conducted exclusively by working people. These schools testified both to cultural autonomy and, partially, to a different type of charity. Without the school-pence paid by their peers, there were families of wives with incapacitated husbands, widows, elderly, maimed or handicapped individuals, colourful drinking companions, etc., who would otherwise often have been subjected to the poor-laws. These two totally different types of school remained clearly distinct. Sunday schools—virtually but surprisingly omitted from English literature—did not.[11]

Sunday Schools

Some Sunday schools remained under an individual's—say an Anglican clergyman's—control. Many, perhaps originally non-denominational, eventually became linked to a specific congregation. Even in the 1780s, however, when Robert Raikes, Sarah Trimmer (with the Queen's approval) and Hannah More founded and propagated the merits of Sunday schools under middle-class jurisdiction, working people, male and female, autonomously founded and maintained Sunday schools. The latter's proliferation stemmed from the initiatives of impecunious, peripatetic preachers of 'new' dissent and individual working people. These schools, technically illegal until 1811, disconcerted the established lay élite, established clergymen, 'old' dissenters, and even the government between 1799 and 1800 because they escaped their supervision. From the 1780s working people made it impracticable for richer people to control the Sunday school movement comprehensively through the power of the purse. Increasingly from 1800 workers' religious activities and willingness to act as unpaid teachers and officials greatly weakened constraints richer people would otherwise have exercised about an institution's foundation, location, size, ethos, curriculum and—while recognising that for about five decades only workers' children were in attendance—its social composition.

The propertied classes primarily sought children of the poorest of the poor for Sunday school instruction. When Town Meetings, usually summoned by magistrates, requested support, subscriptions and officials for the establishment of Sunday schools, they had them in mind. Managers then appointed paid teachers, visitors and inspectors and compiled regulations that often required parents to establish their deserving-poor status and abide by the institution's regulations. Results tallied with ascertainable objectives in qualified ways. Social problems often increased; less impecunious children tended to replace the poorest; middle-class interest and subscriptions waned; the inputs and influence of working people might increase—or schools might close. Within a decade no-one at Gloucester would aid Robert Raikes's Sunday schools; none existed there before his death in 1811; but six poor men later re-introduced them.[12] From the 1830s, the Ragged school movement indicated the failure of richer people to induce the poorest children to attend Sunday (or day) schools.

In many Sunday schools, class cooperation and local participation of a type unknown in day schools emerged. If their voluntary teachers, many of whom were working people, had received modest payment, the cost would have exceeded that of the national contribution to day schools until 1859. Expenditure, as for accommodation, printed material, etc., increasingly depended upon numerous small donations after 1800. Annual gatherings at 'owr sermons' for what were implicitly 'owr' schools facilitated this change. They became associated with processions of teachers and pupils, the latter of whom sang in a public place at Sheffield from 1813. Three years later each school there began to carry banners which became larger and more elaborate—and probably inspired later trade union practice.[13]

Regional efforts of organisations such as the Sunday School Union increased foundations and indicated the strength of and varied balances within social collaboration. At Newcastle upon Tyne heated discussions commenced in 1814. Two years later 35 schools with 600 teachers, by 1831 142 schools with 2,826 teachers, indicated this organisation's achievements in the north-east. The Sunday School Union's protagonists circularised every church and dissenting chapel. Its members met, tried to persuade and counselled congregations that would receive them. If successful, its visitors, who travelled 3,000 miles annually in pairs at their own expense, gave regular advice. Many schools, backed by the organisation's bookshop and book depository, created clothing and benefit societies to facilitate poorer children's attendance.[14]

Notwithstanding crude methods, appalling use of the Bible, and sometimes long hours, children inundated Sunday schools where, especially in nonconformist establishments, a 'considerable working-class takeover of control' occurred. Children attended primarily because of parental directives. Working people's initiatives and efforts helped them to transform and utilise numerous Sunday schools for their own purposes. Many became 'vehicles of a domesticated, internalised, working-class evangelicalism for teaching a mixture of religious beliefs and more practical lessons'. The schools' values of orderliness, punctuality, industry and cleanliness reinforced those which respectable workers instilled at home. Less than 4 per cent of Sunday school pupils were ever attached to a denomination and subsequent obligations remained light. For fifty years less than 1 per cent of pupils in Birmingham returned to immediate membership of church or chapel. Young adults were nevertheless known to sing hymns learnt in Sunday school while they worked in factories. Anniversary celebrations showed how thoroughly the culture of working people had incorporated many Sunday schools—the only religious institution that the majority of them patronised—and how acceptable this form, presumably because so much of it came from themselves, was.[15]

Sunday schools helped meet other aspects of the demand of the poor for education noted by parliamentary investigators in 1818. Until 1870 it would be difficult to determine what basic skills their children gained from day and from Sunday school. Numerous schools as at Leeds, Sheffield, Manchester, etc., taught reading and writing from their inception. By the 1830s writing came to be regarded as a wrongful use of the Sabbath and its teaching contracted perceptibly. Evening instruction in writing and arithmetic, sometimes supplied by Sunday schoolteachers in pupils' homes, often increased. Some nonconformist establishments, however, did not change and numerous children, as at Bolton, switched Sunday schools *en masse* for continued tuition in writing.

The contribution of Sunday schools to basic literacy was nevertheless impressive for almost a century. Pressure upon some Sunday schools was so great that once children could read the Bible they had to leave immediately to make room for others. In Birmingham more than three quarters of all the teaching of reading and a smaller proportion of writing was apparently effected in Sunday schools until 1868. The teaching of basic skills by these institutions continued there after the passage of the 1870 act. Many children's day-school experience was discontinuous, irregular and remarkably brief. Their early age of entry into the rigours of employment or apprenticeship virtually guaranteed the loss, in part or entirely, of whatever skills had been attained previously. Sunday schools enabled these skills to be regained, improved and increased. Edward Baines asserted excessively than an 'average of about *eight years* of Sunday instruction for every child of the working classes' supplemented their brief day tuition.[16]

Between 1818 and 1851 the population increased by 54 per cent: but the attendance of children at Sunday schools quintupled and at day schools doubled. Other features of Sunday schools augmented their greater acceptability. Particularly in urban districts the choice of schools allowed parents to exercise their social or religious sensitivities and have their children taught with the similarly situated or the like-minded. Although the established church had 671,224 more day pupils than its rivals in 1855, it had 497,225 fewer Sunday school pupils. In rural districts, where social supervision was more practicable than in towns, the chapel and its Sunday school were the only means by which working people and their children could avoid some of the injunctions of squire and parson.[17]

For several generations no middle-class children attended Sunday schools. Thenceforth they rarely entered establishments which workers' children overwhelmingly dominated: they tended to be concentrated in the Sunday schools of prosperous congregations. Consequently, they neither distorted the Sunday school tuition of workers' children nor alienated their parents. These consequences became discernible in the 1840s when middle-class children began to attend day schools founded for workers' children and received markedly preferential treatment. Sunday school classes of about ten pupils were a far cry from monitorial schools in which one adult could allegedly teach a thousand children. Sunday schoolteachers, moreover, were more likely to be homely and zealous, to empathise with their charges, and to use local dialects than were the staff in middle-class provided schools. Voluntary day schools frequently gave 'No admittance except to Officials, Teachers and Scholars'. They too often treated parents, whose wishes they disregarded, as pernicious influences upon their children. The Sunday School Union meanwhile emphasised the importance of enlisting parents' full sympathies. Only a proportion of schools were in connection with this organisation but its attitude towards parents appears to have been widespread in nonconformist establishments from the 1820s. Numerous Sunday school buildings were unsatisfactory but were analogous to those of day schools run by working people. They were probably warmer and less intimidatory to workers' children than purpose-built voluntary schools.[18]

Voluntary Day Schools

Day schools the upper and middle-classes provided for workers' children had features more intimidatory than their buildings. Their charitable basis constituted a major deterrent. Workers felt 'strong aversion', a 'universal repugnance to the humiliation of gratuitous education' because it affixed a stigma to everyone who accepted it. Workers found demeaning the obsequious deference and gratitude that pupils had to display publicly to the schools' benefactors. Perceived in the 1840s as 'savages in the midst of civilization' whose education was essential to protect persons and property, they had one offered stamped with 'the brand of pauperism'. Consequences that stemmed from schools' original orientation persisted beyond the commencement of state involvement in education (1833) and the education act of 1870. Governmental aid to schools was arguably a 'species of outdoor relief [i.e. not in the workhouse] administered by a central office'. In some districts the poor-law authorities denied parents relief if they had a child at school. In others, impecunious parents received school fees not exceeding three pence a week per child from the poor rates in the late 1870s. Conversely, local vagaries sometimes rated poor rural people 'to give the pauper children in the workhouse an education they could not give their own'.[19]

Charitable schools offered a 'modicum of learning which they think fit for the children of working people, and in which parents have no voice'. Religious organisations, the Anglican National Society and the nondenominational British and Foreign School Society (BFSS) from the 1810s and other denominations later, established schools that concentrated overwhelmingly upon religious education until the 1830s. National schools had prescribed readers replete with references to God, the Commandments, the Thirty-Nine Articles and eternal life. British schools used scriptural extracts exclusively as reading material until 1839. All their teaching was 'strictly subservient to the communication of scriptural knowledge'. Both types of voluntary school admitted that they emphasised religion 'lest they [children] should know anything else'. Both inculcated obedience to constituted authorities, inured children 'to habits of order and subordination' and, allegedly, prevented idleness and intemperance, reduced crime and poor rates, and made their pupils 'faithful and honest in their service to others, and happy and contented in themselves'. Until about 1840 many schools supplied no secular instruction other than reading. They appeared to discern 'something evil in knowledge, which required to be counteracted by bad theology'. Some offered 'nothing that could be of use either in this world or the next'.[20]

Voluntary schools initially gave free tuition. Many began to charge small weekly payments in the 1820s—to prevent some schools closing when subscriptions declined and, ostensibly, to encourage more regular attendance. Parents' fees supplied about a third in 1836, three times more than state expenditure in 1853, and more than a quarter in 1861 of voluntary schools' costs. Horace Mann and other analysts nevertheless claimed in the 1860s that 80 per cent of the population depended for its instruction upon the charity of the richer classes. Parents' payments similarly went unrecognised by committees of management upon whom they continued to have neither representation nor influence. No working person was a school trustee in 1842. Educationalists and Her Majesty's Inspectors (HMIs) did 'immense harm to the development of ... parents as promoters of education'. HMIs had to be acceptable to schools' lay and ecclesiastical patrons and to the leadership of the denominations.

They promoted substantial curricular and methodological improvements. They also reinforced existing managements' authority over parents too often burdened with increased fees as middle-class subscriptions and interest waned. Warwick's National schools' income from voluntary contributions declined from 83 per cent in 1847 to 15 per cent in 1879.[21]

The richer classes' notion that the schooling of workers' children was a charity, a privilege graduated by social position, and was best supplied by them persisted until the 1870s. If these certainties rested upon the premise that ignorance should defer to knowledge, the basic issue was different. Although children in voluntary schools received a subsidised education, most parents paid. Payers normally selected payees and expected some consideration from, and influence over, them. The richer classes, socially and progressively separated geographically from people whom they regarded as degraded by their dependence upon daily labour, refused to ascertain their educational needs, elicit their opinions, or consider their prejudices. They treated parental representations as impertinences. Parents, reduced to a 'state of pupillage', had to accept what was offered or 'keep their children at home'. From 1880 even this option was withdrawn.[22]

Isolated middle-class arguments recommending parents' inclusion on schools' committees appeared from the late 1850s and even in the Newcastle Commission's report but were completely ignored. Parental cooperation, the principal cause of a school's success consequently remained largely absent. Numerous managers tried to sever natural familial bonds. Frequently, a teacher's first lesson, 'a sad necessity', warned children to beware of their parents and 'look with disgust, if not horror, at the filthiness and abominations of their own homes'. Managers also excluded 'a large mass' of children by over-strict regulations. National schools, for instance, required girls as well as boys to have short hair. The shearing of beautiful curls preceded admission—and indicated a beneficiary of semi-charitable instruction.[23]

Schools' managers selected and directed teachers and stood between them and parents. National organisations with which most of their schools were eventually associated trained the fully qualified teachers, a minority. From the mid-1810s, residential training triumphed. It more thoroughly facilitated the inculcation of appropriate religious principles and the removal of presumption from trainees. Yet in Francis Place's opinion, the BFSS could have produced better educated teachers much more cheaply by soliciting available, more advanced, non-residential applicants. Schools' managers frequently regarded teachers as missionaries. They opted for inferior ability and attainments to secure religiously oriented staff. Pupil-teachers (from 1846) had their religious and moral development guided by the trained teachers to whom they were apprenticed and, by the terms of their five-year indentures, reviewed annually by clergymen, schools' managers and inspectors. Male teachers in National schools were reputedly masters in every sense of the word. Most voluntary-school teachers apparently did not mix socially with parents.[24]

Parents loathed the cheap and allegedly efficient monitorial system which prevailed in many voluntary schools until the 1850s and thereafter survived with considerable tenacity. Parents withdrew children because 'a parcel of boys' taught them. The average age of monitors never exceeded eleven in the 1840s. Reluctant, neither necessarily trained nor paid, they frequently left, to be replaced by others. Encouraged by parents, pupils often stayed at home or left school when monitorial duties loomed. Parents 'didn't wish theirs to teach t'others; they wanted them to learn'. Monitors reportedly hit, misrepresented other children, and promoted bribery, corruption and favouritism by soliciting presents. A 'positive hindrance' to schools' effectiveness and attendance, they also 'communicated religious truths in a manner ... calculated to make religion permanently distasteful'.[25]

Social changes made some voluntary schools inaccessible, others less attractive to working people. By the late 1850s, British schools, in Matthew Arnold's opinion, recruited mainly from the middling classes of society. Most had also become dominated by a specific nonconformist congregation. Wesleyan Methodists were an extreme case of congregations that became prosperous and whose schools excluded workers' children by charging high fees, the highest of all in the 1870s. They nevertheless continued to receive governmental money, originally intended to assist the poor, even when they 'really did not know what to do with it'. From the 1830s, some voluntary schools began to attract middle-class children because they offered the best and cheapest available instruction. Amongst working people were those who objected to this phenomenon even when tuition remained free or fees for their children remained unchanged. In most Derbyshire schools, for instance, labourers' children did not receive the same treatment as those of farmers or tradesmen. Many teachers devoted a 'large portion of their time' to the instruction of the latter's children—who paid more and remained longer—in grammar, arithmetic and other subjects. In one school elsewhere they sat: the others stood. Children taught gratuitously were 'only set to read during a few odd fragments of time that can be spared from teaching the rest.... It is no wonder that the poor feel the injustice of this, and withdraw their children'. Teachers' propensity to concentrate upon the most advanced, predominantly children of superior artisan and middle-class parents, to address the latter as 'master' or 'miss', and make placement in higher classes entirely dependent upon the amount of fees paid, alienated poorer parents further. Other social sensitivities were affronted. A skilled mechanic refused to send his children to a National school, the best in the vicinity, because he did not want them to mix with middle-class children.[26]

Some parents, for whom the chapel was their life, considered it a 'far greater sin to send children to the National School than to let them remain uneducated'. Some would not 'on any account' send children to institutions that taught any religion other than their own. Others aspired to non-denominational schools. A canvas at South Shields ascertained that parents would send 900 children to a non-denominational but only 47 to a National foundation. Others were utterly indifferent to such considerations. Amongst them were those who were absolutely convinced that they could transmit their own religious beliefs to their children as effectively as their dialects.[27]

Parents' reluctance to accept free schooling for their children remained constant until 1891 when it became a qualified right and 'not a concession to poverty'. Some parents were not prepared to receive charity and also pay school pence. Others certainly utilised free schools that failed to teach reading properly after six years' attendance because in no other school could their children 'get so well clothed gratis'. Where charitable schools competed parents were also known to withhold children in the hope that they would obtain clothing etc. from the schools' benefactors—and to change schools for additional benefits. The weight of evidence, however, supports the view that most workers abhorred 'any form of dependence'. Some exceptionally impoverished people objected to free schools 'except in extreme cases'. At Morpeth, parents accepted free schools' tuition lightly and conditionally—and lightly relinquished it. Parent attitudes were more extreme than the claim that if 'in any degree raised above want, they would sooner forego the pecuniary advantage' than accept free schooling. Free schools within a hundred yards of people's homes failed to persuade numerous impoverished parents to send their children to them. This reluctance was perhaps even more pronounced when schools also charged fees. A vicar paid the school-pence for a penniless widow's children, but she loathed accepting it. A family that paid National school fees for two children kept the third at home rather than ask for the school-pence. A poverty-stricken Londoner with five school-age children intermittently could not pay fees for them all. He then reluctantly kept some at home rather than apply for free instruction. An extremely poor mother, with one child at school for whom she paid and four withheld, preferred to see her children 'run in the street than receive the school-pence as charity'.[28]

Governmental policy ensured voluntary schools' 'entire dependence' upon local resources, i.e., resident parochial property-holders. Richer neighbourhoods supported most schools, the poorer the least and worst: distribution remained uneven until after 1870. Places existed for 40 per cent more children than attended in 1851 and 60 per cent more in 1870. In 1846, 142 children attended one school built for 980. The 'frequent irregularity of attendance', lack of punctuality, and the 'very early age' at which a 'fearfully large' proportion of enrolled children left school were matters of common notoriety. An estimated two million children remained unschooled in 1851.[29]

Workers' Private Schools

Some parents only sent their children to voluntary schools when they faced exceptionally severe financial difficulties. Like so many of their social peers they clearly preferred private paying day-schools totally untainted by the charity, values and jurisdiction of other classes. Basic issues of provision, access, method, curriculum, freedom and independence were at stake. Private schools, moreover, 'are often … but proofs of the inefficiency of public ones'. The names bestowed on these schools by middle-class commentators changed, denigrated, and misleadingly oversimplified varied, responsive educational agencies. Although best comprehended as workers' or working-class private schools, misleading middle-class terminology of the 1830s and 1840s is also utilised here on grounds of its familiarity. Dames' and common day schools were depicted as dens of ignorance that misinstructed or failed to instruct perhaps slightly more than a third of the labouring classes' children in the 1830s and a little less in the late-1860s. These parents' preference strengthened the conviction of voluntary schools' protagonists that working people were incorrigibly benighted and totally unfitted to make valid educational choices. Historians of education, overwhelmingly whiggish in favouring the triumph of inspected voluntary and board schools, have also with rare unanimity unjustly maligned schools run by working people.[30]

These schools had neither the inclination to keep nor the facilities to store records and left none. Evidence about a 'very small proportion' of their 'real number', usually held in the teacher's home, even if a one-room familial home, has survived. In London it was 'almost impossible to find many of them' in the 1870s. Because teachers there, like those at Bristol and Kingston upon Hull, were 'most jealous of any enquiry ... little information' could be obtained about the functioning of those located. Middle-class investigations and official documents provide most information about these schools. Childhood recollections in the comparatively few memoirs left by working people are particularly valuable. They, however, are brief, individualist, overwhelmingly male, 'respectable', and no more likely to be correct than anyone else's.[31]

Dames' schools—less commonly all-age, single-sex or co-educational—supplied the infant education of the 'mass of the people' in 1848 and took 'more than their share' of children with accessible voluntary schools. Charging up to five times as much as dames' schools, common day schools often attracted the 'choicest specimens' of workers' children. This situation persisted even in less prosperous decades. By the 1860s, notwithstanding the 'somewhat unfair competition of schools assisted by Government' private schools had 'scarcely, if at all, diminished'. Like voluntary schools, their number had probably increased. Private-school supporters included mechanics and labourers above receiving a charitable education for their children, or allowing them to mix with 'low company'. Educational officials could not understand why parents sent children to be taught, allegedly badly, 'most frequently in a poky, ill-ventilated and over-crowded room ... ill-furnished with books and apparatus, when they can at generally a less cost send them to a well-conducted school ... where teachers and material are alike thoroughly efficient'.[32]

Parents were not necessarily gulled as easily as middle-class contemporaries, with axes to grind, and historians by comparisons that misrepresented the inadequacies of numerous voluntary schools. There were districts with higher illiteracy rates amongst those who had attended day schools than amongst those who had not. It was a 'subject of wonder', the Newcastle Commissioners recorded, 'how people so destitute of education as labouring parents commonly are, can be such just judges as they also commonly are of the effective qualification of a teacher'. 'No greater mistake is made than in supposing the working classes to be indifferent to the state of the schools. They watch with a very critical eye every defect both in the management of schools and the instruction of the scholars.' In any case, the assertion of independence and exercise of traditional educational rights in traditional and completely autonomous agencies of instruction clearly outweighed other considerations. Established in pre-industrial society, this highly diversified educational network had none of the features of voluntary schools in which 'everything partook of a air'. Private schools, moreover, had 'wonderful elasticity in adapting themselves to the requirements of all times' and all familial circumstances.[33]

Apart from a small minority of adolescents, private schoolteachers were adults. Fully experienced in the hardships and other aspects of working people's lives, necessity generally drove them into an occupation that, particularly for women, usually supplied only the 'bare means of subsistence'. Their financial circumstances were generally incomparably worse than those of qualified voluntary schoolteachers. An unknowable proportion of these teachers—71 per cent in Birmingham in 1838—simultaneously pursued another occupation. Variations were pronounced. Hetton Colliery, population 5,887, had a National school and fourteen others conducted by masters whose average fees were twice those of the voluntary school. Leeds had three female teachers for each male teacher and more than half of their schools were perceptibly cheaper than at Hetton. Finsbury had an 'immense preponderance' (9:1) of female teachers, incidentally of 'good moral ... decidedly religious character'. Private schoolteachers had diversified backgrounds that voluntary schoolteachers could never possess and offered parents more meaningful choices. When William Morris left Miss Noad's dame school he went to two of the other three schools nearby. One of their schoolmasters had been a man-of-the-world and an excise officer, one a wool-stapler and soldier with service in Egypt and at Waterloo, and one was a 'nice kind old gentleman, scrupulously exact'.[34]

Individuals apparently often became private schoolteachers at the suggestion of 'kindly neighbours' or friends or relations who promised to send their children. In one case an informal association, not all of whose members were parents, met on Saturday evenings in a public house. After a few hours' drinking they raised a subscription and handed it to the schoolmaster who was expected to spend part of it regaling the subscribers. Fully integrated into the immediate local society, private schoolteachers responded wholeheartedly to parental wishes. One teacher briefly introduced cheap, subsidised, Religious Tract Society and Society for the Promotion of Christian Knowledge publications. Parental aversion to 'anything that might be regarded as charity' effected 'immediate withdrawal' of children. Teachers complied with parental requests that their children be untroubled with learning, not even the needlework that often commanded half of girls' time in voluntary schools. In such cases they supplied semi-parental care for children who could not be looked after at home and prevented them mixing with undesirable companions on the streets. One third of wives in a Birmingham study fulfilled home duties. The others had paid employment in forty-seven different occupations. Unless instructed otherwise, however, private schoolteachers concentrated upon the basic educational skills. Specialisation existed. Separate schools for reading and for writing coexisted in urban districts with those that offered both or the 3Rs. Flexibility prevailed about attendance and punctuality, with tuition and fees specifically suited to familial circumstances. One school's fees, for instance, were 50 per cent higher if children wrote on paper.[35]

Private schoolteachers, like a proportion of Sunday school teachers, neither maintained the type of order nor instilled all the specific values that richer people deemed essential. In their concentration upon the 3Rs they, unlike Sunday school teachers, gave little attention to religious and moral education. Theirs were reputedly 'merely *secular schools*' in the north-east. From a different perspective, little harmonious blending of denominations occurred except in workers' private schools: voluntary schools were usually sectarian because one denomination predominated in them. Diversity prevailed in these small, perhaps 20–30 pupil, schools. Children, for instance, often read, and sometimes learnt to read from, books brought from home. Teachers gave children personal assignments and supplied guidance, help and tuition when necessary. This individual method received interminable criticism on grounds of its inefficient, formless disorganisation. It could not incorporate efficient educational innovation: that is, the prescribed systematic texts, standards, class, and (subsequently castigated) monitorial or pupil-teacher systems of teaching and training. Private schools could not keep pupils in the same standard for 'two, three, four, and in one case even six' years—and thus destroy the confidence of slow learners. Their overcrowded pupils were compared to playful puppies. In inspected schools 'luckless, little' infants, 'frequently packed away in a dark corner', entrusted to a 'dull monitor' merely gained the 'opportunity of learning how, without crying, to sit still for hours together with dangling legs and aching backs'.[36]

If private schoolteachers applied corporal punishment it had no association with conflicts of class, religion or culture. The 'injudicious, if not unprincipled, way in which punishments are frequently administered' in voluntary schools had such a connexion and persisted as a principal obstacle to their improvement. Private schoolteachers did not share educational officials' obsessive insistence upon single-sex tuition wherever practicable and the provision of separate playgrounds for boys and girls. It is highly unlikely that they would have considered inflicting eighteen lashes on the bare back of a schoolboy for speaking to a girl in the 'airing grounds' (which they, of course, lacked). The inadequacies of private school premises merely reflected those of working people's housing. Relativity, however, has its place. Decades after Newcastle upon Tyne's dames' schools were found to be 'more clean and orderly than expected, considering the dirt and disorder that surrounded them', its School Board sanctioned the use of toilets as premises for teaching purposes.[37]

Observations

With sacrifices 'grievously underestimated', working people managed 'somehow or other to get much more knowledge than would appear probable from the difficulties in their way'. Very 'few of their children were completely uninstructed' in 1851. Almost all working people appreciated the importance of education. In view of their pressing constraints of time and money, they required expeditious and effective tuition in basic educational skills. Voluntary schools 'invariably' removed parental indifference and were 'filled with pupils', even those of badly-paid farm labourers, when they supplied it. For such schools parents 'always and everywhere' paid willingly while managers often had difficulty in maintaining subscriptions. An emphasis on the 3Rs, however, fell 'manifestly' short of subscribers' insistence upon specific types of religious and moral training and socialisation. Middle-class individuals who testified to the validity of parents' judgement of voluntary schools rejoiced that they withdrew children to spare them unimaginable boredom and waste of time.[38]

The secular component of voluntary schools' curricula tended to increase slowly from the mid-1830s; and the gradual replacement of monitors with pupil-teachers and changes in the training of teachers somewhat improved the effectiveness of tuition. Yet the Newcastle Commissioners found in 1861 that the 'great majority' of children 'do not learn, or learn imperfectly, the most necessary part of what they came to learn—reading, writing and arithmetic'. Under the prevailing patterns of attendance 60 per cent of children ought to have mastered the 3Rs but only 25 per cent did. The Revised Code of 1862 related inspected schools' grants unequivocally to effectiveness in teaching the 3Rs. Greater concentration upon teaching the basic educational skills gradually secured more parental support for the voluntary schools. For the schooling of every three children assisted by governmental grants in 1860, incidentally, four remained unaided.[39]

Working people's allegiance to their private schools remained tenacious. It resisted varied forms of suasion to attract their children into voluntary schools. Provided that their children were 'unobjectionable', for instance, they were allegedly 'never refused admission into the paying schools merely because the parents cannot pay'. The education act of 1870 neither withdrew parental educational liberties nor abolished private schools but its consequences and subsequent indirect initiatives rendered parents' use of them impracticable. The act remedied deficiencies in voluntary school provision through elected School Boards empowered to levy rates. Surveys ascertained officially acceptable schools. Private schoolteachers who failed to complete the required return had their schools declared unacceptable. Tuition had to be efficient, and accommodation adequate by official determination. Inspections, 1870-1871, closed thousands of schools on the latter grounds alone.[40]

Private schoolteachers and parents whose children they taught thenceforth experienced warnings, threats, harassment and endless conflicts with local educational officials. Many surviving private schools withstood this, but not the next onslaught. Without a certificate of proficiency in the 3Rs or a certificate of two years' attendance awarded by a certified efficient school—a novel category—no child over the age of ten could legally enter the workforce after the passage of Lord Sandon's act of 1876. This indirect compulsion effectively made privately instructed children between the ages of ten and thirteen legally unemployable and played a decisive role in the final destruction of workers' private schools. Compulsory 'efficient' schooling between the ages of five and ten (1880) and free instruction (1891) delivered their *coup de grace*. The Education Department estimated that more than a million children were missing from inspected schools' registers in the early 1880s. E. G. A. Holmes, HMI, was certain that three quarters of them were in 'schools which are inefficient in every conceivable respect. This is no random assertion'.[41]

Meanwhile, the teaching of language—the 'most perfect instrument of empire' (1492)—was also being transformed. Standard language became almost completely identified with the accents of authority from the 1840s. By the time workers' private schools were destroyed it had become a class dialect, the language of the educated.

> The educated classes spoke English correctly, and in their possession of this capacity they were also guardians of the language, preservers of the cultural tradition, and masters of the national history. Official schooling aimed at obliterating class and regional dialects as part of the creation of a 'standard' language that was distinctly non-standard in origin. The result often took the form of an alienating split.[42]

Workers' private schools, which impeded this process, had never been an educational wasteland. From the 1780s, they and cognate traditions helped to make workers' contributions to the Sunday School movement substantial and effective. This involvement prevented it from becoming an exclusively middle-class agency. Workers' private school traditions were perhaps also a seed-bed for the isolated individual enterprise of the few members of congregations that often founded Sunday schools and kept them alive. A nineteenth-century congregation tended to take little cognisance of its Sunday school (usually for *workers' children*) and treated it as a servant rather than as a child. This in turn accounts for a presumably welcome feature of Sunday schools to parents —the otherwise inexplicable lack of obligation or pressure upon children to adhere to a denomination. Sunday schools also complemented workers' private and other schools by supplying a 'large amount of elementary instruction' (1854) too commonly in premises widely criticised from the 1870s and which HMIs would have condemned.[43]

Workers' private schools had helped working people to gain the widespread late pre-industrial literacy that made their subsequent political activity possible, to overcome, as in Lancashire, deteriorating standards of literacy caused by rapid industrialisation, and then to improve literacy generally. 'Most men struggling for a living', moreover, 'knew well enough that for them literacy bought no bread.'[44] The richer classes meanwhile established voluntary day schools sluggishly in the first third of the nineteenth century despite their protagonists' conviction that they would promote social stability. From 1792 politicisation moved down the social scale decisively. Governments faced a powerful concentration of radical political thought and activity from working people. They imposed repressive legislation to curtail workers' diverse challenges to the established order. Part of this repression attacked the 'seditious' and 'blasphemous' press that articulated and disseminated working-people's grievances and proposals. Through fiscal measures and prosecutions particularly onerous between 1819 and 1835, governments tried to price its publications beyond workers' reach and to destroy that part of the press. Parts of the repressive legislation and the intended curtailment of publications that working people wished to read *inter alia* impeded the extension of literacy amongst them.

A premise upon which the censorship of working people's reading rested was that they, unlike the differently educated richer classes, were '*destitute* of all means of arriving at the truth'. Although the soundness of working people's judgement about voluntary schools received some recognition, this alleged characteristic accounted—to richer people— for many parents' private-school preference. They had 'very inadequate means of judging different schools.' Even prospectively, many doubted that they would ever be 'fit judges' of the 'proper duration' of their children's schooling. Workers gained the freedom of the press but later lost the freedom to use their private schools. From the 1780s the dice were loaded. These schools received no equitable assessment, no understanding, and no recognition of their importance to working people's lives and culture. They never received fair competition from voluntary schools' associates or fair treatment from the state. Its power, influence, and resources were used against them, often indirectly. HMIs only examined voluntary and board schools which alone received governmental grants. The state, voluntary school managers, and School Boards had interlocking financial and, as they saw it, incomparably preferable educational interests in securing the private schools' elimination.[45]

HMIs, diocesan inspectors and others frequently criticised the workings of individual voluntary schools but richer people rarely questioned their widespread assumption that they should control the schooling of workers' children. Different denominations, conservatives, whigs, liberals and middle-class radicals shared this view. Classical economists otherwise often *laissez-faire* advocates—in Adam Smith's case as a prophylactic against 'the most dreadful disorders'—and utilitarians keen to promote a 'happiness' attainable only through the inculcation of their tenets also favoured directed instruction for workers' children. Controversy, compromise and the richer classes' ordering of their priorities dogged and delayed the implementation of this objective. Parliament had accepted in principle the need for national elementary education in 1807.[46]

A clear distinction nevertheless existed between the state's 'enforcement of education' and its assumption of the direction of that education. If government had merely required 'for every child a good education', it could have saved 'itself the trouble of *providing* one'.[47] A certificate of proficiency in the 3Rs and enforcement of an age limit for the commencement of work would have sufficed—but not have given all workers' children a religious, moral and social training approved by richer people. Application of such a policy would also have raised attainment standards in workers' private schools.

Quite exceptionally, glimpses appear of private schools' potential. Many children who had learnt nothing from tuition in class blossomed under individual tuition. Men of 'high class' were private schoolmasters as well as 'persons of inferior attainments'. A full-time dockyard labourer gave extremely successful preparation for competitive examinations in his evening school. The advantages of drawing children from dame and common day schools into one with a charitable basis were 'very questionable'. Dames' schools at Leeds warranted the sympathy and help of the public. A diocesan inspector praised dames' schools at Lichfield for their 'parental feeling', criticised only their lack of the 'interrogative element', and suggested that a little guidance from the clergy could remedy this defect. If it were remedied, this inspector would 'infinitely prefer' three dames' schools to one large infants' school. Working people, moreover, a third of whom at Hull belonged to benefit societies, had collaborative, self-help traditions and organisational skills. With the assistance of a building society but without governmental aid, miners at a Northumbrian colliery built a commodious school and a schoolmaster's house to overcome their children's lack of adequate instruction. Every adult miner, regardless of marital status or paternal prowess, made the same substantial contribution towards the capital expenditure and thenceforth paid three pence weekly for current expenditure.[48]

The insatiable demand for child labour, curbed tardily and partially by the state from the 1830s, persisted in the bishop of Manchester's opinion of 1873 as the 'most capital fault' in all endeavours to school workers' children. The damning indictment of their exploitation in the Children's Employment Commission, 1842—instances of children starting work aged 3 or 4 years, 'not infrequently' at 5, more generally 7 and 8, and working usually twelve but up to eighteen hours a day—showed continuity as well as greater diversity of inhumanity. For the previous half century boys of poor families were being sent down pits between the ages of 6 and 8.[49]

From the 1830s factory legislation was extremely limited and extended slowly—to branches of silk-manufacturing, for instance, in 1874. Its part-time educational provisions secured unenthusiastic implementation: six of two thousand mill-owners acted upon those of the 1833 measure by 1836. A factory inspector repeatedly highlighted the few good factory schools and the lamentable failures of the great majority. Because there was 'evidently no disposition, in any quarter, to have the glaring defects in the law corrected', he refused, in his final year of service, to enlarge any further upon the adverse educational consequences of factory legislation in 1859. Legislation relating to workshops, often domestic (and which produced half of Birmingham's manufactured goods in the 1850s), was even more belated. Youngsters in such enterprises remained unprotected for many decades. Working people's powerful pressure for the regulation of child labour, shown in Samuel Kydd's *The History of the Factory Movement* (1857), had strictly circumscribed results. Proposals to extend schooling by fining anyone who employed a child under the age of 10 without a certificate of educational proficiency went unheeded until the 1870s.[50]

The testimony of HMIs, diocesan inspectors, and officials of voluntary schools points unequivocally to a more widespread exploitation of child labour as its curtailment in certain mines and factories commenced. Juvenile labour was essential to employers 'in a vast number of manufactures, trades and occupations'. Demand for it, which increased yearly throughout the country, was greater in 1861 than in 1839. The labour of the child tended to '*supersede the labour of the parent*' with 'every improvement of machinery'. Parents, driven by poverty, were engulfed by fierce competition and the 'absolute necessity which has been created for the employment of children at too early an age and for too long a time'. Employers' insistence that they '*must* have the children' usually acquired 'irresistible force' when accompanied by the intimation that if parents withheld their children their own services would no longer be required. The demand for juvenile labour was known to triumph even when parents were neither indifferent about their children's schooling nor too poor to pay for it. Consequently, the age reached by children in schools and the regularity of their attendance had been 'gradually but steadily diminishing' for more than a decade of mid-century prosperity.[51]

Children at Sheffield had a longer, less fragmented school life when trade was neither very good nor very bad. The schooling of children with parents in regular moderately-paid employment was least affected by prosperity or reduced economic activity, and that of those receiving daily payment less than those of pieceworkers. Intermittent or unpredictably sustained high wages did not ensure the protection of children's schooling. The commonplace deduction that schooling was 'more likely ... in periods of prosperity for the family' is logical but not necessarily valid generally. Derbyshire ironstone miners' occupational practices differed greatly from those of skilled artisans in

Birmingham or Sheffield but they all curtailed their children's day schooling during periods of prosperity. A study of six agricultural and six manufacturing districts drew the same conclusion: prosperity increased demand for child labour. Children's wages—sometimes all a mother received if her husband spent his wages entirely upon himself—contributed significantly to domestic income. A third of a farm labourer's, and more of an artisan's, familial income disappeared if he sent two children, aged 9 and 11, to a paying school. In numerous workshop trades and crafts children were often employed by or apprenticed to working people, perhaps their fathers or mothers. They earned wages. They also increased male and female skilled and unskilled pieceworkers' productivity and income significantly, perhaps by relieving them of time-consuming tasks that required little skill or strength. Pieceworkers in various occupations also had a powerful incentive to increase the number of their apprentices or juvenile employees during periods of vigorous economic activity.[52]

Dostoevsky witnessed the 'triumph of Baal' when he first visited England in 1862. The 'contrast between the "colossal facade" of riches, luxury and general prosperity of the few and the abject poverty of the many and their "coolie-like" acquiescence in their fate' struck him forcefully. The schooling of working people's children was one of England's 'gigantic' social problems but many parents showed little acquiescence in their grappling with it. These problems were related to 'the increased luxury of the opulent, the widening chasm and diminished sympathy between class and class, the struggle between wealth and poverty, and the wide destitution of one portion of the poor' which had allegedly 'robbed them of all heart, and mind, and power'. The struggle also generated the 'habits of intemperance and sensuality in another portion, in imitation of the luxurious living of their social betters'. In 1857, when demand for child labour was increasing daily, Rev. W. J. Kennedy, HMI, was unusually explicit. He doubted whether England could 'undersell all other nations, and yet educate duly our youthful labourers'. He believed that 'we must make up our minds to sacrifice the one object to the other'. As he did not see any preparedness 'to part with any portion of our manufacturing and commercial greatness', the promotion and improvement of school attendance ought to continue '*within the limits compatible with our commercial pre-eminence*'.[53]

Notes

1 Neil McKendrick, 'Home Demand and Economic Growth: A New View of the Role of Women and Children in the Industrial Revolution', in *Historical Perspectives: Studies in English Thought and Society in Honour of J. H. Plumb*, ed. Neil McKendrick, London, 1974, p.157; P. J. Waller, *Town, City and Nation: England 1850–1914*, Oxford, 1983, p.126.

2 John Belchem, *Industrialization and the Working Class: The English Experience, 1750–1900*, Aldershot, 1990, pp.11–13, 153, 156, 207.

3 G. Kitson Clark, *The Making of Victorian England*, London, 1962, p.147; Samuel Couling, *Our Labouring Classes: Their Intellectual, Moral, and Social Condition Considered*, London, 1851, pp.50–2.

4 Stephen Yeo, *Religion and Voluntary Organisations in Crisis*, London, 1976, p.119; L. R. Haggard, ed., *I Walked by Night: Being the Life and History of the King of the Norfolk Poachers*, London, 1974, p.113.

5 Belchem, *Industrialization*, p.33; Robert Roberts, *A Ragged Schooling*, London, 1984, p.23; Peter Keating, ed., *Into Unknown England 1866-1913: Selections from the Social Explorers*, London, 1976, p.191; James H. Treble, *Urban Poverty in Britain, 1830–1914*, London, 1979, p.188.

6 Nassau W. Senior, *Suggestions on Popular Education*, London, 1861, p.85; Michael E. Rose, *The English Poor Law 1780–1930*, Newton Abbot, 1971, p.204; Sidney Webb and Beatrice Webb, *English Poor Law History in English Local Government*, London, 1963: 7 i 327; 8 ii 1.

7 Geoffrey Taylor, *The Problem of Poverty 1660–1834*, London, 1969, p.85; William Dodd, *The Labouring Classes of England*, Boston, 1847, pp.69–70, 86.

8 E. P. Thompson, *The Making of the English Working Class*, Harmondsworth, 1977, p.295; F. M. L. Thompson, *The Rise of Respectable Society: A Social History of Victorian Britain, 1830–1900*, London, 1988, pp.343, 351–2; *Journal of the Statistical Society of London* (hereafter *JSSL*) 5 (1842): 77; Charles Shaw, *When I was a Child, by 'An Old Potter'*, London, 1903, pp.135–7; Keating, ed., *Unknown England*, p.168.

9 John Dufton, *National Education, What It Is, and What It Should Be*, London, 1847, p.32; Dodd, *Labouring Classes*, p.28; Earl of Shaftesbury, *National Association for the Promotion of Social Science*, London: 12 Oct. 1858, p.7.

10 As early as 1816, the Spitalfields Association organised 8,460 visits to 3,366 families in an eleven-week period. Phillip McCann, ed., *Popular Education and Socialization in the Nineteenth Century*, London, 1977, p.26; David Roberts, 'Dealing with the Poor in Victorian England', *Rice University Studies* 67 (1981): 60.

11 Phil Gardner, *The Lost Elementary Schools of Victorian England*, Beckenham, 1984, p.98; Eric E. Rich, 'The Passing of the Education Act of 1870', Ph.D. diss. London University, 1932, pp.10–11.

12 See Robert J. Hind, 'Working People and Sunday Schools: England, 1780–1850', *Journal of Religious History* 15.2 (1988): 199–218; see also *idem*, 'Elementary Schools in Nineteenth-Century England: Their Social and Historiographical

Contexts', *Historical Reflections/Reflexions Historiques* 11.2 (1984): 189–205.

13 David Wardle, *Education and Society in Nineteenth Century Nottingham*, Cambridge, 1971, p.44; Philip B. Cliff, *The Rise and Development of the Sunday School Movement in England 1780–1980*, Redhill, 1986, pp.91–92, 100; see also Thomas W. Laqueur, *Religion and Respectability: Sunday Schools and Working Class Culture, 1780–1850*, London, 1976; Malcolm Dick, 'The Myth of the Working-Class Sunday School', *History of Education* 9.1 (1980): 27–41.

14 Cliff, *Sunday School Movement*, pp.88–90.

15 Thompson, *Respectable Society*, p.141; Cliff, *Sunday School Movement*, p.5; David Hempton, *Methodism and Politics in British Society, 1750–1850*, London, 1984, p.89; *Minutes of the Committee of Council on Education* (hereafter *MCCE*), 1844, 1:151.

16 Cliff, *Sunday School Movement*, pp.116, 129; Laqueur, *Religion and Respectability, p.*124; Alfred Hill, ed., *Essays upon Educational Subjects Read at the Educational Conference of June 1857*, London, 1857, p.53.

17 Committee of the Sunday School Union, *The Census and Sunday Schools*, London, 1854, p.6; *JSSL* 18 (1855): 154.

18 Less than a quarter of Sunday school pupils were middle-class children by the 1850s. *The Report of the Proceedings of the Sunday School Convention*, 1–5 September 1862, p.162, affirmed that children of labourers, artisans and smaller craftsmen attended but not those of clerks, large traders, professional people and persons of independent means; Marion Johnson, *Derbyshire Village Schools in the Nineteenth Century*, Newton Abbot, 1970, p.204.

19 *Parliamentary Debates* (hereafter *Parl. Deb.*), 3rd ser., 20 (30 July 1833):150; *ibid.*, 91 (19 April 1847): 1008; *ibid.*, 137 (2 May 1855): 2118; *JSSL* 1 (1838): 458; *JSSL* 42 (1879): 458–9; Jelinger Symons, *School Economy*, London, 1852, p.11.

20 *The Educator*, 3rd ser., 1.6 (London, 1863): 177; 1st *Annual Report of the National Society for Promoting the Education of the Poor in the Principles of the Established Church, 1812*, pp.51–2; *21st Annual Report of the British and Foreign School Society, 1826*, p.69; *ibid.*, *40th Report of the BFSS, 1845*, p.39; *MCCE, 1847–48*, 1:4; *Educational Record* 1 (1849): 27, 64; *ibid.*, 2 (1853): 184; *Parl. Deb.*, 3rd ser., 48 (20 June 1839): 595; *ibid.*, 116 (22 May 1851): 1247, 1251–2.

21 Frederic Hill, *National Education*, London, 1836 1:76; *Parl. Deb.*, 3rd ser., 125 (4 April 1853): 528; *Parliamentary Papers*, XXI, part 1, 1861, *Report of trhe Commissioners Appointed to Inquire into the State of Popular Education in England* (hereafter *Newcastle Commission*), 1:20; *JSSL* 5 (1842): 308; *JSSL* 25 (1862): 52; Horace Mann, *National Association for the Promotion of Social Science*, 1862, p.269; *Educator*, 3rd ser., 1.6 (1863): 158; Robert James, 'The Development of Education in the Borough of Warwick during the Nineteenth Century', M.Ed. diss. Warwick University, 1971, p.163.

22 *MCCE, 1847–1848*, 1:24; F. B. Zincke, *Why Must We Educate the Whole People?*, London, 1850, pp.39–41, 43; *Parl. Deb.*, 3rd ser., 138 (11 June 1855): 1789.

23 *Newcastle Commission* 1:320; *MCCE*, 1845, 1:256 ; *ibid.*, 1846, 1:260, 443; *The Educator*, 3rd ser., 1.6 (1863): 148.

24 British Library, Francis Place Papers, Add. MS. 27823, fos. 43–5, 49–50; *JSSL* 1 (1838): 456; *MCCE*, 1839–40, pp.111–12; *ibid.*, 1842–43, p.33; *ibid.*, 1845, p.245; *Newcastle Commission* 5:163.

25 John Armitstead, *On the Means Possessed by the Church for the Education of the People*, London, 1847, p.21; *MCCE*, 1842–43, p.437; *ibid.*, 1844, 2:138, 510, 523; *ibid.*, 1845, 2:114, 180; *ibid.*, 1853–54, pp.673–7; *Central Society of Education, Second Publication*, London, 1838, pp.363–4.

26 *Central Society of Education, First Publication*, London, 1837, pp.59–60; *JSSL* 15 (1852): 116; *MCCE*, 1842–43, p.52; *ibid.*, 1858–59, p.344; Matthew Arnold, *Reports on Elementary Schools, 1852–1882*, ed. Sir F. R. J. Sandford, London, 1889, pp.8–9, 79; *Educator*, 2nd ser., 26 (1860): 27, 40; *ibid.*, 3rd ser., 1 (1862): 50; *Leeds Mercury*, 13 April 1869; Public Record Office (hereafter PRO), Ed 24/13A/3, W. E. Forster (copy), 3 April 1878.

27 John Burdett, ed., *Destiny Obscure. Autobiographies of Childhood, Education and Family 1820s to 1920s*, London, 1982, p.38; George C. T. Bartley, *The Educational Conditions and Requirements of One Square Mile of the East-End of London*, London, 1870, pp.23, 48, 53; *Educational Record* 8 (1867): 94; *Educator*, 3rd ser., 1.6 (1863): 159.

28 William W. Mackenzie, *A Treatise on the Elementary Education Acts, 1870–1891*, London, 1892, pp.130–42; *Central Society, Second Publication*, pp.340–1; *16th National Society Report*, 1827, pp.12–13; *JSSL* 1 (1838): 455; *ibid.*, 25 (1862): 61; Bartley, *One Square Mile*, pp.43, 45–8, 51–2; *MCCE*, 1844, 2:444.

29 *Parl. Deb.*, 3rd ser., 111 (5 June 1850): 785; Rich, 'Education Act, 1870', pp.220–1; *MCCE*, 1844, 2:12, 141; *ibid.*, 1845, 1:154–5, 2:175; *ibid.*, 1847–48, 1:xcv.

30 Phil Gardner, *The Lost Elementary Schools of Victorian England*, pp.1–80; *Central Society of Education, First Publication*, London, 1837, p.59.

31 Bartley, *One Square Mile*, p.15; *JSSL* 4 (1841): 156, 250.

32 *MCCE*, 1845, 2:114; *ibid.*, 1846, 2:11; *JSSL* 1(1838): 455; *ibid.*, 25 (1862): 60; *Report of the CCE (England and Wales), 1882–1883*, p.110; *Educator*, 3rd ser., 1.6 (1863): 199.

33 *Newcastle Commission*, 1:175–6; *JSSL* 1 (1838): 73; *Educator*, n.s., 16 (1858): 86; Richard W. Hiley, *Sundry Attacks on Private Schools and Strictures Thereon*, London, 1884, p.33; Edmund H. L. Willes, *Elementary Education in Leicestershire*, Leicester, 1869, p.12.

34 *JSSL* 2 (1839): 348, 416; *ibid.* 3 (1840): 29–31; *ibid.* 4 (1841): 160; *ibid.* 6 (1843): 31; William Morris, *Swindon Fifty Years Ago*, Swindon, 1885), pp.285, 290–2.

35 Gardner, *Lost Schools*, p.95; *JSSL* 1 (1838): 457–8; A. Hill, ed., *Essays upon Educational Subjects*, p.69. The growth of female employment shown by the census of 1851 was one of its most significant features.

36 Gardner, *Lost Schools*, p.165; PRO, Ed 21/12634/14320, Wesley Road Junior Mixed School, Middlesex, Report by H. H. Piggott, HMI, 22 June 1914; Symons,

School Economy, p.6; *Report of CCE (England and Wales), 1882–1883*, p.88.

37 *MCCE*, 1845, 2:234–5; *Report of CCE (England and Wales), 1882–1883*, p.91; *Northern Liberator*, 1 November 1839; *JSSL* 1 (1838): 358, N. E. Dennis, 'The Provision of Schools in Newcastle upon Tyne during the School Board Period, 1870–1903', M.Ed. diss., Newcastle upon Tyne University, 1969, p.58.

38 Nassau Senior, *Popular Education*, p.3; *Educator*, 3rd ser., 1.6 (1863): 198; JSSL 25 (1862): 50; *MCCE*, 1842–43, p.472; *ibid.*, 1844, 2:88, 187; *ibid.*, 1845, 1:257.

39 *Newcastle Commission* 1:168, 295; *Educator*, 3rd ser., 1.1 (1862): 8.

40 *Newcastle Commission* 1:394; Gardner, *Lost Schools*, pp.188–210.

41 *Report of CCE (England and Wales), 1882–1883*, pp.114, 124.

42 Rod Mengham, *The Descent of Language: Writing in Praise of Babel*, London, 1993, pp.102, 128, 130.

43 Anon., *Sunday School Reform*, London, 1871, pp.3–4; Committee of Sunday School Union, *The Census and Sunday Schools*, p.2; Cliff, *Sunday School Movement*, pp.178–9.

44 For an introductory bibliography on literacy see Phil Gardner, *Lost Schools*, pp.186–7, n.148; Robert Roberts, *The Classic Slum*, Harmondsworth, 1980, p.167.

45 Stanley Harrison, *Poor Men's Guardians: A Survey of the Struggles for a Democratic Newspaper Press, 1763–1973*, London, 1974, p.73; *Parl. Deb.*, 3rd ser., 76 (19 July 1844): 1079; *ibid.* 141 (11 April 1856): 930.

46 Adam Smith, *The Wealth of Nations*, London, 1950, 2:272.

47 John Stuart Mill, *On Liberty*, London, 1963, pp.129–30.

48 *Report of an Educational Conference of Parochial Clergy and Schoolmasters*, Oxford, 1856, pp.35–6; *JSSL* 2 (1839): 416; *ibid.* 6 (1843): 31; E. G. West, Education and the State, London, 1965, p.167; *Report of CCE (England and Wales), 1863–1864*, p.93; *Educator*, 3rd ser., 1.6 (1863): 198.

49 Bishop of Manchester, *A Great Demonstration in Favour of Religious Education*, Manchester, 1873, p.13. This commission of 1842 showed that children under the age of five were employed primarily by working people, often their parents.

50 Hill, *National Education*, 1:129; Nassau Senior, *Popular Education*, p.185; *Essays, 1857*, pp.69, 76. See also P. W. J. Bartrip, 'State Intervention in Mid-Nineteenth Century Britain: Fact or Fiction?', *Journal of British Studies* 23 (1983): 63–83.

51 *Parl. Deb.*, 3rd ser., 148 (11 February 1858): 1229; *MCCE*, 1844, 2:283; *ibid.*, 1846, 1:256; *Newcastle Commission* 1:39; *Essays, 1857*, pp.14, 20, 128, 170, 277.

52 *Essays, 1857*, pp.72–3; John Rule, *The Labouring Classes in Early Industrial England, 1750–1850*, London, 1986, p.230; Sunday School Union, *Census and Sunday Schools*, p.12; Nassau Senior, *Popular Education*, p.4.

53 *The Best Short Stories of Dostoevsky*, trans. David Magarshack, New York, 1992, p.xviii; *Essays, 1857*, pp.236, 264.

Splitting Time's Arrow: Cultural History and the Robin Hood Myth

Stephen Knight

1

In a recently published book I have attempted to describe the many formations in the Robin Hood tradition, and to give some account of their interrelationship, both with themselves and with the social contexts that produced and consumed them.[1] As a result of that work there are two residual and interrelated issues I want to pursue separately. One is methodological, one is thematic. In methodological terms I want to reflect on the appropriate ways to conduct an analysis of this kind in cultural history, especially what type of history or historicising is most appropriate. And secondly, and as a result of settling on an answer to that question, I want to give some overall account of the main formative forces in the Robin Hood tradition, how they have changed over time, and in particular how they were re-formed at the start of the nineteenth century, and so reshaped the myth into its lively modern form.

My title refers to both of those two areas. In thematic terms, the moment when Robin splits the arrow is a compulsive motif in the tradition, and also a key instance of the re-formation of the myth in acceptable terms for a new context. But in addition, methodologically speaking, I refer in that title to what I see as a need to split up the simple progress of ongoing chronography, that line of time which is so commonly taken as an unconsidered basis in literary as well as historical writing. To understand the elements and the operations of this myth it is necessary to perceive something more than a steady plod from ancient forest laws to modern television, and to do that various elements of co-temporal and contra-temporal movements will need to be focused upon, various overlaps, gaps and recurrences. There are two ways of splitting an arrow: longitudinally into strips as Robin does in his improbable moment of heroic archery; and latitudinally, into many separate short pieces, that is into separate periods and contexts. I will do the latter in the process of seeking historical meaning in the complex and often contradictory structures of the Robin Hood tradition.

The actual (that is, imaginary) arrow splitting is a good place to start. We all know the scene. The Sheriff's brutish chief archer has shot in the final for the golden arrow. His shaft stands quivering in the centre of the target. The heavily disguised opponent steps quietly forward. His friends look anxious. Prince John, or perhaps the Sheriff, smiles meanly. But our incognito hero draws, pauses, and lets fly. His arrow sweeps through the sky and, with a crack, lands on the very tip of his opponent's shaft, splits it into waving fronds, and plunges right into the heart of the target, through the point of the other arrow.

The crowd goes wild; the heroic archer smiles, just a little. Robin Hood has won the archery contest.

But why did he win? Why wasn't it a draw? When I used to play darts, you would occasionally stick one dart in the plastic or wooden tip of the other, but you would always get the same score as the original dart. Did Robin win for hitting dead centre when it was obscured? Or did he actually win for splitting his enemy's arrow?

A date may help. This compulsive motif is not in fact medieval, or even renaissance, like some major re-formations of the Robin Hood tradition. It comes from the hands of Sir Walter Scott, that deadly narratological marksman. It is in *Ivanhoe* Chapter 13 that the arrow splitting first occurs as far as I am aware and Scott's main source, here as elsewhere, is none other than himself; there is a scene in *The Lady of the Lake* (V.22) where the Douglas splits his own arrow in this kind of way. The origin is presumably in a misinterpretation of the phrase 'to split the peg' or 'to split the wand', different mechanisms of archery perfection from an earlier period, which are mentioned in early ballads that Scott would certainly have known, including *The Gest of Robin Hood* and 'Adam Bell, Clim of the Clough and William of Cloudesly'.[2] The meaning of the incident is not hard to find, in competitive masculine self-consciousness: Robin apparently is represented as being more powerful in phallic terms than his enemy, and the compulsive nature of the motif is parallel to the popularity of Arthur's capacity to withdraw the sword from the stone, or as mythographers would have it, withdraw the phallus erect.

The wider significance of the arrow-splitting moment is that it suddenly appears and then becomes a compelling motif, as the myth that is renovated in the early nineteenth century is mediated in many popular sources, through to modern film and television. I will return to the period and the elements of that renovation towards the end of this paper. The point about opening with this incident is to stress methodologically that historicising the Robin Hood myth does not necessarily start with year one in the tradition; it starts by studying the relation between elements of the tradition and the contexts in which they appear or are fully developed. Time's arrow, that is, should not be simply followed, but neither should it in this case be simply reversed, as Martin Amis masterfully did in his novel of that name, in order to suggest that the holocaust was not in fact a historical necessity, but a wilful creation by people in their own fragment of time. In the case of this study, time's arrow needs to be split laterally into fragments, because the myth itself has never been simple or single, but has always had multiple interpretations, often of quite contradictory political character; by splitting the tradition into notionally disconnected moments an analysis can comprehend how each interpretation has presented the hero's inherent resistance to authority as being of a specific kind and with a specific purpose.

2

One major attempt to assert, and ideologise, linear time in the tradition, which I wish to controvert for several reasons, has occurred in our time, namely the attempt to read Robin Hood as a historical character. In referring to the tradition as a myth I am evidently rejecting this notion by denying it the name of legend, and before elaborating on the contradictory and complex character of the myth, I should specify my reasons for rejecting the historical simplicity of a notionally real Robin Hood whose legend has been exfoliated in various ways, with ideological purposes.

Most of the Robin Hood bibliography items in recent years have been in this mode of biographical historicism; it is a main, though by no means only, interest in the long introduction to *Rymes of Robin Hood* by the historians R. Dobson and J. Taylor.[3] It is the only focus of the book by John C. Bellamy and a major emphasis of J. C. Holt's book.[4] Several recent articles have returned to the question of who was the original Robin Hood. The premises are both empiricist and individualist, of course, and in that way they replicate two of our culture's basic concerns. Ironically, this mode of historicism is itself located inside history—whereas most of its practitioners would feel they are outside the myth and its processes, and so feel they can speak on behalf of history itself, rather than their own self-constructive practice.

This 'real Robin Hood' industry, or ideology, goes back some way. We can perhaps overlook the early attempts to find a biography for the hero as being less (or perhaps more) than empirical—Stukeley's famous genealogy, for example, which connected the outlaw with the conqueror's own family, as Robert Fitz Ooth.[5] The first true hero of empiricism was Joseph Hunter, a Yorkshire archivist, who in 1852 published the remarkable fact that Edward II had in 1321–22 employed a valet of the chamber called Robin Hood.[6] Hunter connected this with the story in the *Gest* of Robin serving, for a while, an unnumbered King Edward. But intriguing as the detail is, this Robin was never an outlaw or a fugitive.

Equally incomplete are other contenders—the fugitive found by Crook in the Reading court rolls from 1261–62 can with some strain be seen as a reference to an earlier figure:[7] he may, the historicists argue, have been connected with the outlaw just because he was a fugitive named Robert and so the quest goes back earlier, to the man found by L.V. D. Owen in York in 1226 called 'Robert Hood, a fugitive'.[8]

The implication has been that a careful enough empirical search will find the real figure from whom the legend spreads, and Holt is satisfied that Owen's man is the source.[9] But to construct a pleasingly historico-individualist stemma of this kind involves excluding evidence. For example, why pass over the slightly earlier and evidently different Robert Hood, an abbot's servant who killed a man in Cirencester in 1213. He is regarded by Holt as a 'less likely possibility'[10]—but why? The West can be quite fertile Robin Hood territory, at least for plays and place names, and there are early instances of the outlaw defending the church against its enemies, as in Walter Bower's continuation of John of Fordun's *Scotichronicon* from the 1440s.[11] More tellingly, why does Holt also name as 'less likely' the certainly historical Robin Hood who was arrested for breach of a royal forest at Rockingham in 1354?[12] This is an area quite rich in Robin Hood associations, apart from being only a long day's walk south-east from Sherwood.

It is the linear nature of this concept of history and the individualised basis of the implied ontology that are central to the problem. The empiricist historians have their own version of time's arrow, which privileges themselves as capable of knowing that one other person of importance: here stand proudly, side by side, the true Robin Hood and his true historian.

On the contrary, the records imply that the name Robin Hood is a *nom de guerrilla*: it is taken up by people who are fulfilling the role of anti-authoritarian activities, whether in game or criminal earnest. It is a name like Santa Claus, which people bear when they are fulfilling an appropriate role. The reality of Robin Hood, that is, lies in his mythic function. Where that function and that name came from is obscure, but it certainly seems that the youthfulness implied by the diminutive 'Robin' and the elusive mystery implied by 'Hood' as a cognomen are central. Some scholars, such as Robert Graves and Margaret Murray, have taken 'mystery' much further, wanting to see Robin Hood as fully connected with magic, witchcraft, the old religion.

That mantic reading of the hero is not strongly supported in the surviving evidence, but it is clear enough that some elements of a natural force are part of the myth, as is strongly realised in recent film versions, especially the television series 'Robin of Sherwood' made for Harlech television, starting in 1984. But the myth is more specifically centred on a notion of resistance to wrongful authority, and it is in those circumstances that most of the 'real' people appear to have taken up the name, or to have been given it. The impact of Robin Hood's mythic functions in history becomes clear if attention is paid to the genre in which the early tradition is both most widespread, and also most obscure.

3

The Robin Hood plays and games belong to a genre which I would like to bring to the fore in the tradition, both past and present, namely performance. This is partly because it appears that drama is the genre central to the tradition, through to modern television and film versions, but also because of the remarkable popularity of performance in the early period. In the appendix to my book, there appear some 260 references to the hero by 1600. A few are texts, others are proverbs, topographical connections and general comments about the hero. But the largest single group by far, more than half of the 260, are specific references to the staging of the Robin Hood play-game, a title I use to indicate how this is at once a semi-formal play and a communal game or ritual activity. The usual term 'plays and games' is too vague and suggests they are separate, rather than a continuum of kinds of socialised performance. None of the play-game texts survive, presumably because they were never written down or, more likely, had no fixed verbal form. Some descriptions of the activities are recorded, and quite a few accounts for costumes, props, entertainments and so on. This is because these play-games were very often semi-official, supported by the town authorities, and so their accounts at least were written down. In keeping with that status, the play-game is often a communal celebration, where Robin Hood both represents natural forces and brings them to the advantage of the local community.

A typical Robin Hood activity is when he and supporters will walk through the woods to a nearby village or small town and collect money. Robin Hood of Finchamstead arrived in Reading in 1505 and collected for the village. A few weeks later Robin Hood of Henley arrived for the same purpose. The natural connections are sometimes symbolic—Robin might ride in a cart decorated with blossomy boughs, and he often wears green. The natural connections are not only topographic and symbolic: the season is crucial. One of the recurrent mistakes about the Robin Hood play-game is that it takes place on May Day. It is clear from the evidence, and clearly stated by David Wiles (whose book, brief though it is, is the best authority on the topic) that the date of the Robin Hood play-game is late May or early June, and Whitsunday is the focus.[13] As anyone living in the English countryside will know, by the end of May the hedgerows and woods are white with blossom, showing full early summer, not the more uncertain promise of late spring. Robin Hood is associated with functioning nature, not with fertility rites towards that function.

But the natural symbolism and the money collected were directed towards the local community (not toward the poor—that comes in another part of the mythical forest, as we shall see). The churchwardens often controlled the play-game income, though it might be spent on civic not spiritual matters, like improving the roads. But the play-game was not always so communally coherent. The ritual can be a force for conflict in two possible connections. One is when there is rivalry between communities. There was a serious riot in the West Midlands in 1498 when the men of Wednesbury came to Walsall on Robin Hood's day in spite of legal prohibitions;[14] they came for mischief, not just merriment, and we know about this because of legal intervention to keep the peace.

Other violent versions of the Robin Hood play-game occurred when the local authorities, particularly in Scotland, sought to contain the carnival whose values they now disavowed; new religious attitudes rejected older forms of ritual, and other conflicts occurred when the size and complexity of a town meant that the space of natural communality had become a site for class dissension, as in Edinburgh in 1561 when the tradesmen, their apprentices as usual acting as shock troops, clashed with the legal authorities over Robin Hood activities.[15]

The play-game, however, only briefly suggests a version of the conflicts which are elsewhere more fully realised through the authority-resisting figure of Robin Hood in the ballads. This pattern does, though, appear more clearly in a few early written plays which are close in narrative to the more widely available early ballads. In these genres, which appear related to rapidly developing craft towns, particularly Nottingham, there is a central strain between a sense of local authority, itself seen as natural in some way, and the threat of external governmental forces, seen as foreign and constricting. Poacher versus royal forester is an obvious version of this, as is free local figure versus the force of the king, as mediated by the sheriff. Resistance to a distant authority, whether it is clerical in the person of monk or abbot, or secular in the role of sheriff or forester, is the central mechanism of the early Robin Hood myth, especially in the ballads: clearly a historical and social conflict being played out here.

The notion of local, quasi-natural value represented by the hero appears to be always associated with a specific place. Robin Hood it is striking to notice, is always strongly localised in the early period. He is Robin Hood of Sherwood, or Barnsdale, of Inglewood or even Richmond Park. And he is equally strongly connected—often negatively—to the small towns growing up beside these attractive open spaces of liberty and imaginedly natural life. The ultimate authority, whether King or St Mary, is regarded with respect; but the officers who imposed authority in their names are far from admired. Much of the thrust of the early ballads and the surviving early plays is exactly of this kind, acting out a conflict between local community and wider, national forces of legislation.

4

In the previous section I have been referring to early plays, a few of which still exist, and early ballads, quite a number of which survive. They essentially tell the story of Robin Hood the social bandit, this figure who is essentially local and natural in his values, and who is more or less resistant to authority, depending on the context. However, this pattern should not be read as simple. In its sense of resistance to distant authorities this material can have quite different political implications in the same period. Around 1450 two narratives are preserved. One is told by Walter Bower, a Scottish chronicler who adds to Fordun's *Scotichronicon* an example of Robin Hood's outlaw activities; he dates the events in 1266, just after the time of Simon de Montfort, whom Robin supported, according to this account.[16] For Bower, what is memorable is that Robin, though knowing the sheriff was in the forest looking for him, refused to interrupt mass before sallying out to defeat this representative of an external, and in this case anticlerical authority. But at just the same time is also recorded the long ballad of 'Robin Hood and the Monk',[17] in which Robin goes alone to Nottingham to worship Mary, is betrayed by a 'great-headed monk' and imprisoned by the sheriff. In revenge Little John and Much behead the monk and humiliate the sheriff: both church and state are punished for their anti-natural and anti-local activities.

If the early Robin Hood is, within his social bandit range, quite varied, greater variety was to come. This is not a simple process of historical change—the radical local figure remains in story and especially song, and can be traced in many ways through to the present—including in Michael Tippett's Marxist ballad opera from 1933.[18] But that figure of early resistance was overlain with another of more conservative character, as new social and cultural formations reconstructed Robin Hood: more fragments broken from the shaft of time's arrow needed to be scrutinised to historicise further patterns in the myth.

It was the sixteenth and seventeenth centuries which saw the development of the gentrified version of the myth of Robin Hood. Only now was the hero dated in the chaotic time of King Richard I, turned into a lord, provided with a lady, and made a hero of charity who steals from the rich to give to the poor: such condescension did not belong to the social bandit, who stole to give to his own class fraction only. All these new formations come together in the figure of the dispossessed Earl of Huntingdon. Once the authority he resists is itself wrongful, the outlaw can clearly represent good rule focused on royalty and aristocracy: he has become a figure of hierarchical conservatism, where before, and sometimes after, he has been a figure for variously radical local authority. This is a major change in the thrust of the myth, a conservative incorporation of considerable impact that is still to a large extent present in modern versions. In this formation, it is usually bad royal officials and corrupt Catholic churchmen who are resisted (not yet bad King John), and Robin has an automatic right to lead the outlaw band because of his birth, where in the social bandit version the leadership is a difficult matter, sometimes negotiated in the stories, and all non-local authority was suspect.

The agencies of this gentrification seem multiple. They certainly include renaissance historians anxious to be thought well of by the powerful, the first of whom has the not inappropriate name of John Major. In his *History of Greater Britain*, published in 1521, he set Robin firmly in the days of bad King John and stressed the outlaw's humane and chief-like character, so appropriating his power for the nobility. On the basis of this remodelling of the hero, in his *Chronicle at Large* (1569) Richard Grafton speculated that he might have been an earl, and by 1592 John Stow's *The Annales of England* gave the full story of dispossession in the days of Richard. A dramatist joined in when in 1598–99 Anthony Munday, in two five-act plays (*The Downfall* and *The Death of Robert Earle of Huntington*), fleshed out the story, matching Robin the Lady Matilda Fitzwater to provide the lineage that such a lord would expect.[19]

But the gentrification was not immediate, complete or even artistically potent. The memorable conflicts of the early plays and ballads, already well known by the 1590s, are almost completely absent from the gentrified tradition. What followed in that lofty mode was aesthetically enfeebled in many ways as a result of ignoring this theatrical vivid material. Robin Hood masques, playlets, harlequinades and ballad operas through the seventeenth and eighteenth centuries brought little life to the story of the genteel outlaw. Ennobled in rank but largely bereft of interesting narrative incident, Lord Robin struggled on in various half-effective, action-starved modes, until another major change, itself relating to a new fragment of history, came over the tradition after 1800 and shaped it for modern interests.

5

Without the rejuvenating imagination of Scott, Keats and Peacock early in the nineteenth century, it seems likely that the myth of Robin Hood would be as lost as are the stories of Guy of Warwick, Bevis of Hampton, Johnnie Armstrong or other late medieval heroes who have not engaged the modern imagination. The ancient notion of a natural force resistant to wrongful authority is reconstructed in the late eighteenth and early nineteenth century period of revolutions, social, industrial and poetic, and the force of the outlaw figure becomes a focus of modern concepts of the self and state. In part, the energy is derived from the fact that the old ballad materials were linked with the gentrified tradition through the anthology of Joseph Ritson, who in 1795 gathered almost all the early stories, recognised their radical force strongly and favourably, but also celebrated Robin as a displaced Earl. However, the old material also had its vigour directed in fresh ways. New history made new forms in the old myth.

Scott, in splitting the arrow, made Robin a competitive male. But the arrow he split was fired by a certain Hubert, whose grandfather shot at Hastings. Scott also inscribed in the myth a structure that is usually called nationalist, though it is, in fact, basically racist. Much has been written on Scott's success in creating a national image for both Scots and English in his historical fictions, and the nationalist potential of the Robin Hood material has been crucial in its power over the last two centuries—indeed it was as a part of the materials for the distinctly nationalist new curriculum of English that Robin Hood ballads, plays and anthologies were published in large numbers from 1910 to 1930, in both England and America; many of the film and television forms derived directly from those materials.[20]

But that nationalist appeal is itself bound up with another element that is new in the romantic period. Keats and his friend John Reynolds exchanged Robin Hood poems, and Leigh Hunt in particular developed stories in verse. These set the tone for the later treatment of the myth by Tennyson in *The Foresters* (1892) and by most of the minor Georgian poets, as well as many forgotten authors of bulky Victorian novels. Throughout these texts, a major element of Robin Hood's power is summed up in the word 'greenwood', which is a site alternative to the modern city: the thrust of the myth has become that of heritage. The forest, that natural place of old, has special new consoling power now that distant authority is not that of sheriff or abbot, but plainly that of mercantile capitalism and its unpalatable urban consequences. Poem after poem, novel after novel, rather thin plays, often for schoolchildren, all celebrate Robin and Marian as the spirits of a freer, cleaner, more natural England. There is a strong nationalist false consciousness in this heritage idea, a view of a trüer nation in the past, in the greenwood.

To Scott's nationalist and masculinist renovation is added a political nostalgia which Keats presents most sharply, but is widely disseminated—most extensively, to give credit where it is due and rarely given, from the work of Thomas Love Peacock. His *Maid Marian* (1822) may be the least reprinted of his prose, but in the stage version by J. R. Planche, it was extremely well known, much imitated (and in pantomime, pastiched) throughout the nineteenth century. Here Scott's story was combined for the first time with the idea of greenwood heritage, creating a mixture of national self-satisfaction, nature-focused false consciousness and aristocratic individualism.

This particular arrow has a long flight and considerable penetrative power. It was a potent ideological weapon both to entertain our period and also project its most conservative features. But that conservative development has not silenced earlier and more radical modes: the myth is never simple or single. It remains historically and politically multiple, and can include moments of modern leftism that recall original aspects of resistance. Errol Flynn's Robin of 1938 is evidently the enemy of Normans cast in the mould of Nazis. Michael Praed in the 1984 TV series is a telling combination of Robin the working class student radical and also the new age visionary. Kevin Costner in 1991 brought international liberalism to the myth, having as assistant a literal Black Muslim.

Like Hubert's arrow, the Robin Hood myth splits into many elements, and they can be read for their immediate significance in terms of the politics and history of their time of production and consumption. Some remain strange, unique, and even less than heroic: in the remarkable Nottingham playlet *Robin Hood and his Crew of Souldiers* (1661)[21] Robin yielded readily to the messenger of the newly crowned king. In the 1990s we can watch *Maid Marian* on BBC television: the genre is feminist farce and Robin is no more than a 'go-for-it boutique owner', who has designed the costumes: all real leadership is, for once, found in Marian. We will hear more from feminism yet, as at least one novel in that mode is now being written.

No doubt we will hear more too from the limited voice of biographical historicism, but however much that mode may retain an empiricist self-confidence, it is in reality just a part of the ongoing pattern of finding in Robin Hood a figure of what is in any period felt to be appealingly natural and liberatingly heroic—a process which may include a mapping of the whole forest of outlaw tradition, like the one I have just completed.

But I would claim for my study a methodological self-awareness. Whether they know it or not, all who study the outlaw hero also operate across the multiplicities of both myth and history, as I hope to have elucidated them—or at least some of them. To think of capturing all the features would be an ambitious folly worthy of the Sheriff. Whether it is a simple matter of defending late medieval local rights, or of re-shaping the modern hero of heritage, or the more elusive matter of writing a book about the whole myth and its significances, Robin Hood remains a moving target.

Notes

1 *Robin Hood : A Complete Study of the English Outlaw*, Oxford, 1994.

2 To be found in F. J. Child, ed., *The English and Scottish Popular Ballads*, 5 Vols, reprint edn, New York, 1965; see Vol.3.

3 London, 1976.

4 Bellamy, *Robin Hood: An Historical Inquiry*, London, 1985; Holt, *Robin Hood*, revised edn, London, 1990.

5 *Paleographica Britannica*, Stamford, 1746, Vol.2, p.115.

6 'The Great Hero of the Ancient Minstrelsy of England: Robin Hood, his Period, Real Character, etc., Investigated', *Critical and Historical Tracts* 4 (1852): 28–38.

7 'Some Further Evidence Concerning the Dating of the Origins of the Legend of Robin Hood', *English Historical Review* IC (1984): 530–4.

8 'Robin Hood in the Light of Research', *The Times: Trade and Engineering Supplement* 38, No.864, p.xxix.

9 Holt, 1990, pp.48–9.

10 Holt, 1990, p.54.

11 See Knight, 1994, pp.33–5 for a translation and discussion.

12 See Dobson and Taylor, 1976, pp.12–13.

13 *The Early Plays of Robin Hood*, Cambridge, 1981, p.4.

14 Holt, pp.148–9.

15 Knight, p.109.

16 Knight, pp.33–6.

17 Child, *English and Scottish Popular Ballads*, No.119, pp.94–101.

18 Knight, p.214.

19 Munday's Robin Hood plays are discussed in detail by M. A. Nelson, *The Robin Hood Tradition in the English Renaissance*. Salzburg Studies in English Literature, Salzburg, 1973, pp.124–88.

20 See Knight, Chapter 6, 'We Saxons Aren't Going to Put Up with these Oppressions Much Longer', pp.218–27.

21 See Stephen Knight, 'Robin Hood and the Royal Restoration', *Critical Survey* 5 (1993): 298–312.

Personal Freedom in Twentieth-Century China: Reclaiming the Self in Yang Lian's Yi *and Gao Xingjian's* Lingshan

Mabel Lee

A common assumption is that China's traditional culture had no place for the 'self', an awareness of which is critical for the emergence of the notion of personal autonomy and for the generation of demands for the right to personal freedom and the corollaries of social and political equality. The propaganda, including the literature, produced during the Cultural Revolution (1966–76) would seem to support such an assumption. However, this paper will argue that such an assumption is incorrect and that while the Chinese notion of 'self' may differ significantly from its Western counterpart, it has had a long history of development and that the period of greatest development has in fact taken place in the present century, during which time Western philosophies with strong resonances in traditional Chinese philosophy have been eclectically embraced. The awakened 'self' and its demand for freedom was then *consciously* put aside because of the perceived need for mass action in patriotic struggles first against Western imperialism, then against Japanese territorial encroachment and finally full-scale invasion in 1937. Such threats to the nation had been clearly removed by the late 1970s and, as Deng Xiaoping's ascendancy to power signalled the end of the Cultural Revolution to a still nervous population, the call for the affirmation of the self resurfaced in the voice of the young Beijing poets during the Democracy Wall Movement, 1978–79.

As China opened to the international world in its push to establish itself as one of the modernised nations of the world, foreign works of literature, philosophy, politics, and economics flooded in alongside the technological and scientific works. In the first half of the 1980s translations of Western literature were being published at registered publishing houses in vast numbers and despite the periodic singling out for criticism of individual writers, particularly during the 'anti spiritual pollution' campaign (1983–84), the more relaxed political atmosphere of the 1980s made it possible for the resurgence of demands for personal freedom and also the right to personal freedom, and in the first instance to freedom of expression. Such demands escalated with growing momentum in the latter half of the 1980s and culminated in the tragic events of Tiananmen on 4 June 1989. Significantly, the year 1989 was the tenth anniversary of the Democracy Wall Movement as well as the Seventieth Anniversary of the May Fourth Movement of 1915–1919, the latter being the first mass student movement demanding national freedom and equality for China and personal freedom and democracy for the individual.

It was in this political context that the following two literary works, which are clearly explications of the self, were written in China during the 1980s: Yang Lian's collection of sixty-four long poems entitled *Yi*[1] and Gao Xingjian's 81-chapter novel *Lingshan*.[2] These works, each considered by the respective authors to be his major work to date, are deeply philosophical and represent several years of writing and serious reflection on the self and the place of the self in society, traditional culture, history and in literary creation. Importantly, both works are regarded by the authors as expressions of the self.

As the role of the self is crucial and highly pronounced in creative literature, these two works will serve to demonstrate how both Yang Lian and Gao Xingjian have invented unique constructs and extended the confines of language and literature to reclaim the self as author. Although two different genres are concerned, both writers have employed various artistic strategies to endow the author with more than a single voice. Such strategies have allowed *Yi* and *Lingshan* to successfully reveal several facets of the authorial self.

Before turning to discuss specific aspects of the conceptual framework of *Yi* and *Lingshan* the following comments on the development of the notion of the Chinese self in modern times, its linkages with traditional Chinese philosophy as well as with Western philosophy, will serve as a critical context for understanding the core philosophy of the self of both writers which despite their readings in

Western literature, remains distinctly Chinese. The self portrayed in *Yi* and in *Lingshan* has discernible genealogical ties with the traditional self described below, but it is also identifiably the self of two reflective writers of China pondering on existential issues and the place of the self in society and in the cosmos during the 1980s. In the case of each, the perceptions of the self are enriched by strong intellects, powerful observational skills and imaginations, and highly developed aesthetic visual, auditory and kinetic sensitivities. Wide reading in China's classical and modern literature, philosophy and history as well as in Western literature and history have deepened their critical abilities, as have their individual experiences of personal trauma because of their acute awareness of self and obsession for creative writing. Last but not least both writers are highly skilled in the effective use of language.

Early traditional Chinese notions of an autonomous self have their origins in the Daoist writings attributed to Laozi and Zhuangzi. Embedded in the Daoist tradition is the opposition to restriction on the freedom and autonomy of action of the individual, both to the physical body and to the spiritual self. That the basic premise of human life was the individual's freedom to expression in speech and action, was a dominant feature in the writings of independent thinkers in China's past, and was developed and expounded unambiguously in late pre-modern times by Li Zhi (1527–1602) of the Ming dynasty who fought unrelentingly for the freedom of intellectual enquiry. His critical dissertations on Buddhist, Moist and Daoist texts incurred the wrath of orthodox Confucian scholars who vilified, slandered and silenced him.[3] The Confucian scholar bureaucracy of the Ming (1368–1644) and Qing (1644–1911) dynasties with its strong emphasis on orthodoxy ensured that such heretical ideas were stifled, until some centuries later, when Li Zhi was upheld as an exemplar by modern Chinese anarchists and hailed as China's Bakunin in the early years of the twentieth century.[4]

It was only when the ruling Confucian scholar class clearly perceived its failure to respond effectively to the threat imposed by the modern industrialised West that the authority of orthodox Confucianism was severely and effectively challenged from within. In the late nineteenth century the value and importance of the individual's autonomous self came to be promoted, initially as a construct for national salvation. Pro-Western Confucian scholars such as Wang Tao, Yan Fu and Tan Sitong in the 1880s and 1890s argued that democratic institutions had made Western nations wealthy and strong because through such institutions each individual was charged with the responsibility for the well-being of the nation.

Yan Fu (1855–1921)[5] who brought to the Chinese John Stuart Mill's *On Liberty* and *System of Logic*, and Montesquieu's *L'ésprit des Lois* with his translations of these works, argued perceptively in a series of essays in 1894 that the Chinese civil service examinations since the Song dynasty (960–1279) had made scholars impotent with the possible but uncertain prize of a position in the bureaucracy. The examinations had sapped scholars of intelligence, corrupted their morals and reduced them to a parasitic existence in society. Whereas the people of the West were their own masters those in China were slaves. Could slaves be expected to fend off nations governed by masters? In Yan Fu's view it was the lack of freedom in China which had prevented the development of science and technology in China: personal freedom was feared by the sages of China whereas in the West all laws were aimed at the preservation of personal freedom. Applying Darwin's 'struggle for existence' and 'natural selection' to society and social phenomena, as espoused by Spencer, Yan Fu concluded that if modernisation were to take place in China the Chinese would probably not cope, just like people in poor health cannot cope with strenuous exercise.[6]

At this point it would be relevant to draw attention to Neo-Confucian thought which remains active to this day at the core of Chinese culture, despite the enormous political and social changes which have taken place during the twentieth century. It is in the Neo-Confucian concept of sagehood, that the crucial difference between the individualism of the West and China may be seen most clearly: sagehood, ie. perfection of the self or self-realisation lay in the elimination of differences between the self and others. This is diametrically opposed to the individualism of the West which seeks to emphasise differences between the self and others.[7]

In *An Exposition of Benevolence* (Renxue, 1898), Tan Sitong (1865 –1898) indicted traditional Chinese political strategy: rulers exercised authority by keeping the masses ignorant. The institution of an autocratic ruler had brought about moral degeneration in which sycophantic behaviour was an integral part: it was named 'loyalty' by those who joined the ruler in oppressing the common people. Thus the original intent of Confucius had been progressively eroded over the centuries and his teachings had been reduced to being instruments for preserving the authority of the ruler and the ruling class.[8]

By the early years of the twentieth century Western anarchist thinking was to provide Chinese intellectuals with the vocabulary and conceptual framework for a dynamic modern political and social philosophy which consistently argued that the individual was the most important and basic unit of society. Through the publications of Chinese anarchists grouped in Tokyo and Paris, anarchism was established as a crucial part of Chinese radical thinking and action, and as an integral and powerful voice in revolutionary discourse. The anarchist emphasis on the individual and social concerns, the denigration of all existing past and present traditions and institutions, demanded the transformation of the Chinese psyche through the process of anarchist education: in other words, cultural revolution. Power and authority, epitomised by the government, had resulted in the distortion of the primitive instinct of mutual help in social man. The lust for power had brought about this distortion through the coercion of punishments and the inducement of rewards (money, status, honours and fame). In the Chinese anarchist search for a more noble and meaningful form of human existence, social classes and the lust for power were isolated as the main sources of the contagious hypocritical morality rampant in human society.

Chinese anarchist thinking[9] was most dramatically expressed and widespread in the New Culture Movement of the May Fourth period, 1915–1919.[10] Then, following the events of the May Fourth Incident in 1919, anarchist thinking filtered into the Chinese communist movement as many former anarchists gradually joined the ranks of the Chinese Communist Party (CCP) which was established in 1921.[11] Important anarchist achievements in the education of labour and the peasantry, mass mobilisation and the strategy of cultural revolution, also, were conveniently appropriated by the CCP. Dirlik perceptively observes that the prevailing mood of the May Fourth period 'was not reflective discrimination but an euphorious revolutionary eclecticism that could imagine a basic unity in diverse ideas so long as these appeared progressive, democratic and scientific' and that 'under the circumstances the ideas anarchists contributed to the New Culture Movement were not easily distinguishable as anarchist ideas, especially since the anarchists did not claim them explicitly for anarchism.'[12] Indeed the immense amounts of anarchist literature available in Chinese translation at the time together with the writings of Chinese anarchists themselves appeared regularly in mainstream publications by 1919, indicating that certain elements of the anarchist ideal had become widely accepted in China. The works of Kropotkin, Bakunin, Goldman, Tolstoy, Grave, Reclus, Louis Blanc, and Malatesta were available in Chinese at the time and some editions ran to five thousand copies.[13]

The rejection of politics and political alignment inherent within anarchist thinking had turned idealistic youth away from involvement in the blatantly political reality of early Republican China. Many of the younger generation of intellectuals, not only those who had embraced anarchism as a total social philosophy, had internalised those elements of anarchist thinking which extolled the importance and value of the individual. These elements were familiar and found resonances in the traditional culture, particularly in the philosophy of the *Zhuangzi* as well as in the literature influenced by that work.[14] By the second decade of this century the anarchist movement had rapidly declined in the West and the younger generation of Chinese intellectuals who had become committed to the ideals of freedom and autonomy of the individual and the affirmation of the self no longer acknowledged their anarchist sources. However, the work of the anarchists had prepared the minds of Chinese youth so that they passionately embraced Nietzsche's pronouncement 'God is dead!' which concisely summed up their aspirations for personal freedom by ending with one stroke all authority external to the individual self.

In this period Chinese creative writers moved to the vanguard as the heroes of the May Fourth movement.[15] The new literature of the period, written in the vernacular language, represented a break with the classical literary traditions of the past and a shift to the issues and concerns of the present, but more importantly it represented both a new awareness of the meaning of the creative act and the literary process as well as the beginnings of a maturing in the Chinese understanding of the literatures and concerns of other peoples of the world.[16] The May Fourth spirit, with its emphasis on the individual and the self, was consciously established as the tradition for China's modern literature. Although it would not be difficult to substantiate that many of the masterpieces of Chinese literature of the past were pure expressions of the unfettered self, it was Western literature, philosophy and psychology which in this period provided the language and modern perspective for theoretical discussions of literature. Creative literature was now acknowledged as the expression of the untrammelled self, as possessing an intrinsic worth and as having an existence other than that of simply being a vehicle for transmitting some political teaching or ideology.[17]

It is the literary excellence of the *Zhuangzi*, as much as its philosophy of the untrammelled self, which has inspired creative writers for countless generations. Chinese writers of this century have been drawn to Nietzsche's writings for precisely the same reasons. Particularly attractive for Chinese writers, and all Chinese reflective thinkers, was Nietzsche's reinforcement of the importance of the self in the context of the modern industrialised world: his harsh indictment of the dehumanising effects of modern Western civilisation issued a strong warning against uncritical imitation of the West at a time when there were severe pressures for China to modernise. The works of Japanese writers such as Kuriyagawa Hakuson (1880–1923) which acted as conduits of Nietzschean thinking to the Chinese added the dimension of immediate relevance by addressing actual problems of the times and his *Symbols of Suffering*, *Out of the Ivory Tower* and *At the Crossroads* were well known from Chinese versions published in the early 1920s.[18] The titles of Kuriyagawa's books speak for themselves: in times of national crisis the eremitism of Daoism was an option for only a few, and for Chinese intellectuals who had largely internalised the Confucian sense of social responsibility,[19] Zarathustra's decision to return to human society was a poignant message. Modern Chinese literature in the May Fourth tradition which accredited the importance of the self in the creative process and embraced the perceptions of contemporary Western literature, emerged first in fiction through the works of powerful writers such as Lu Xun and Yu Dafu, and later in the works of poets such as Guo Moruo, Xu Zhimo, Wen Yiduo, Dai Wangshu, Bian Zhilin and Li Jinfa.[20]

The events in China's history since the May Fourth period, however, denied all but a tenuous development to a literary tradition where the creative self would play the pivotal role. From the early years of the twentieth century a conscious willingness to deny the self for patriotic reasons had begun to emerge in China alongside anarchism with its emphasis on the self and the individual. This renunciation of the self was to grow as foreign powers continued to exert their will upon a weak and impoverished nation ruled by an inept and corrupt government. Territorial encroachment and events leading up to the Japanese invasion in 1937 made the denial of 'self' imperative and this was particularly painful for creative writers with ingrained anarchist leanings and a strong commitment to literature of the self.[21] After the brief civil war which transferred the mantle of government to the CCP in 1949, further demands for 'self' denial were made on individuals. A population conditioned by half a century of 'self' denial, easily succumbed to political tyranny: the denial of an individual's autonomous self was progressively institutionalised by the meticulous implementation of the 'mass line' promoted zealously by party ideologues. An aggressive propaganda machine, with powerful disciplinary and reward mechanisms, effectively silenced dissenting thinkers who dared so much as to voice expressions of the self. Their gradual silence ensured that less independent minds would fall prey to carefully designed propaganda. The Cultural Revolution saw the total denigration of the individual (and of the self) whose role, value and function were reduced to that of being a cog in the socialist machine driven and directed by those in power within the Party. Compelled by socialist public morality the population became accessories to the gross distortion and deletion of basic human instincts. Hypocrisy and deception under the mask of socialist public morality became the established tradition of the times.[22]

The extreme self-alienation of the Cultural Revolution was initially externally-induced but the institution of a socialist public morality allowed it to become a perpetually internally-induced self-alienation. The blatant and exaggerated nature of the excesses of hypocrisy and deception exercised during the Cultural Revolution and the resulting distortion of human thinking and behaviour presents a stark lesson for the world. However, the phenomenon of self-alienation is not exclusive to the Cultural Revolution, nor even to China, it exists in all human societies. As described in the poetry of Yang Lian, habit and tradition anaesthetise the pain of lobotomy and castration for unknowing victims but for those who are aware of these operations taking place, and who therefore do not respond to the anaesthetics, there is excruciating agony. It is this perception of human existence which haunts the poems of Yang Lian's *Yi*. Self-alienation is tragic for all human beings but human society nevertheless continues to perpetuate this process because the instinctive impulse to preserve the species continually results in an obsessive desire to procreate. There are rituals and festivals to glorify the proliferation of the physical self while people who have been reduced to walking corpses remain oblivious to the fact that the spiritual self is being progressively annihilated from the day of birth.[23]

The underlying philosophy of Yang Lian's *Yi* is the unity of heaven and man, a dominant feature of traditional Chinese culture. However, Yang Lian's interpretation of that unity is radically different. Whereas man in traditional culture was subservient to heaven and therefore obeyed heaven, for Yang Lian man is an integral part of heaven. Thus change occurs simultaneously in both man and heaven: as the experiences of the self increase, a richer world is experienced. The unity of heaven and man therefore constitutes ever-changing unities in the world as perceived by the self; poetry is the verbalisation of the self's ever-changing perceptions. This view of the self and the world of the self has its roots in traditional Chinese philosophy: in Daoism and in Neo-Confucianism which incorporated elements of Daoism and Buddhism. In the West it is to be found in the Monadology of the seventeenth-century German philosopher Gottfried Wilhelm Leibniz whose treatise on the monads was in fact developed under the influence of Chinese philosophical works.[24]

The framework of *Yi* is the *Book of Changes* and its intention is the liberation of the self of the individual from the constraints of tradition-bound perceptions of reality. Yang Lian argues that this ancient shamanistic book was the symbolisation of nature by primitive man. People who have annotated the work through the ages have distorted its meaning to suit their own religious and philosophical viewpoints. What were originally scattered and fragmented divinational signs were linked to form a system for expounding some teaching of a later time. However the *Changes* far excel the later interpretations precisely because they are ineffable in their primitivity and simplicity. The *Changes* are primitive man's emotional responses and summing up of the surrounding natural environment. Heaven, earth, mountain, marsh, water, fire, thunder and wind are the natural features of the Yellow River basin, the birthplace of the Chinese civilisation; these images of nature therefore became the earliest symbols of Chinese civilisation. Hence the *Book of Changes* with its trigrams formed from the Yin (female) and Yang (male), and the hexagrams formed from the trigrams, did not intend to transmit a 'theory of changes', but simply to depict the environment inhabited by the Chinese people of ancient times, its changes and mankind's increasingly complex observations of these. The poetic sense of the *Changes* is inherent in this interpretation for it imposes no restrictions and refers to direct perceptions.

The *Changes* which symbolise nature, like nature are also free; they are neither tied to fixed definitions nor to ossified temporal or spatial boundaries. Heaven, earth, mountain, marsh, water, fire, thunder, wind, do not specifically symbolise anything yet together symbolise everything. They neither belong to antiquity which documented them nor to the present which has rediscovered them. They are the products of human hands, spatial demarcations of knowledge. They constitute a miniature of the cosmos which changes with time and with the individual. The spirit of poetry is similar: its objective is not to explain, its objective is solely its existence.

Sixty-four is a hypothetical construct. *Yi* is divided into four books, each containing sixteen items. The abstract symbols of the *Changes* are not used but certain images and numbers are indicated to preserve the primitive free symbolisation of the *Changes*, like the forms in nature. The arrangement and pairing of the trigrams to form hexagrams is also free. Each trigram is placed in the top position and in turn are placed Heaven, Earth, Mountain, Marsh, Water, Fire, Thunder, Wind. Through this poetic structure there is a return to the spontaneity and freedom which are basic features of the *Changes*.

In internal structure, Heaven and Wind, Earth and Mountain, Water and Marsh, Fire and Thunder, are used to construct the four books of *Yi*:

1. 'The Untrammelled Man Speaks': Man confronts nature.
2. 'In Symmetry With Death': Man confronts history.
3. 'Living in Seclusion': Man confronts the self.
4. 'The Descent': Man's transcendence.

The four books of *Yi* form an interconnected whole. Each book has its own particular structure, form of language and content: these too are inter-related, deepening in layers as concentric circles. The circles represent the poet's perceptions unfolding at different levels but have the same centre: man's existence. In poetic creation, Yang Lian is conscious of plunging deeper and deeper into the abyss of existence and, in the process, discovering a 'more profound' language for dialogue with the world. Or, one might say, by sinking deeper and deeper into oneself, man instead envelops the world. This is the path to 'what is beneath the phenomenal, ie. the metaphysical'. For him it is like 'Dante's return to the pure world from Hell or Nietzsche's Zarathustra's going down from the mountain'.[25]

Although prior to 1978 Yang Lian had written some two hundred classical poems, he did not keep any of these after he had decisively turned to writing Modernist poetry. However despite its modern imagery and use of the Modernist concerns, the music of classical poetry continues to reverberate in his poetry. His training in classical Chinese encourages him instinctively to maximise dynamic emotional effect in his writings through the rigorous choice of words; it also allows him to continue to read widely in the masterpieces of Chinese literature of the past while simultaneously expanding his knowledge of world literature. These experiences of continued heightening of the awareness and sensitivity of the self to the linguistic expressions of the finest minds of the world allows for sharper perceptions of an ever-broadening poetic world.[26]

Yang Lian's reading of Nietzsche's *Thus Spoke Zarathustra* and *The Anti-Christ*, confirmed and reinforced the Zhuangzean perspective on human existence afforded in classical literature, particularly poetry. There was a Nietzsche craze in China during the May Fourth period when China's modern literary traditions were first established, and another one in the late 1970s and early 1980s when Yang Lian began to establish himself as a poet. Nietzsche was invoked on both occasions to break the shackles of tradition. On the second occasion 'tradition' referred to that of the remote past as well as that of the immediate past. It is interesting to note that whereas Nietzsche was extolled during the May Fourth period by intellectuals in China, in the West he was at the same time being condemned as the perpetrator of an ideology which had brought about the human carnage and suffering of the First World War. The second Nietzsche craze in China during the late 1970s and 1980s coincided with the exoneration of Nietzsche from associations with the Nazi movement and Nietzsche's subsequent influence on Postmodernist thinking in the West.[27] From 1978 Yang Lian began greedily to consume world literature, reading vast pages of hand-written rough translations of various Western authors which circulated amongst like-minded youth who had no interest in reading Chinese authors.[28] Recalling his intensive reading of world literature in those times, Yang Lian states that he 'devoured' these works; and of these he expresses special admiration for Dante, Beckett, Eliot, Yeats and Pound. His reading of foreign works dwindled after 1986 as he became totally engrossed with completing *Yi*.[29]

As mentioned earlier, Western Modernist writings slipped in alongside Western scientific and technological publications as the Cultural Revolution drew to an end with the death of Mao Zedong in 1976. However, as Pollard points out, Modernist writings posed a serious problem because of the standard Chinese understanding of it. 'Modernism was spawned in Europe at a time when European civilisation had collapsed from within.... The First World War then confirmed the end of civilisation. Writers and artists came to see the world as chaos or wasteland, and, mistrustful of or repelled by objective reality, turned in on themselves. The only thing they could be sure of was the subjective truth of what went on in their own heads. Various forms of irrationalism dominated philosophical thought: Nietzsche's 'the world as will and idea', Bergson's vitalism, and Freud's theory of the libido. Hence the works of Modernism are marked by self-aggrandisement, or a sense of vacuity, isolation, gloom and doom, or anarchy. Existentialism, the theatre of the absurd, the French *nouveau roman* were regarded as later broods from the same nest.[30]

For young Chinese who had been breast-fed on propaganda 'literature' for decades, access during the late 1970s and early 1980s to the masterpieces of world literature, including that of China's past, produced a dynamic effect. Such literature had the effect of affirming the value, worth and integrity of the self, which was essential as a salve for the all but atrophied emotions, imaginations and intellects of the Chinese people in the aftermath of the Cultural Revolution. The young Beijing poets grouped around the *Today* magazine were sensitised by their reading of Modernist literature and were seized by an obsessive need to self-expression which is essential to the act of all literary, artistic and philosophical creation, and to the lives of all reflective human beings. The poets were first to move into the vanguard for the movement to redefine literature and to speak through their poetry to inspire both young and old. In the first issue of *Today* magazine, the editorial board boldly invoked the authority of Marx's 'Comments on the Latest Prussian Censorship Instruction' (1842) to support their rejection of the existing cultural despotism which demanded that all literature produce only black flowers: 'What we need are the unfettered flowers from the depths of people's hearts', the young *Today* poets declared.[31]

The written Chinese language is a unique and extreme form of intellectual and literary repression, yet this very repressiveness enhances the emotional impact of Chinese literary expression. Repression is strongest in the poetic genre and it is interesting that it has been Chinese poetry in the terse classical language which has succeeded in achieving international recognition for almost a century through the translations of Arthur Waley, David Hawkes and A. R. Davis. Even more interesting is the fact that the poetry of writers such as Ezra Pound, which drew inspiration from the imagery of classical Chinese poetry and philosophy, was in the 1980s to provide a strong source of inspiration for young Chinese poets such as Yang Lian. The Beijing poets captured the imaginations and the spirit of the times as their souls spoke out to address the concerns of the self after its virtual annihilation during the Cultural Revolution.

Yang Lian's poetry was barely comprehensible to his critics but his unabashed references to basic human instincts and to parts of the human body, particularly the genitalia, were clearly subversive in China which had for more than half a century nurtured clearly prudish and puritanical traditions. On the publication of *Norlang*[32] in the May 1983 issue of *Shanghai Literature*, Yang Lian became a target for criticism as part of the 'anti spiritual pollution' campaign and none of his poems was published in China during the whole of 1984. However, his infamy brought him to the notice of China scholars such as John Minford, Alisa Joyce and Sean Golden, whose translations in the Hong Kong journal *Renditions* in 1983 and 1985 first brought Yang Lian's poetry to international audiences. Yang Lian left China in 1988 to take part in two major Australian literary arts festivals, Spoleto in Melbourne and Carnivale in Sydney. He subsequently travelled to New Zealand in early 1989 and is now a New Zealand citizen. He has continued to write poetry, most of which is published mainly in Hong Kong and Taiwan. Since then Yang Lian's poems have been published in German, English, French, Italian and Swedish. He has read his poems at poetry festivals in various parts of Europe, the USA, England, Australia and

New Zealand. In 1994, while Copeland Fellow at Amherst College he presented readings at Amherst College and Bard College, and was honoured with an invitation to present readings with Derek Walcott, José Balza and Joseph Brodsky at the United Nations for the Twenty First Anniversary Celebration of the Translation Center at Columbia University.

The playwright and novelist Gao Xingjian graduated from the Beijing Foreign Studies Institute majoring in French literature and he had already begun to read widely in foreign literatures before the beginning of the Cultural Revolution. Criticism of modern Western literature and those who had associations with it intensified as the Cultural Revolution developed: Gao spent five years working as a peasant in the countryside. Born during the Japanese invasion, fifteen years earlier than Yang Lian, Gao was to suffer for twenty years because of his irrepressible urge to write literature of the self. He persisted in writing even while in the countryside and survived detection only by carefully and ingeniously hiding his manuscripts. However, as the absurd human tragedy of the Cultural Revolution unfolded, anxiety periodically overcame him and he committed to flames some scores of manuscripts. In the more relaxed post-Mao period he suddenly emerged as a controversial figure in the Chinese literary world. In 1981 his book *A Preliminary Discussion of Contemporary Narrative Techniques* provoked much criticism and sparked off a heated debate on Modernism vs Realism.[33] He was not deterred and continued to provoke criticism with his experimental plays and is renowned for having introduced the theatre of the absurd to China. *Warning Signal* was performed at the Beijing People's Art Theatre in 1982 and *Bus Stop* in 1983 to a restricted audience at the same venue before it was closed by the authorities as the 'anti spiritual pollution' campaign came into swing. Gao was prohibited from publishing during the whole of 1984. In 1985 *Wild Man* was performed at the People's Art Theatre again stirring up controversy and in 1986 *Other Shore* was stopped during rehearsal. His plays have not been performed in China since.

Gao Xingjian accepted an invitation to Germany and France in 1987 and subsequently settled in Paris where he continues to write. His novel *Lingshan* which he had started to write in 1982 was completed in Paris in September 1989 and published in 1990 by Lianjing in Taipei. Most of his plays have been translated into Swedish and several have been performed at the Swedish Royal Theatre. A number of the plays have also been translated into French, English, German, Italian, Hungarian, Polish and Japanese and have also been performed in theatres of Germany, France, Austria, England, USA, Yugoslavia, Australia, Taiwan and Hong Kong. In 1992 he received the French award of Chevalier of the prestigious Ordre des Arts et des Lettres for distinguished contribution to the field of the arts and literature.

Gao's *Lingshan* bears the stamp of a mature writer. He is an excellent storyteller and his playful persona permeates the entire eighty-one chapters of the novel despite the serious philosophical and ethical issues addressed in it. A masterly prose writer with unique visual acumen, he captures the spirit of isolated, remote villages and the countryside of the Chinese hinterland in black, white, and greys, as in artistic photography. This is the setting for *Lingshan* but it is not a static setting and the specifics are detailed as he travels, both in fact and in memory, to the many places he had visited in childhood as a refugee, as well as in dream. Gao's creative techniques in drama are effectively transferred to the novel. The space within the various settings is used to maximum effect and allows for the rich portrayal of minor characters from an amazingly wide spectrum of Chinese society both of the past and of the present, and from history, mythology, and literature.

However, *Lingshan* (Spirit/Soul Mountain) is essentially an exploration of the self, of the self in history and specifically the self of Gao Xingjian as a representative of the human species with basic instincts, emotions and the capacity to think and reflect. It would seem that Gao's need to expiate the tension of documenting the history of the Chinese self was precipitated by his stark confrontation with death in 1983. X-rays taken at two separate hospitals on two separate days provided irrefutable evidence for the diagnosis that he had lung cancer and had only a few months to live. Seeming to confirm the diagnosis was the fact that his father had died of the disease a couple of years earlier. The result of a third X-ray some months later brought him back from the brink of physical death only to restore him to the reality of constant criticism and harassment by the authorities for his Modernist views on literature and his dogged persistence in experimenting with theatre of the absurd.

Gao Xingjian left Beijing to avoid the attacks of literary critics and commenced a long journey lasting five months during which he investigated the remnants of early Chinese civilisation as preserved in the customs and practices of Han, Miao, Yi and Jiang groups living in remote, inaccessible regions of Sichuan and Yunnan. The author with his ever-curious mind captures with artistic sensitivity the fine details of the encroachment of centuries of socialisation (and government) on humanity and on the natural environment alike. The authorial comments are muted and minimalist and challenge the readers to respond. These chapters are related in the first person singular, 'I'. The use of the plural form of the self, 'we/us' is anathema for Gao: he insists on the use of the singular self for to do otherwise would be to compromise the self and perceptions which can only be unique to the self.

However, the author is travelling alone and experiences cold, hunger, and acute loneliness; this leads to the creation of 'you' in the author's own image as the ideal partner for discourse. Then 'you', experiencing the same loneliness, create 'she/her'. The 'you' chapters contain many beautifully executed depictions of the primordial black and grey world of the pre-self erotic consciousness; these are surrealistically conveyed as dream, nightmare and lustful fantasy through the persona of 'you' and 'she'. The technique of creating 'you' and 'she' is one which ingeniously provides the author simultaneously with many lenses for exploring a number of man-woman relationships which are compounded by these two protagonists relating stories about others as well as those of themselves.

Finally 'he' is created in the person of 'you' turning and walking away. 'I' and 'you' are too closely related to allow for objective comments on the self. It is through the creation of the third person 'he' that critical distance is achieved and permits for yet another dimension for the expression of the authorial perceptions of the self.

Literature of the unfettered self, like the work of all creative thinkers, is potentially seditious. Inevitably, under repressive governments, if publication is possible 'seditious elements' are usually more obvious in the works of writers and artists who are subjected to, or are witness to, violent and blatant forms of social or political repression. But after stripping back the surface overlay which is the immediate response of the writer or artist to the violence and repression there should remain an underlying stratum with relevance to broader human concerns.[34]

Chinese literature under the Cultural Revolution carried the political messages of the dominant political faction of the party. The slogan 'literature should serve politics' was clearly stipulated and the role of the author and reader were totally negated. Only politically chaste and puritanically pure writings could get past the censors: editors who approved the publication of politically unsound writings were held responsible and the labour camps and cadre schools were strong deterrents to write or to publish anything but what was politically safe. As a result the human characters in writings of the period were not unsurprisingly simplistic clear-cut black and white villains and heroes lacking in 'human smell'.[35] It may be argued that since the 1980s, the self has been reclaimed in Chinese literature and that generally speaking freedom and autonomy in all aspects of the literary process, to a certain degree, exists in 1990s China much as it does in the various democracies of the world. In fact it would appear that the literature published in 1990s China indeed exudes a positively strong 'human smell'. However, literature of the self is a personal concern and is unaffected by any form of coercion, including that of market forces. Provided that the existing political authority permits a minimal basic level of personal freedom, literature of the self will flourish. However, the attainment of that threshold of personal freedom and the existence of a literature of the self only indicates the freedom and autonomy of individuals engaged in the creative process (writer and readers). The existence of a literature of the self cannot be regarded as an indicator of the achievement of social equality and justice which remain elusive in human society. These lofty ideals have been sought by philosophers in various cultures throughout history but the translation of philosophy into political action and then the establishment of ideologies and institutions have not necessarily brought about the realisation of these ideals: sometimes the result has simply meant greater equality and justice for one or some social group at the expense of others.[36]

Notes

1 Yang Lian (b. 1955). The collection *Yi* is included in Yang Lian and Yu Feng, *Taiyang yu Ren*, Sun and man; Changsha, 1991, and in Yang Lian, *Yi*, Taipei, 1993. Discussions of Yang Lian's *Yi*, as well as selected translations from the collection, are contained in the following works: Mabel Lee, 'The Philosophy of the Self and Yang Lian', Yang Lian, *Masks and Crocodile: A Chinese Poet*

and His Poetry, Sydney, 1990, pp.9–36, 'Before Tradition: The *Book of Changes*, Yang Lian's *Yi* and the Affirmation of the Self Through Poetry', eds Mabel Lee and A. D. Syrokomla-Stefanowska, *Modernization of the Chinese Past*, Sydney, 1993, pp.94–106, and 'Man Confronts History: Six Poems From Yang Lian's 'In Symmetry With Death', *Ulitarra* 3 (1993): 57–66.

2 Gao Xingjian (b. 1940). The novel *Lingshan* was published in Taipei, 1990. Goran Malmqvist's Swedish translation of the novel, *Andarnasberg*, Stockholm, 1992, and Noel and Liliane Dutrait's French version, *La Montagne de l'Ame*, Paris, 1995, have received many favourable reviews. See the summary and analysis of *Lingshan* in Torbjorn Loden, 'World Literature with Chinese Characteristics: On a Novel by Gao Xingjian', *Stockholm Journal of East Asian Studies* 4 (1993): 17–39, which includes an extensive bibliography on Gao Xingjian's writings. See also Mabel Lee, 'Without Politics: Gao Xingjian on Literary Creation', *Stockholm Journal of East Asian Studies* 6 (1995).

3 Wm Theodore de Bary, 'Individualism and Humanitarianism in Late Ming Thought' in Wm Theodore de Bary and the Conference on Ming Thought (eds), *Self and Society in Ming Thought*, New York, 1970, pp.145–247, examines the meaning of 'individualism' in traditional Chinese thinking as well as the key elements in the individualism espoused by the late Ming thinkers Wang Yangming, He Xinyin and Li Zhi. See also Mark Elvin, 'The Double Disavowal: The Attitudes of Radical Thinkers to the Chinese Tradition', ed. David S. G. Goodman, *China and the West: Ideas and Activists*, Manchester, 1990, pp.5–6, where Elvin warns that it would be a mistake to view the disintegration of 'the surface structure' of Chinese tradition in the twentieth century as merely the result of external pressures and stimuli and cites Wang Yangming, He Xinyin and Li Zhi as independent thinkers contributing to this disintegration long before modern times.

4 See Bugong Chou (Enemy of Injustice), 'Li Zhuowu xiansheng xueshuo' (On the teachings of Mr Li Zhuowu), *Tianyibao* 1 (Tokyo, 10 June 1907), reprinted in Yang Tianshi, 'Shehui Zhuyi Jiangxihui ziliao' (Source materials on the Association for the Discussion and Study of Socialism), *Zhongguo zhexue* 1 (August 1978): 434 –5.

5 Yan Fu's translations include John Stuart Mill, *On Liberty* (1898) and *System of Logic* (1900), Montesquieu, *L'esprit des Lois* (1900–1905) and E. Jenks, *A History of Politics* (1903). These translations had a powerful effect on Chinese intellectuals who were preoccupied with the quest of discovering the secret to the wealth and power of Western civilization. Yan Fu soon began to feel that he had made a mistake, that he had set in motion the demand for radical changes which he in fact opposed. While he had become a reactionary soon after the turn of the century, his translations were important in forming the ideals of the new generation of Chinese intellectuals who emerged after the abolition in 1906 of the state civil service examination system. See B. I. Schwartz, *In Search of Wealth and Power: Yen Fu and the West*, Cambridge, Mass., 1964, and Y. C. Wang, *Chinese Intellectuals and the West*, University of North Carolina Press, 1966. It should be noted however that the state civil service examination system had in imperial times given the scholar class access to political power; its abolition meant that the modern Chinese intellectuals were alienated from political power.

6 See Wang, *op. cit.*, pp.195–211.

7 The Chinese scholar's equating of self-fulfilment with discharging social responsibilities is examined in Thomas A. Metzger, *Escape from Predicament: Neo-Confucianism and China's Evolving Political Culture*, New York, 1977.

8 See Chan Sin-wai, trans., *An Exposition of Benevolence: The Jen-hsüeh of T'an Ssu-t'ung*, Hong Kong, 1984. Significantly also, as Elvin points out, Tan's work aimed to fuse Neo-Confucianism and Mahayana Buddhism 'by implicitly equating the achievement of *ren* ('sensitive awareness of all other people') by the totality of mankind, with the collective attaining of nirvana understood not as the total obliteration of the self, but as the stripping away of all the accidental specificities of the self that made it in any way different from any other self.' See Elvin, *op. cit.*, p.7.

9 In recent years three excellent definitive studies on Chinese anarchism have been published; they are complementary and invaluable for their contribution to research on the intellectual history of China in the twentieth century: Peter Zarrow, *Anarchism and Chinese Political Culture*, New York, 1990, provides a solid analysis of the indigenous origins of modern Chinese anarchist thinking; Arif Dirlik, *Anarchism in the Chinese Revolution*, Berkeley, 1991, provides an excellent and comprehensive analysis of modern Chinese anarchism in the context of the whole spectrum of revolutionary discourse in the twentieth century; and Ming K. Chan and Arif Dirlik, *Schools into Factories: Anarchists, the Guomindang and the National Labor University in Shanghai, 1927–1932*, (U. S. A.), Durham and London, 1991, provides an examination of the most significant case of political alignment by the Chinese anarchists in establishing the National Labour University in Shanghai.

10 See Dirlik, *op. cit.*, chapter 5 and Chow Tse-tsung, *The May Fourth Movement: Intellectual Revolution in Modern China*, Stanford University Press, 1967.

11 The politicization of Chinese intellectuals following the May Fourth Incident and the gravitation of large numbers of Chinese intellectuals to communism are detailed in works such as Maurice Meisner, *Li Ta-chao and the Origins of Chinese Marxism*, Cambridge, Mass., 1967.

12 See Dirlik, *op. cit.*, pp.160–1.

13 See Dirlik, *op. cit.*, pp.154–5.

14 Studies on various aspects of the impact of Nietzsche in China may be found in works such as David A. Kelly, 'The Highest Chinadom: Nietzsche and the Chinese Mind, 1907–1989' and Chen Guying, 'Zhuang Zi and Nietzsche: Plays of Perspectives', both in Graham Parkes, ed., *Nietzsche and Asian Thought*, Chicago, 1991; Yue Daiyun, 'Nietzsche in China', *The Journal of the Oriental Society of Australia* 20 & 21 (1988–1989): 199–219; Mabel Lee, 'From Chuang-tzu to Nietzsche: On the Individualism of Lu Hsün', *The Journal of the Oriental Society of Australia* 17 (1985): 21–38.

15 Cf. Ezra F. Vogel, 'The Unlikely Heroes: The Social Role of the May Fourth Writers' in Merle Goldman, ed., *Modern Chinese Literature in the May Fourth Era*, Cambridge, Mass., 1977, pp.145–160. See also Leo Ou-fan Lee, *The Romantic Generation of Modern Chinese Writers*, Cambridge, Mass., 1973; M. Galik, *Milestones in Sino-Western Literary Confrontation, 1898–1979*,

Wiesbaden, 1986, which examines the interliterary process of confrontation in Chinese literature in the period 1898–1979, and discusses connections with ancient Greek literature and mythology, Russian, French, English, German, Norwegian, American, Japanese and Bengali literature; and also the selection of articles in M. Galik, ed., *Interliterary and Intraliterary Aspects of the May Fourth Movement 1919 in China*, Bratislava, 1990.

16 Western literature was introduced to Chinese intellectuals from the turn of the twentieth century through Chinese translations and through the reading of the works in either the original or in Japanese translation by the vast numbers of young Chinese studying in Japan, France, Germany, England and the United States. See Galik, *op. cit.* (1986).

17 Cf. Liang Qichao's promotion of the political novel to argue the reform cause just a decade earlier, in works e.g. Mabel Lee, 'Liang Ch'i-ch'ao and the Political Revolution of Late-Ch'ing' in A. R. Davis and A. D. Stefanowska, eds, *Search for Identity: Modern Literature and the Creative Arts in Asia*, Sydney, 1974, pp.203–24, and 'Chinese Women and Social Change: A Theme in Late-Ch'ing Fiction and its Subsequent Development' in Wang Gungwu *et al.*, eds, *Society and the Writer: Essays in Literature in Modern Asia*, Canberra, 1981, pp.128–38. For the development of modern literary theory during the May Fourth period see Bonnie S. McDougall, *The Introduction of Western Literary Theories into Modern China, 1919–1925*, Tokyo, 1971, and Marian Galik, *Mao Dun and Modern Chinese Literary Criticism*, Weisbaden, 1969.

18 These works by Kuriyagawa Hakuson have been summarised in Mabel Lee, 'Suicide of the Creative Self: The Case of Lu Hsün', A. R. Davis and A. D. Syrokomla-Stefanowska, eds, *Austrina: Essays in Commemoration of the 25th Anniversary of the Founding of the Oriental Society of Australia*, Sydney, 1982, pp.140–67. See also in Goldman, ed., the following: Ching-mao Cheng, 'The Impact of Japanese Literary Trends on Modern Chinese Writers' , pp.63–88, Leo Ou-fan Lee, 'Genesis of a Writer: Notes on Lu Xun's Educational Experience, 1881–1909', pp.161–188, and Harriet C. Mills, 'Lu Xun: Literature and Revolution—from Mara to Marx', pp.189–220.

19 Cf. T. A. Metzger, *op. cit.*

20 For comprehensive studies on Lu Xun in the context of May Fourth writings see Leo Ou-fan Lee, *Voices From the Iron House: A Study of Lu Xun*, Indiana University Press, 1987 and *Lu Xun and His Legacy*, Berkeley, 1985. The following studies focus on the anarchist, Zhuangzean and Nietzschean influences on the writings of Lu Xun and Yu Dafu: Mabel Lee, 'Suicide of the Creative Self: the Case of Lu Xun' and 'From Chuang-tzu to Nietzsche: On the Individualism of Lu Hsün'; Beate Rusch, 'Yu Dafu's House of Mirrors: A Few Notes on the Remaking of Self in Yu Dafu's Philosophy of Life and Blue Smoke', M. Galik, ed. *Chinese Literature and European Context*, Bratislava, 1994, pp.55–62.

21 See for example the anguish expressed in Lu Xun's prose-poems written 1924–1927 and published as the collection *Yecao* in *Lu Xun quanji*, Beijing, 1981, Vol. 1, pp. 159–223. He understood the importance of the self to the creative act and his writing of these prose-poems represents a conscious abandonment

of creative literature as he knew and loved it. See Lee, 'Suicide of the Creative Self'.

22 I have examined the concept of tradition with special reference to Yang Lian's treatment of the topic in 'Before Tradition: The Book of Changes, Yang Lian's *Yi* and the Affirmation of the Self Through Poetry'. See also Ginger Li, trans., Yang Lian, 'Tradition and Us', *Renditions: A Chinese-English Translation Magazine* 19 & 20 (1983): 69–73.

23 The following comments have been summarized from Yang Lian, 'Guanyu *Yi*' (About *Yi*; unpublished manuscript written in Auckland, New Zealand, 16 July 1991).

24 See David E. Mungello, *Leibniz and Confucianism: The Search for Accord*, The University Press of Hawaii, 1977.

25 'About *Yi*'.

26 The influence of classical literature on Yang Lian is noted in detail in Lee, 'The Philosophy of the Self and Yang Lian'. Cf. Sean Golden and John Minford, 'Yang Lian and the Chinese Tradition', Howard Goldblatt, ed., *Worlds Apart: Recent Chinese Writings and Its Audiences*, Armonk, N.Y., 1990, pp.119–37, which provides an analysis of Yang Lian's poetry of the late 1970s and early 1980s, drawing attention to specific classical Chinese works as well as historical sites which have directly influenced Yang Lian's early poems. See also the following articles in Jeffrey Kinkley, ed., *After Mao: Chinese Literature and Society 1978–1981*, Cambridge, Mass., 1985, which together provide a detailed description of the literary context in which Yang Lian commenced his writing of modern poetry in the late 1970s: William Tay, ' "Obscure Poetry": A Controversy in Post-Mao China', pp.133–57; and Pan Yuan and Pan Jie, 'The Non-Official Magazine *Today* and the Younger Generation's Ideals for a New Literature', pp.193–219.

27 See Graham Parkes, 'The Orientation of the Nietzschean Text', Graham Parkes, ed., *op. cit.*, pp.3–20, which incisively pinpoints the Euro-American bias of Nietzsche studies. Parkes' volume is aimed at rectifying this bias, focussing on the significant impact of Nietzsche on Japanese and Chinese thinkers into present times. Deliberate distortions in the posthumous editing and publication of parts of Nietzsche's writings by his sister in the Nachlass led to Nietzsche's philosophy being associated with both the fascist and Nazi movements. The voluminous research publications of the past decades on this issue have been summarized in Cheung Chiu-yee, 'Lu Xun and Nietzche: A Comparative Study' (Ph.D. thesis, University of Sydney, 1994) which is an exhaustive study of affinities between Lu Xun and Nietzsche. See also Raoul David Findeisen, 'A Sino-German Venture of the 1940s: Fascist Reception of Nietzschean Philosophy and the Zhanguo Group', M. Galik, ed., *Chinese Literature and European Context*, pp.73–81 and Michael Godley, 'Politics From History: Lei Haizong and the *Zhanguo Ce* Clique', *Papers in Far Eastern History* 40 (1989): 95–122, which examine the use of Nietzsche's writings to justify the fascist activities of the Guomindang government during the 1930s.

28 Prior to 1978, foreign literature was the exclusive domain of two publishers in Beijing, People's Literature Publishing House and People's Publishing House, and their provincial branches. In 1978 two major publishing houses specialising

in foreign literature translation were established to meet growing demands in the more liberal atmosphere of the times: the Shanghai Translation Publishing House with a brief to publish representative works of well-known 'bourgeois' schools and contemporary works reflecting important trends in literature, politics and economics; and the Foreign Literature Publishing House in Beijing to publish exclusively foreign literature in translation or in the original language. From 1980 these two publishers jointly published the *Twentieth Century Foreign Literature Series*. In 1981 there were twenty specialist foreign literature magazines and 437 registered literary magazines with foreign literature columns. Apart from single volumes of foreign authors, several important collections and volumes of foreign literature also appeared from various presses through the country indicating the scope and widespread interest in foreign literature. Important works include: Yuan Kejia, ed., *Selection of Foreign Modernist Writings*, 4 vols, Shanghai Literature and Art Publishing House, 1981; Luo Jiashan, ed., *Selection of European and American Modernist Writings*, Yunnan People's Publishing House, 1982; Feng Yidai, *Collected Translations of Modern Foreign Literature*, 3 vols, Guangdong People's Publishing House, 1982; *Collection of Contemporary American Short Stories* and *Collection of Modern and Contemporary English Short Stories*, Shanghai Translation Publishing House, 1981; *Selection of Modern World Short Stories*, 4 vols, Anhui People's Publishing House, 1981; *Selection of Modern English and American Poetry*, *Selection of Modern French Poetry*, *Selection of Poetry From Germanic Countries*, Hunan Publishing House, 1982; *Collection of Theatre of the Absurd*, Shanghai Translation Publishing House, 1981; *Selection of Black Humour*, Fujian People's Publishing House, 1983. See Zhao Qianyi, 'Western Literary Influences on Contemporary Chinese Literature: With Special Reference to Fiction and Poetry in the 1980s' (MA thesis, University of Sydney, 1994).

29 See Lee, 'The Philosophy of Self and Yang Lian', pp.16–17. It was in the rich and stimulating environment of the Beijing literary scene of the late 1970s and early 1980s that Yang Lian read works by authors which were to leave indelible imprints on his poetry. Names like the following immediately sprang to his mind when I questioned him about foreign authors he had read at the time: T. S. Eliot, Dante Alighieri, George Orwell, Dylan Thomas, William Blake, Ezra Pound, Saul Bellow, Walt Whitman, William Golding, Thomas Hardy, W. B. Yeats, James Joyce, Franz Kafka, Friedrich Nietzsche, Marcel Proust, Samuel Beckett, Eugene Ionesco, Charles Baudelaire, Vladmir Mayakovsky, Boris Pasternak, Alexander Solzhenitsyn, Fyodor Dostoevsky, Milan Kundera, Czeslaw Milosz, Rabindravath Tagore, Octavio Paz and Gabriel Garcia Marquez. Cf. Golden and Minford.

30 See D. E. Pollard, 'The Controversy Over Modernism, 1979–84', *China Quarterly* 104 (1985): 641–56, for an analysis of the political implications of the introduction of Western modernist writings into China during this period.

31 The Editorial Board of *Today*, 'To Our Readers'. See the translation with notes in David S. G. Goodman, *Beijing Street Voices: The Poetry and Politics of China's Democracy Movement*, London, 1981, pp.162–63.

32 See Alisa Joyce with John Minford, trans., Yang Lian, 'Concerning *Norlang*', *Renditions: A Chinese-English Translation Magazine* 23 (1985): 162–63 as well

as translations of Yang Lian's poems in the same volume.

33 Gao Xingjian, *Xiandai xiaoshuo jiqiao chutan*, Guangzhou, 1981. See also the comments, translations and summaries on the debate in *Renditions: A Chinese-English Translation Magazine* 19 & 20 (1983): 41–80; and also Josephine Riley and Michael Gissenwehrer, 'The Myth of Gao Xingjian', Josephine Riley and Else Unterrieder, *Berichte des Ludwig-Boltzmann-Instituts für China-und Südostasien-Forschung Number 27*, Bonn, 1989, pp.129–51.

34 Over the past few decades, Marian Galik has published many studies on modern Chinese literature dealing with the impact of a wide range of foreign literary and philosophical influences spanning a century of development until present times. In 'Metamorphosis in Modern Chinese Intellectual (and Philosophical) Consciousness: Musings Over Its "Coming to Be" ', *Asian and African Studies* 1.2 (1992): 132–145, Galik examines some theoretical and practical aspects of modern Chinese intellectual history and philosophy from the end of the nineteenth century to the 1980s, analysing the works of Wang Guowei, Lu Xun, Mao Dun, Qu Qiubai and Liang Shuming. He draws attention to the theoretical construct of 'interliterariness', put forward by Dionyz Durisin in *Theory of Literary Comparatistics*, Bratislava, 1984. Durisin indicates that development of thought about literature has led to the endeavour to understand 'not just the work of literature and its constituent parts but also the inner laws of the development of literature, ie. the literary process.' The result has been that 'a characteristic feature of poetics of recent times is the surmounting of the static approaches to the interpretation of the literary phenomenon'. The 'nature of the artistic fact is not merely the summation of those elements and procedures given a constant form by history, but also a living organism subject to transformation by history, showing many-sided affinities to the surrounding historical and social reality, with the cultural background of the artist and society, with the preceding literary traditions, with different branches of art etc.' (p.11). Durisin's comments would support a holistic approach to the study and evaluation of modern Chinese literature in the context of world literature. See also Galik's 'Interliterary and Intraliterary Aspects of the Study of Post-1918 Chinese Literature', Goldblatt, ed., pp.231–45.

35 Liu Zaifu, a member of the official literary establishment, joined in supporting the young poets' cause to promote the importance of the self in creative literature; he complained of the lack of 'human smell' in modern Chinese literature. See Mabel Lee, 'Rethinking Literature in the Post-Mao Period: Liu Zaifu's Theory of the Subjectivity of Literature', *The Journal of the Oriental Society of Australia* 18 &19 (1986): 101–25.

36 This is a revised version of a paper entitled 'The Individual and the Meaning of Personal Freedom in Twentieth Century China: A Century of Development' presented at the Ideas of Freedom in Asia Conference held at the Humanities Research Centre of the Australian National University, Canberra, 4–6 July, 1994.

Language and Culture: a Translator's Perspective

Marian Maddern

I first met Soumyen Mukherjee about a quarter of a century ago. I was then doing postgraduate work, in the Indian Studies Department that Melbourne University used to have, on the nature of Bengali and the process of literary translation from it into English. Dr Mukherjee was looking for a translator for a project he had in mind: a collection of essays by the great nineteenth-century Bengali novelist and essayist Bankim Chandra Chatterjee. My teacher and supervisor, Professor Sibnarayan Ray, thinking that I might be interested in such a project (as I was), introduced me to Dr Mukherjee—and off and on we have been collaborating ever since: first on that initial project, and more recently on translating a volume of three short novels by Bankim Chandra.

Literary translation is an activity that has been seen by different people as problematic in all sorts of ways, though this has never discouraged people from engaging in it and other people from reading its results. Rather than discuss theories of translation I have presented here some of my experiences in literary translation—experiences which have thrown light on certain aspects of the languages and cultures concerned, or have highlighted similarities and differences between them or, indeed, have thrown into relief certain intransigences, certain blind spots, as I peered into Bengali and its literature.

To 'learn' another language (however impossible it may be to do this completely) is to find a whole new area of cultural constructs opened (at least partially) to one's enquiring eye. And the very act of seeing these constructs of a different language and culture fosters a new awareness of one's own language and its constructs. Often small, specific examples can illuminate or bring home general ideas in very clear-cut ways. Bengali is a member of the (large) Indo-European family of languages as is English. We often read about how cognate words in the two languages (and their predecessors) demonstrate their common ancestry. But to come across in a general Bengali-English dictionary entries such as:

' "tri"—(1) n. three (2) a. & in comp. three, tri- ... "tripad"—n. (math.) a tripod' [the derivation here is from the Sanskrit "tri" = three, and "pada" = foot], and

' "ma"—(1) n. mother; mamma, mama, ma', and

' "matri"—n. (in comp.) mother' (i.e., matri-)

is to feel this common ancestry with a new force. (The dictionary in question is the Samsad Bengali-English dictionary, roughly the size of the Concise Oxford.) On the other hand, there are fascinating divergences. Both English and Bengali have words which are made up of a combination of a negative and a word for 'one'—in English, 'none', in Bengali, "anek" (made up of the privative prefix "a-", from Sanskrit and cognate with the Greek privative 'a-', plus "ek" = 'one'). The English word, as we all know, means 'not one', and has a negative force, indicating no example of, not any, nothing. But the Bengali word, also meaning 'not one', equally logically, yet differently, indicates 'many'. (Interestingly, Bengali has no single word for the meaning of the English word 'none', instead constructions such as 'anything ... not', 'anyone ... not' are used.

The Bengali words quoted here have been transliterated (enclosed in double quotation marks): Bengali and English use different scripts. A comparison of the two script systems could in itself go on for quite a long and fascinating time, but I shall restrict myself here to just a few comments. Bengali uses no capitals. This means that, among other things, proper names are not marked off from other words in any way. Also, many Bengali personal names are words with meanings. This is not just in the sense that they derive from words with meaning in other languages, as is the case with English names such as Helen (Greek), Jeremy (Hebrew), Vera (Russian), Lawrence (Latin), or that they are (sometimes modified) forms of words from an earlier stage in the language, as is the case with such English names as Edgar and Harold (Old English), but in the sense that they, or the individual words they are made up of, are ordinary words. Thus the name "Charulata" is "charu" = 'graceful' plus "lata"= 'a creeper, a climbing plant'; the name

"Ashok(a)" means 'free of grief'; and the name "Bankim Chandra" means 'curved moon'—and so on. But all this can mean certain pitfalls in certain contexts. I well remember the experience, in the early days of my acquaintance with Bengali, of working on a sentence which seemed to be about a thick green, or deep-green, pandit—only to realise from the dictionary that 'deep-green', or 'dark-complexioned', an appellation of Krishna, was actually the pandit's name.

This kind of experience is salutary, and keeps one humble—but there is another kind of experience which can be equally salutary, and can keep one humble in almost an opposite way. As one continues to learn, always aware that there is more to learn, one begins to feel in an inarticulate way that total knowledge of Bengali is not only what is expected of the translator, but that it is what every educated, literary-minded Bengali has. As well as not using capitals, Bengali has not used script modifiers such as italics to carry meaning. This means that (in all but very recent printed Bengali) there is no marking off of foreign language words. A couple of years ago I was translating a poem by a contemporary Bengali poet, a poem which used, as so many contemporary poems do, fairly elliptical combinations of images. One line in particular baffled me, and I asked a Bengali friend, a poet and essayist living in Bengal, for help. My friend suggested, though without certainty, that the line referred to the return in popularity of a popular singer by the name of Pyaralal. But the poet herself later explained to me that the line referred to the return in popularity of the parallel cut in trouser styles. She had used the English word 'parallel', and this is spelled in Bengali as "pyaralal". None of us, after all, know even our own language completely. (Not all of us, for example, know that 'none' in English can take a plural verb ... Bengali, interestingly, does not distinguish singular and plural in any of its verb forms, but uses the one form for both singular and plural subjects.)

This last experience was also an example of a case where questions could and did elicit understandable answers. But this, too, is not always so. (Indeed, the belief that gaps in understanding can of course always be filled in by research and the asking of questions is probably a specific culture-linked belief in itself.) I remember many years ago working on a chapter (in my doctoral thesis on the structure and grammar of Bengali) on Bengali systems of number and measurement. As I worked, the outlines of a particular gap became clear: in the matter of quantities, fractions and mixed numbers, it was obvious enough how formal or written Bengali expressed things like 'one-sixth', 'two and one-sixth', 'two yards' and 'one-sixth of a yard'. But, apart from a construction which my sources assured me was only used in fairly rough, colloquial speech, there seemed to be no way of saying 'two and one-sixth yards'. I tried to put this difficulty to two educated Bengalis. After a certain amount of seeming non-communication, I finally asked, 'Well, how would *you* ask for two and one sixth yards of cloth?' One of them shrugged amiably; the other replied, 'I would ask for three yards of cloth.' Yet a third Bengali speaker, some time later, said, much struck, that he had never before realised it, but that as far as he could see, there was a real gap in the language here—which is an interesting comment in itself.

The transliteration of English words or names into Bengali can present pitfalls of different kinds. In the case of the confusion between "Pyaralal" and 'parallel' there were two factors operating: the confusion about whether the word was a name or not, and the confusion about whether the word was of foreign origin or not. But either one of these is enough in itself to produce errors. Not so long ago, I managed to misread a couple of famous English writers as classical Sanskrit poets: a character in a novel, discussing in a letter the nature of different kinds of love, says that 'Kalidasa, Vayarana, Jayadeva' are the poets of one kind of love, and 'Shekshapiyara, Valmiki' are the poets of another kind. Misled by the context, and the other names in the lists, and aware that my knowledge of Sanskrit authors is far from complete, I failed to recognise the second and fourth of these names as Byron and Shakespeare.

Novels offer their own windows into culture. The same nineteenth-century novel, Bankim Chandra's *The Poison Tree*, in which those lists of writers occur, has as a central element of its plot the evil results of the ill-considered marriage of the male protagonist with a young widow. The man is married already—but it is not bigamy which constitutes the moral issue here so much as widow-remarriage, which had been socially unacceptable in Hindu society for centuries (though not specifically forbidden by any religious texts or scriptures), and which social reformers were newly debating and questioning. 'Other times, other customs'—or, as a Bengali proverb has it, 'Customs differ in different countries/regions'.

The kind of 'traditional wisdom' expressed in proverbs offers another set of examples of intriguing similarities and differences: similarities and differences in images, messages and values. Bengali has a rich collection of proverbs, many of them still in vigorous use. The poem mentioned earlier, in the course of forthrightly addressing thoroughly contemporary issues such as the overuse of tranquillisers and the existence of test-tube babies, refers to two different traditional proverbs in its eighteen lines. One line runs 'Nine of us could not sit on a tamarind leaf'—a reference to a proverb which says 'Nine good people can sit on a tamarind leaf': that is, good people are quiet enough, well-behaved enough for a number of them to be able to fit without trouble into a small space. And another line runs 'We ginger-sellers *do* know the news of the ships'—a reference to a proverb which says 'Why should ginger-sellers know the news of ships': that is, don't expect people to know of things beyond their own business; or even, people should stick to their own business. (The quoted lines are from my as yet unpublished translation of a poem by Gita Chattopadhyay.)

Some Bengali proverbs and sayings are pretty much direct equivalents of some English ones, in both images and meanings: for example, 'playing with fire', 'If there's a wish/will there's the means', and 'a thunderbolt with no cloud' (a bolt from the blue). Others have messages similar to some English ones, but express these in different images, for example, 'An uncle with only one eye is better than no uncle at all' (Half a loaf is better than no bread); or 'If he/she/they get/s to sit, he/she/they want/s to lie down' (Give him an inch and he'll take an ell); or 'If he/she/they doesn't/don't know how to dance, the courtyard is at fault' (A bad workman blames his tools). Bengali, as well as not having separate forms for plural and singular verbs, has no gendered pronouns, and often omits pronouns anyway. Sometimes, though, a seeming similarity can be misleading: 'It doesn't rain as much as it thunders' might suggest 'His bark is worse than his bite', but this would be to ignore (conditioned by English rather than Australian images?) the effect of a climate in which the rains are eagerly awaited: a nearer equivalent would usually be 'Much cry but little wool', or in a fuller form of the proverb, 'Great cry and little wool, as the Devil said when he sheared the hogs'. (This saying, derived from a medieval English miracle play, is known to Bengali writers of 'Teach Yourself Bengali' books, but, I find, unknown to most of my Australian friends and colleagues.) We could note here, too, the Bengali expression 'Water/ rain without clouds', referring to an unexpected good or benefit.

Other proverbs again translate easily enough, but may need a degree of explanation: 'On whose shoulders are there two heads?' means, more or less, Who has a head to spare? Who can afford to take this risk? and 'Brothers, places' (actually, word for word, 'brother brother place place') means Brothers tend to go different ways; and 'You go from branch to branch, I go from leaf to leaf' means I have more knowledge of the details. And then there are the proverbs which do not have equivalents (though this is not to say they are beyond understanding), which are in one way or another more different, more culturally specific: for example, 'There's no trusting a tusked animal or a drunkard', or 'Slandering (your) guru leads to (your) rebirth as an inferior creature', or, with all the (Hindu) resonances of the word dharma, 'The drum of dharma sounds of itself'.

I continue to find the links and similarities across cultures endlessly fascinating—but equally fascinating are the unpredictable and irreducible differences. I thank Bengali, and my Bengali-speaking teachers, colleagues and friends for helping to sharpen my awareness of both.

World-Systems before Capitalism

M. N. Pearson

Within the broad category of radical history, which seems to be the same as political economy, there is no question that the dominant paradigm has been laid out by Immanuel Wallerstein in his world-system model. Since the first volume appeared in 1974 his work has set the agenda, leaving orthodox Marxists, let alone modernisation theorists, liberal market analysts and empiricists floundering in his wake. It even seems that post-modernists, after their brief florescence, have returned to the obscurity they deserve. Wallerstein's work produced a host of rebuttals, modifications, and elaborations. Yet from the beginning even the most trenchant critics have never questioned the value of his enterprise; rather they have been concerned to improve it, to a greater or lesser extent modify it, but they still recognise its seminal importance.

I propose in this short tribute to Soumyen Mukherjee, himself well known for his promotion of 'radical' history, to sketch some recent trends in world-system research, and then to present a very sketchy analysis to show how these recent works may have some utility for looking at the history of East Africa and India in the early modern period.

This is not the place to provide a detailed overview of Wallerstein's model of the modern world-system.[1] Very briefly, Wallerstein believes that from about 1500 there evolved in western Europe a modern world-system, which is to be seen as a new sort of world-economy because it was capitalist. For this reason it has lasted much longer than previous examples of world-economies, and since the late nineteenth century has incorporated the whole globe. This then is a dynamic system in which change occurs, unlike A. G. Frank's rather static dependency theories of nearly three decades ago. Indeed, the model may even be predictive, for Wallerstein believes and hopes that this capitalist system will collapse within the next century or so, leading to a socialist world government.

Within the modern world-system Wallerstein delineates three

zones, linked by unequal exchange designed to extract a surplus and convey it to the dominant areas. These three zones, which are primarily differentiated by different labour systems, are the dominant cores to which the surplus flows, the peripheries from which it is extracted, and the semi-peripheries which act as a cushioning or mediating zone between the two extremes of core and periphery. Here is another element of dynamism, for areas can rise and fall, enter and then leave the core, move from semi-peripheral to core, or to peripheral, status. The three types of zones are not necessarily conterminous with particular states, though from time to time there have been hegemonic states within the cores.

Outside this modern world-system there were, until it incorporated the whole world in the late nineteenth century, areas which were deemed to be external. Trade between external and modern world-system areas was in luxuries, and unlike necessities these cannot create systemic relations. This distinction has been one of the most criticised of all aspects of Wallerstein's work, yet while he has shown openness and flexibility in some other areas, here he stands firm. In a recent essay he retains the distinction, and stresses that it is a key one analytically.

Wallerstein's grand design is not yet completed, for the fourth volume has yet to appear. Nevertheless, he has been active in responding to criticisms, and producing elaborations of this schema.[2] There are several overviews of early critiques of his work.[3] I intend now to look at some of the more important modifications and critiques which have appeared in the 1990s. But this is a fertile field indeed; space and my own no doubt only partial reading mean I can only sketch a few recent pieces which have struck me as interesting, or indeed merely have come to my attention. Just as the sketch above of the fundamentals of Wallerstein's work is far too brief and does little justice to the complexity of his model, so also my survey of the recent literature will reveal huge gaps and ignore many other no doubt seminal contributions.

Right from the start some critics have claimed that the modern world-system is too 'economist', for it ignores other ways in which people and societies have been linked. Chase-Dunn and Hall, whose work we will return to later, note that there are all sorts of exchanges—in trade, information, military exchanges for example. Even if one only looks at material exchanges, these can be gifts, tribute, commodity trade, etc. A more sustained attempt to look at non-material ties has been put forward by Voll. He starts, as is usual, by noting 'the luxuriant productivity of this [world-system] perspective'.[4] He wants to describe non-material elements that tie places together; his example is the Muslim world c. 1000–1800. He finds that Dar al-Islam is 'a special example of a large-scale human group' and quotes McNeill on this: 'What is common to all groups, surely, is a pattern of communication among members, sufficiently frequent and sufficiently standardised as to minimise surprises and maximise congruence between expectation and experience so far as encounters within the group are concerned.' Voll says: 'This pattern of communication in the Islamic world is not primarily based upon exchange of goods, coordination of means of production, or a large network of economic activities. Instead, it is built on the shared sources of the Islamic experience, which provide the basis for mutually intelligible discourse among all who identify themselves as Muslims within the Dar al-Islam.'[5] 'The Muslims might be said to have created the "Islamic world-system", identified by a distinctive set of sociomoral symbols for the definition of proper human relationships.... I am suggesting that both [the modern world-system and the Islamic world-system] are relatively comprehensive social systems that can qualify as world-systems, even though the primary identifying characteristics are drawn from different dimensions of the social system as a whole.'[6] Thus the modern world-system is not the first long-lasting world-system without a world-empire, and yet the Islamic world-system was not a world-economy.

On the one hand, in the light of my recent work on the integrating function of the hajj in the early modern period,[7] this is a perspective with which I am very sympathetic. Nevertheless, a rigorous political economist, and I think we could include Wallerstein here, would merely say that these links, while they exist no doubt, have no important consequences. Or, to put it another way, any Marxist or neo-Marxist would still insist that we are talking here about superstructure, not base. Were we to look at the material base we would find a very different sort of world-system, more likely systems, in the very area Voll is describing, and of course this base, or these bases, determine the superstructure.

Wallerstein saw the creation of capitalism in western Europe from the sixteenth century as the decisive event in recent world history. The problem is that, like it or not, capitalism did develop first in this area, not somewhere else, and this process did expand to affect the whole world and leave the rest of the world in a subordinate material position vis-à-vis Europe. Yet this sometimes leads to charges that he is 'Eurocentric'. Attempts to rectify this, notably by Abu-Lughod and Frank and Gills, are implicitly, sometimes explicitly, aimed to avoid this perceived bias, for they aim to identify world-systems before (European) capitalism.[8] This seems to be an ill-conceived complaint. Wallerstein and his followers stress Europe not for racist reasons but because objectively this is where the portentous development of capitalism did occur, and for the last 500 years this has been the one seminal fact in world history. There is however a related matter, which is that Wallerstein has sometimes, and with some justice, been criticised for knowing more about Europe than about the areas which Europe peripheralised. This however, it seems to me, can easily be rectified by accumulating more empirical data. It is hardly a central flaw of perspective.

The main thrust of recent world-system work (or maybe this statement merely reflects my own pre-modern research interests) is devoted to investigating the nature of world-systems before capitalism, that is before say 1500. However, it is of course possible to have world-systems existing after this in areas not yet incorporated, for example East Asia before the nineteenth century. The idea is to look at connections within and between societies, to challenge any idea of discrete states making their own history unaffected by other areas. All this is of course a direct contradiction of older modernisation 'theories'. A very successful early attempt to do this was Eric Wolf's well known text, which stressed connections in the world at 1400.[9]

Wallerstein's contributions here are at best sketchy, for they play little role in his main concern, which is with the nature of the modern world-system. He found two sorts of earlier world-systems, namely world-empires and world-economies, the latter of course being non- or pre-capitalist. Both were inherently unstable. World-empires sooner or later collapsed, as their rulers lacked the capacity to enforce their will over their vast territories and also because as rulers they had to defend their whole domain. World-economies were destined to be taken over by world-empires. World-economies are more or less a residual category; he noted early on that there are world-empires, and then for 'convenience and want of a better term', there are world-economies. 'Prior to the modern era [and the modern world-system], world-economies tended either to be converted into empires or to disintegrate.' However, we must give him credit for being aware that this is unsatisfactory. He noted in 1990 that the new challenge for world-system theorists is the 'elaboration of world-systems other than that of the capitalist world-economy.'[10] Earlier he said that we 'shall have to rework our knowledge of world historical data (as well as expand it) in order to analyse coherently how pre-capitalist economies functioned, which will—I believe—open many doors for us'.[11]

The master then is sympathetic, and indeed he himself, sometimes in collaboration with others, has contributed here. As one example, of relevance to my own empirical concerns, with Ravi Palat he wrote on India as a pre-capitalist core. They sketch the growth of trade, and the subsequent accumulation of riches in the two most commercialised areas, Coromandel and Gujarat, and in an innovative way tie this in to wet-rice cultivation. But this of itself does not have to mean there was 'an increasingly singular divisioning of labour to which we refer when we use the concept of a world-economy'. It could just show an exchange of preciosities between two autonomous systems, such as between India and Europe in 1500–1750. However, in fact this trade 'represented a transfer of the products of lowly-remunerated labourers located elsewhere along the Indian Ocean littoral to South Asia'. This was especially to be seen in the huge rise of coarse cotton cloth production in Gujarat and Coromandel, and the consequent 'deindustrialisation' of other regions in the Middle East and Southeast Asia. Indeed, in this pre-capitalist world-economy there are semi-peripheries too. Bengal exported rice to Coromandel and raw silk to Gujarat, but at the same time it sent cloths to Indonesia, and has the janus-faced character of a semi-periphery. The emerging core zones of Gujarat and Coromandel 'progressively drew upon sources of subsistence and raw materials for artisanal manufacture from increasingly distant regions—leading to the incorporation and subsequent peripheralisation of the latter zones within an emerging world-economy centred around, and integrated by, transport across the Indian Ocean'.

Thus there was 'from the eastern coasts of Africa through the Arabian peninsula and the Indian subcontinent to the Malay archipelago ... an evolving world-economy ....' Yet this was not the same as a capitalist world-economy, in other words a modern world-system, partly because there was no ruthless drive to accumulate, but also because the basis lay in the nature of wet-rice cultivation. Various things flowed from this, including different political structures. Thus what happened after 1400 in the Indian Ocean area was different from Europe, and the result was that in Europe a capitalist world-economy emerged, while in the Indian Ocean area it did not, especially as there was no real subsumption of labour to capital, which is a crucial part of the development of capitalism.[12] This is to be seen as an important step forward by Wallerstein himself as we try to specify more clearly the nature of world-economies before capitalism. Before 1500, their chosen terminal date, there is no modern world-system but there is a world-economy based on India, and no doubt others elsewhere. The question then becomes what is the situation once the modern world-system emerges after 1500. India, we are told, remains external to this until the late eighteenth century, and so presumably the world-economy centred on India continued, until bits were chipped away from it and incorporated in the expanding modern world-system. When the core, India, was peripheralised this world-economy obviously was ended.

Yet at another level this is a familiar story, especially in their view of how capitalism is to be differentiated from capital. Here and elsewhere he stresses the absolute centrality of the 'ceaseless accumulation of capital',[13] though a more orthodox Marxist, such as Eric Wolf at least on this point, would make more of the dramatic difference between capital as money, and capitalism, and would note the key fact that capital must penetrate and control production in order for there to be capitalism.

Several other scholars have produced larger works devoted to describing early world-economies. The results have been mixed. Janet Abu-Lughod's book[14] was sympathetically reviewed by Wallerstein.[15] Abu-Lughod finds a world-system in the century 1250–1350 whose heartland was the Middle East, but which included Europe, China and the Indian Ocean. The linkage at this time of these areas, based on long distance trade, resulted in an economic upturn in them all. This is a world-system which linked a number of world-systems, each of which had cores, semiperipheries and peripheries making up an integrated production system. None of these world-systems was dominant; rather there was co-existence and mutual tolerance and profit within the larger world-system. In short, she finds a benign interacting group of world-systems, or world-economies. There was no single hegemonic power, and this is a contrast with what grew out of it, the capitalist world-system dominated by Europe. One core was the 'Arabo-Persian imperial centres' another 'the towns of developing western Europe'. Thus we can see that world-systems are not all the same, and also that they can change.

All this is well taken, yet she seems to be comparing two different things. She claims that there are different sorts of world-systems, some like Wallerstein's with cores which are dominant, others like hers where there are cores but no hegemony. This may be true, but she neglects to note that Wallerstein's world-system is capitalist, and surely this makes all the difference, for this requires cores to be dominant. Nor indeed does a pre-capitalist world-system necessarily have cores which are not dominant, as we have just noted Palat and Wallerstein pointing out. Indeed, I am uneasy about her whole notion of a core which is not dominant, and what follows from this, the notion that this was a benign, non-extractive, world-system: it seems to me that core and dominance are inextricably linked, indeed one implies the other either in a capitalist system or any other. If areas are linked in a hierarchical world-economy there must be some unequal exchange. Only if there is no hierarchy within the system (and in this case is it a system at all?), or if one looks at relations with areas external to the system, will there be a benign and non-exploitative relationship. Later we will note Chase-Dunn and Hall claiming that there is something which they call core/periphery differentiation, and they seem to imply that this also does not involve inequality. This is one among many areas where more research and reflection is needed.

Returning to Abu-Lughod, one could also point to a less than rigorous use of terminology, yet this is important in this sort of work. She uses 'world economy' and 'international trade economy' interchangeably, and sometimes refers to Wallerstein's 'modern world system' whereas in fact he always has 'modern world-system'. The hyphen is crucial, for it assumes integration and cohesion.

In all this, Abu-Lughod is not denying that something changed in the sixteenth century when capitalism appeared, even if she fails to go into this very much. Her work is important and useful. A. G. Frank's recent work, sometimes in collaboration, is much more dubious. First in an article, very tolerantly published by Wallerstein in his journal *Review* in 1990, and subsequently in a co-edited book, he has put forward the extraordinary notion that the present world-system (not world-system) goes back to at least 2500 BC. There has been only one world-system in all of history. Late in its career this world-system was first joined and then dominated by Europe. However, Frank refuses to see this as marking a major break: 'I will also question the supposed historical uniqueness and perhaps the social-theoretical relevance of the modern capitalist mode of production.' Networks and world-systems have existed long before capitalism, and he quotes Chase-Dunn that 'any regularised and repetitive exchange of material goods which substantially affects the welfare of a population or the maintenance of a power structure constitutes part of a single world-system network'.[16]

Soon afterwards Frank collaborated with Gills to edit a book where the same points are made more strongly. Thus 'the contemporary world-system has a history of at least 5,000 years'. Wallerstein and his followers think that what marks off the period from about 1500 is the process of 'continuous capital accumulation', but they claim to find this long before 1500 in their continuing world-system.[17]

Frank's earlier work on dependency in Latin America was often criticised as being too static, finding essentially the same impact since 1500, and indeed Wallerstein's main contribution was to modify dependency theory to make it more dynamic. Precisely the same comment could be made about Frank's more recent writings. If one finds a world-system for the last 4000 or whatever years, then one really is ignoring change. We need rather to emphasise change, to disaggregate the data (just as needs to be done with Eric Wolf's overly broad notion of a tributary mode of production which encompasses most of world history) to get beyond such general, and so not very heuristic, descriptions. Also, in a maybe unreconstructed way, I still feel capitalism makes a difference; nor is this just an article of faith, it can be demonstrated. More orthodox Marxists have often complained that Wallerstein finds the evolution of capitalism far too early, and indeed I would myself follow Marx and Eric Wolf, among others, in finding capitalism appearing in the eighteenth century, regardless of various proto-capitalisms and whatever before this. Nevertheless, while Frank and Gills, and Abu-Lughod, are obviously right to say there were connections and trade and even accumulations of capital (which however did not intervene in the productive process) long before capitalism—indeed this is a very familiar point indeed—capitalism objectively made a most fundamental difference. To his credit Frank in his edited volume allows both Amin and Wallerstein to say this. It is refreshing to see Wallerstein and Frank both finding space in their own publications for views diametrically opposed to their own!

Amin stresses that there were connections and regional systems in the tributary systems before the rise of European capitalism, but 'capitalism is a qualitatively new age in universal history which started around 1500'.[18] Wallerstein also continues to emphasise the 'dramatic caesura that the creation of a capitalist world-economy imposed on the world'.[19] However, as Wallerstein himself has said we need to specify much more clearly the nature of world-systems before capitalism. Janet Abu-Lughod has contributed here, but I must say that Frank's efforts can hardly be seen as a step forward.

Chase-Dunn and Hall have produced a much more satisfactory and challenging contribution. In the lead chapter for their edited collection[20] they follow the others in saying that there have been world-systems long before capitalism. Some of these are stateless, but most are state-based. However, it is incorrect to assume that in these systems one has to find the sort of core/periphery (this is their usage) relations that one finds in the capitalist system. Rather than assuming this, they ask that scholars look in a fresh way at 'the existence and nature of intersocietal inequalities'. Even though one may well find, in state-based world-systems, a core which accumulates resources by exploiting peripheries, intersocietal hierarchies could also be quite different from those which developed under capitalism.

They also confront Wallerstein's perceived economism by noting that there are all sorts of exchanges: trade, information, presumably, along Voll's lines, even religion. Even if one only looks at material exchanges, these can be gifts, tribute, commodity trade, etc. Here they agree with Schneider and say that exchange of prestige goods is not epiphenomenal at all. They can be very important as elites can use them to get or maintain power. Thus, at least by implication they find that luxuries, as well as necessities, can create systemic relations. Similarly, Braudel's claim that hegemony, even before capitalism, was always based on economic domination is questionable. They claim that more often in these world-systems it was political and military power which created inequality.

As they say, all exchange is not unequal exchange. Thus there are broadly two types of core-periphery relations in pre-capitalist world-systems. First is core/periphery differentiation, where there is interaction between societies in a world-system, as compared with core/periphery hierarchies, where there is domination which can include political domination, extraction of resources, and unequal exchange. One task is to measure degrees of intersocietal exploitation, and this is very difficult, especially when the kinds of resources which are socially valued differ.

Finally, they produce a list of world-system types. They follow Wolf's three modes of production, and find the Indian Ocean to be an example of 'commercializing state-based world-systems in which important aspects of commodification have developed but the system is still dominated by the logic of the tributary modes'. In the core of these commercialising world-systems, in which the core seems to be an empire, there is more use of money, of credit and interest, of wage labour, and of price-setting markets. In the core-empires the rulers use sophisticated means to tax merchants, 'and outside the bounds of empires, in interstitial semiperipheral regions, autonomous city-states controlled by merchant and production capitalists created and sustained market relations between empires and peripheral regions'. They say these centralised empires will be more exploitative towards peripheries than earlier empires, as they are better at concentrating resources at the centre. But of course they are not nearly as efficient at extracting resources as was the later capitalist core in the modern world-system. Nor indeed are peripheries essential in these tributary empires. They claim that in China the mode of production was tributary certainly, but accumulation was mostly accomplished without exploiting peripheral areas. There may be a problem here in that their identification of empires as the cores implies much more integrated and effective premodern empires than may be justified. In other words, empires may in their own territory include the whole range of cores, peripheries, and semiperipheries, as indeed Palat and Wallerstein claimed in the case of India. True, they are writing of India during one of its periods of political fragmentation, but I am sure that when India was united in one empire, say under the Mughals in the sixteenth and seventeenth centuries, there still were core and peripheral areas.[21]

There is a large congruence here between what Palat and Wallerstein have to say, and the Chase-Dunn and Hall model. Both, unlike Abu-

Lughod, are pointing to precapitalist world economies in which there can be exploitation and extraction. Palat and Wallerstein in their case study are explicit on this point, while Chase-Dunn and Hall accept this as being likely, at least in their state-based systems. Empirically there is little question that India, or parts of India, must be seen as the core of an Indian Ocean world-economy. It is for other specialists to apply these insights to areas such as the Middle East or Southeast Asia, the two areas where Palat and Wallerstein find the greatest impact from the Indian core in this pre-modern period. My own contribution will be to sketch in a very preliminary way how these models can elucidate connections in one part of this world-economy, that is across the Arabian Sea between India and East Africa. In particular I will present a little of my on-going research on East Africa to show how we can approach its history in an international context.

East Africa has been subjected to a variety of political economy analyses. In the 1970s Marxists, inspired by Catherine Coquery-Vidrovitch, engaged in what finally turned out to be a rather fruitless debate over modes of production in Africa.[22] More recently the field has been held by *dependista* writings inspired by the early A. G. Frank. Rodney, Sheriff, Alpers and Bhila all produced empirically grounded books which claimed to find a continuous history of underdevelopment in East Africa going back to the fourteenth century, or even earlier.[23] A strong point of their analyses was that they avoided Eurocentrism by finding that the Portuguese in the sixteenth and seventeenth centuries continued an existing system of exploitation rather than initiating a new process. The crucial break came late in the eighteenth century when the East African slave trade expanded very greatly under the auspices of the Omani state of Zanzibar, or even a century later with European colonialism. In other words, when industrial capitalism replaced merchant capital East Africa was subjected to a much more efficient exploitation than previously. But this is seen as an intensification rather than something completely different. Empiricist writers such as Newitt and Austen have found this perception of a seamless web to be unconvincing.[24]

The distinction to be made is between the Swahili coast and the interior of East Africa, and especially between the coast and the states around the Zambezi river on the Zimbabwe plateau, notably Great Zimbabwe and then the Mutapa state. In the early modern period the main exports from these states were ivory and gold (slaves came later). Imports were mostly Indian-made cloths and beads. Ostensibly then we are looking at the export of raw materials, and the import of manufactures, and this seems to show a clear first world/third world situation of exploitation. This perception is reinforced when we note the vast profits that foreign traders were making from this exchange. However when we look at the relative values of these goods we find something different. Both gold and ivory were produced using discretionary, male, labour, and this was not extracted from more 'productive' activities such as embryonic manufactures or food cultivation. Nor was either product highly prized in the interior states. Gold is most valuable in a monetised economy, and these were not. Ivory, culturally so important for jewellery and ornamentation in India, was sometimes used for fencing in the African interior. Elephants were usually hunted for their food, not their tusks. As for imports, low cost beads and cloths from India were highly prized in Africa. This concept of relative values is quite in accordance with Wallerstein's luxury-necessity dichotomy, for he notes that 'each side tends to have different cultural definitions of value.'[25] The result was mutual windfalls for both sides in this most unusual trade between India and the African interior, a benign situation congruent with Abu-Lughod's analysis of a rather different area of research. In the absence of any sign of exploitation of the interior, or any hint of unequal exchange, these areas must be regarded as being external to the Indian core.

The Swahili city states strung along the East African littoral acted in a classic compradorial way as *mediators* between the overseas core and the interior. The coast was linked to the interior through a whole hierarchy of intermediaries. Richard Wilding very aptly noted that we need to distinguish three main trade units: the hinterland network; the coastal interface; and the Indian Ocean network.[26] On the coast foreign traders sold to the Swahili, who themselves at this time never went inland, for both cultural and economic reasons. Rather they negotiated with particular tribes in their *umland*,[27] and these then with long-distance traders who accessed the far interior. There is some evidence of deindustrialisation in these ports: thus Spear claims that 'The weaving industries of Kilwa, Lamu and the Benaadir were severely curtailed by Indian cloth imports'.[28] More generally the terms and conditions of trade and of production were not controlled by these Swahili middlemen.

Thus Kilwa's wealth came from its control of the gold trade through Sofala, and demand for gold fluctuated world-wide and affected very greatly Kilwa's prosperity. Nevertheless, in one of the better periods the early thirteenth century palace complex at Kilwa is described as being 'as spacious as any roofed stone building south of the Sahara until modern times'.[29] In their janus-faced nature, and in their subordination to the Indian core, the Swahili coast can be seen to be a classic semi-periphery, in Chase-Dunn and Hall's terms autonomous city-states controlled by merchant and production capitalists in an interstitial semiperipheral region; they consider that such city-states tie in an imperial core with a peripheral area. However, if we accept the sketch above of the nature of trade and production in the interior, then we have the rather unusual situation of a semiperiphery connecting a core area with an external one. Implicitly at least this may fit precisely with the Palat and Wallerstein sketch, for while they locate the East African coast within the world-economy centred on India, they say nothing about the African interior.

Space precludes a more extended discussion. It is my hope that even this sketchy analysis will at least show the utility of world-system research in any discussion of the history of the Indian Ocean, and in a small way will contribute to one of the most fruitful areas of world-system research today, that is the nature of pre-capitalist world-systems.

Notes

1 The literature is vast indeed. For a full statement of the model see Immanuel Wallerstein, *The Modern World-System*, 3 vols, New York, 1974–89, and as examples of thorough-going but sympathetic critiques Theda Skocpol, 'Wallerstein's World Capitalist System: a Theoretical and Historical Critique', *American Journal of Sociology* 82.5 (1977): 1075–90, and Jane Schneider, 'Was There a Pre-Capitalist World-System', *Journal of Peasant Studies* 6.1 (1977): 20–9, reprinted in Christopher Chase-Dunn and Thomas D. Hall, eds, *Core/Periphery Relations in Precapitalist Worlds*, Boulder, 1991.

2 See Wallerstein's three volumes, or for a synoptic view Terence K. Hopkins and Immanuel Wallerstein, 'Patterns of Development of the Modern World-System', *Review* 1.2 (1977): 111–45. For other summaries see Thomas Richard Shannon, *An Introduction to the World-System Perspective*, Boulder, 1989 and M. N. Pearson, *Before Colonialism: Theories on Asian-European Relations, 1500–1750*, Delhi, 1988, Chapter 1.

3 In André Gunder Frank and Barry K. Gills, eds, *The World System: Five Hundred Years or Five Thousand?*, London, 1993, p.294.

4 For example Ravi Arvind Palat and Immanuel Wallerstein, 'Of What World-System was Pre-1500 "India" a Part?', in S. Chaudhuri and M. Morineau, eds, *Merchants, Companies and Trade*, forthcoming (my thanks to Dr Palat for sending me a typescript); Etienne Balibar and Immanuel Wallerstein, *Race, Nation, Class: Ambiguous Identities*, London, 1991, and numerous articles in his house-organ, *Review*, Fernand Braudel Center.

5 See especially T. R. Shannon, *An Introduction*, M. N. Pearson, *Before Colonialism*, Chapter 2, and the special number of *Review* 12.2 (1990) titled 'World-Systems Theory Fifteen Years On: What Have we Learned?'.

6 Chase-Dunn and Hall, eds, p.9.

7 John Obert Voll, 'Islam as a Special World-System', *Journal of World History* 5.2 (1994): 214.

8 Voll, pp.219–220.

9 Voll, p.226.

10 M. N. Pearson, *Pious Passengers: the Hajj in Earlier Times*, Delhi and London, 1994; and a new edition published as *Pilgrimage to Mecca: the Indian Experience*, Princeton, 1995.

11 On 'Eurocentrism', see for a start Edward Said's *Orientalism*, London, 1978, and *Culture and Imperialism*, London, 1993, and the English translation of Samir Amin, *Eurocentrism*, London, 1989.

12 Eric R. Wolf, *Europe and the People without History*, Berkeley, 1982, Chapter 2.

13 Wallerstein, *Modern World-System*, I, 348.

14 Immanuel Wallerstein, 'World-System Analysis: The Second Phase', *Review* 12 (1990): 291.

15 Immanuel Wallerstein, 'Africa in a Capitalist World', *Issue: A Quarterly Journal of Africanist Opinion* 3.3, Fall (1973): 10.

16 Palat and Wallerstein.

17 For example, in Frank and Gills, eds, p.293.

18 Janet Abu-Lughod, *Before European Hegemony: The World System A.D. 1250–1350*, Oxford, 1989; for a short version see her 'Restructuring the Premodern World-System', *Review* 13.2 (1990): 273-86 and her contribution in Frank and Gills, eds.

19 In *International Journal of Middle East Studies* 24.1 (1992): 128–31.

20 Abu-Lughod, *Before European Hegemony*, pp.5–6, and generally pp.8–40 and 364 et seq for her main ideas.

21 André Gunder Frank, 'A Theoretical Introduction to 5,000 Years of World System History', *Review* 13.2 (1990): 155–248, especially pp.164, 181.

22 Frank and Gills, eds, p.3.

23 Amin, in Frank and Gills, eds, p.247.

24 Wallerstein, in Frank and Gills, eds, p.295.

25 Chase-Dun and Hall, eds, pp.5–44.

26 Chase-Dun and Hall, eds, p.23; by commodification they mean that goods, land,

wealth and labour have become commodities.

27 For my views on the Mughal empire see 'Land, Noble and Ruler in Mughal India', in Sir Edmund Leach, S. N. Mukherjee and John O. Ward, eds, *Feudalism: Comparative Studies*, Sydney, 1985 (Sydney Studies in Society and Culture, no. 2) pp.175–96, and a comparative view in 'Merchants and States', in James D. Tracy, ed., *The Political Economy of Merchant Empires*, New York, 1991, pp.41–116.

28 See Catherine Coquery-Vidrovitch, 'Recherches sur un mode de production africain', *La Pensée* 144 (1969): 61–78, and an English version, 'Research on an African Mode of Production', in Martin A. Klein and G. Wesley Johnson, eds, *Perspectives on the African Past*, Boston, 1972, pp.33–51. For an overview of Marxism in Africa see Robin Law, 'In Search of a Marxist Perspective on Pre-Colonial Tropical Africa', *Journal of African History* 19.3 (1978): 441–52.

29 Walter Rodney, *How Europe Underdeveloped Africa*, Washington, 1982 [first pub. 1972]; Abdul Sheriff, *Slaves, Spices and Ivory in Zanzibar: Integration of an East African Commercial Empire into the World Economy, 1770–1873*, London, 1987; E. A. Alpers, *Ivory and Slaves: Changing Patterns of International Trade in East Central Africa to the Later Nineteenth Century*, London, 1975; H. K. K. Bhila, *Trade and Politics in a Shona Kingdom: the Manyika and their Portuguese and African Neighbours, 1575–1902*, London, 1982. See also Gaudens P. Mpangala, *Major Issues in Tanzanian Economic History*, Part 1, 'Pre-Colonial Economy and Social Formations', Dar es Salaam, 1992.

30 For a short version of Newitt's views see M. D. D. Newitt, 'East Africa and the Indian Ocean Trade: 1500–1800', in Ashin das Gupta and M. N. Pearson, eds, *India and the Indian Ocean, 1500–1800*, Calcutta, 1987, pp.201–23 and for an overview of Austen's see Ralph A. Austen, 'African Commerce without Europeans: the Development Impact of International Trade in the Pre-Modern Era', *Kenya Historical Review* 6 (1978): 1–21 and for a fuller version his *African Economic History: Internal Development and External Dependency*, London, 1987.

31 I. Wallerstein, 'The Ottoman Empire and the Capitalist World-Economy: Some Questions for Research', *Review* 2.3 (1979): 390–1.

32 Richard Wilding, *The Shorefolk: Aspects of the Early Development of Swahili Communities, Fort Jesus Occasional Papers* 2 (mimeo, 1987): 7.

33 Used in the precise sense of an area which is culturally, economically and politically related to a particular town or city.

34 Thomas Spear, *Kenya's Past: An Introduction to Historical Method in Africa*, London, 1981, p.133.

35 J. E. G. Sutton, 'Kilwa', *Indian Ocean Review* 7.4 (1995)10–11.

Multiculturalism, Theatre and the Politics of Liberation: The Melbourne Workers Theatre and the Turkish Community

Maria Shevtsova

Multiculturalism, although not fully defined as a policy in the strictest sense of the term, was nevertheless given official status by the Whitlam Labor government during its brief period in office from 1972 to 1975. This recognition from 'above' was a delayed reaction to Australia's cultural diversity 'below', in civil society, in that the mass immigration of non-Anglo/Celts to Australia had begun towards the end of the Second World War and had continued unabated through the fifties. By the seventies, then, mass immigration had radically altered the ethnic mix of the country whose heterogeneity the existing predominantly British colonial institutions were singularly ill-equipped to handle.

The patterns of immigration were quite clear. The immigrants of the post-war years came from the Mediterranean and Eastern Europe.[1] They were principally from the working class or peasantry and became the industrial, construction or rural workers required for Australia's economic expansion. The immigrants of the sixties were of a similar kind, although they now included better educated and also professional people, some of them recruited under the family reunion program.

The beginning of the seventies saw an influx of Arabic-speaking people, among them Lebanese who went into small business. A variety of Muslim communities appeared at this time. Then followed a whole range of non-European immigrants including South Americans and Turks. The latter, who are of special interest to this paper, provided factory labour above all else. The eighties saw more Turkish and Middle Eastern immigrants of one kind and another, as well as Asian groups, the Vietnamese being the largest of them.[2] Immigration policy towards the end of the eighties focused on Asians, and particularly on those who were supposed to invest their capital in Australian business and thus 'save' Australia from economic recession.

This panorama, while incomplete, at least helps to mark out which major groups besides Anglo/Celts constitute Australia's ethnic-cultural diversity today. Secondly, it shows that the diversity is made up of several layers whose 'texture' is defined by the time and type of immigration involved. Thus talk of multiculturalism in the nineties must include factors and therefore meanings that were weak or even insignificant in the early seventies. Nevertheless, whether we look at the predominantly European-based diversity of the pre-Whitlam period or the wider spectrum since then, what is especially noteworthy is how all the non-Anglo/Celtic groups, past and present, have had to struggle against, come to terms with, embrace or ignore Anglo/Celtic hegemony in all spheres—economic, political, social, linguistic and artistic.

In short, what is at issue here is Anglo/Celtic *cultural* hegemony, the adjective retaining its strongest anthropological meaning; and the prevailing culture is the direct outcome of a colonial history which systematically alienated anyone who was alien, in other words, not English or of English stock, Protestant, loyal to the British Crown, and aspiring to the upper classes. Hence, of course, the problematical relationship between the 'Anglo' and 'Celtic' (notably Irish working class) components of a culture that, by exercising internal control—the Anglo over the Celtic—nevertheless succeeded in maintaining a 'British' profile. Unlike other countries of the New World, whether Second or Third, Australia had never had a war of independence or a civil war. Nor had she developed a 'melting pot' ideology, however fraught with ambiguities and inconsistencies such an ideology may be. Consequently, the mechanisms for ethnic self-definition and pride, on the one hand, and for the integration of different ethnicities, on the other, simply had not been put into place.

Both of these apparently contradictory elements (that is, unicity and integration) are arguably essential for any society that claims to be multicultural in anything other than a purely tokenistic sense of the word. 'Integration' as conceived of here should not be confused with 'assimilation'. The first involves the idea that disparate groups come together without losing their distinctive character. The second suggests

recur across the spectrum. Take, for instance, the relationship between plural cultures. Is one of them dominant? In what sort of minority is a 'minority' culture? Or take again the difficult relationship between art and politics, which is exacerbated in a multicultural situation precisely because the demands *of* power, and the demands *upon* power, are decentred, scattered across various interest groups. Besides which, artists cannot be created by decree. Governments may wish to fill ethnic quotas—X number of artists for Y number of ethnic groups. Even so, there is no guarantee of a direct correspondence between institutional projects and the socioartistic dynamic in which artworks are produced.

In the case of Australian multiculturalism and the theatre, there is a striking disconnection between theatrical creativity, social reality and institutional political programs. This is because pluriethnicity and its formalisation in a 'policy' (albeit several steps behind the former) were both way ahead of the theatre. It was not until the early eighties that productions in tune with the principles of multiculturalism began to emerge from non-Anglo/Celtic communities. There was, notably, the Italo-Australian company, Doppio Teatro, in Adelaide and the Greek-based Filiki Players in Melbourne. Their primary objective was to construct the immigrant experience from the point of view of immigrants so as to give this experience (or, more accurately, lived trauma) appropriate dignity in their own eyes. They culled life-stories from their communities, making performances from them that evoked the performance styles of their ancestors. Performances were in two languages in the same show, and sometimes in three or four—regional languages included. The purpose of performance bilingualism—English always being used—was to help reclaim the culture of origin. It intended, at the same time, to demonstrate this culture's viability to Anglo/Celts, while helping them through the language barriers—irony of ironies, since foreign, 'wog' languages had had a hard time of it, particularly in the fifties when the parents of those who became bilingual performers were usually held in contempt for speaking their native tongue. The aim, overall, was to impose upon the national consciousness the contribution that non-Anglo/Celtic groups had made to the nation, the ethnic identity of these groups being redefined through the theatre so that they could take their rightful place in the nation.

Multicultural theatre as it is known in the nineties (although the euphemistic 'ethnic' is still used) is the outcome of a drive to empower communities that had been virtually disenfranchised. In this lies its political significance. But not all groups under the same banner have militant, explicitly political intentions. Here is where the Melbourne Workers Theatre steps in.

The MWT was founded with the support of trade unions in 1987 in order to close ranks with trade unions and their members. These were now under attack in a society that had long since seen the best and the worst of the Whitlam period and was about to be hit by a backlash against multiculturalism as well as against the relatively liberal immigration policy that had been nurturing it. The company is a professional one in residence, until 1994, in a train maintenance depot in the heart of Melbourne. Its aim, as formulated in a 1991 mission statement, is 'to make theatre for, with and about working class people in a way that reveals the complexities and contradictions of current working class struggles to improve living conditions'. It tours workplaces for lunchtime performances of 25 minutes. Sometimes 50 minutes of performance time is allowed by agreement with employers and unions. Public performances of the longer version are given in community halls. They target a specific, non-English-speaking community which is linked in several ways with the production at hand.

The strongest link is with the working-class component of the designated community. This, apart from being consistent with the MWT's ideological position, is totally logical given the considerable number of non-Anglo/Celts in the Australian working class as a whole. The remaining connections have to do with the preparatory processes of productions, and their content and manner of presentation. Theatre practitioners and liaison officers are chosen from the targeted community so that real-life events pertinent to the community can be staged authentically. The principle of authenticity extends to the use of non-English in productions which, however, is not as extensive as occurs in the bilingual companies referred to above. The aesthetic decisions on form, structure, style, and so on, which are necessarily involved in the company's creative work, are thus sustained by its belief that whichever community is selected for special attention is best served when its members participate in both the preparation and the performance of a production.

The notion of 'service' being evoked here was integral to the community arts movement of the seventies and remained valid for the multilingual theatre of the eighties to which the MWT, for all its distinguishing characteristics, is indebted: what *distinguishes* it most is its goal of political intervention, in a very organised manner, in the processes of society itself. Now, insofar as the MWT is part and parcel of the sociological phenomenon we know as multiculturalism, it shows the difficulties that arise from multiculturalism's incarnations in multicultural *theatre*. Although I am taking the Australian model, I believe that these difficulties are just as relevant to any situation where multicultural theatre or multicultural arts in any shape or form are practised. They are also bound to be pertinent to any situation where the idea of multicultural arts is entertained merely theoretically.

Several main difficulties may be put in the form of the following questions. Let us take the notion of 'service' as redefined by the MWT's work, and which means something like 'facilitating practice'. The question then is: What are the social limits of facilitation through the intervention of someone else? The MWT wishes to empower communities by giving them the means to express problems that are vital to them, but which are not necessarily confined to them. Yet this empowerment is mediated twice over, firstly, through a team of theatre workers who, although sharing a general viewpoint, or who are at least sympathetic to it, are not necessarily deeply in touch with the prescribed community; secondly, presumed empowerment is mediated through a theatre production that, although performed by actors of non-English-speaking background, is not performed by the colleagues of the train drivers, welders and other blue-collar workers (or hospital workers or white-collar workers, as the case may be) who are watching in the audience. This is not, in other words, a case of worker-controlled—because worker-propelled and worker-performed—empowerment.[6] Furthermore, let us assume that empowerment can operate effectively at the consciousness-raising level, that is, at the mental-emotional, representational and symbolic level of apprehension. What, then, is the role of multicultural theatre when it also aspires to being a catalyst for social change? Can it pass from the symbolic level to the level of action? Does a non-English-speaking community, which is also disadvantaged economically (the case of MWT audiences), start to inhabit social space beyond its determined 'ethnic' space by virtue of an objectivised projection of its condition?

The passage from art to reality is full of traps. Theatre workers, especially when professionals (as is the case for the MWT), have artistic criteria for their work, no matter what social meaning is contained in it or imputed to it. When is multicultural theatre merely illustrative? When is it merely a tool in the hands of organisations, governments and administrations for ends that may have little to do with art, let alone with the benefits supposedly reaped by minority communities? And when is multicultural theatre a mere gesture, a technique for skirting around urgent social problems whilst giving the impression that they are being seriously met? What, then, is the role of so-called multicultural artists? Should they be hired because they look and sound like 'wogs', or because they fulfil in some other way whatever ideological aspect of whichever version of multiculturalism is the order of the day? Or are there only *artists*, multiculturalism not being an attribute of artists, but only of the kind of *works* they create?

With all these questions in mind, let us turn to my survey of audiences for the MWT's 1991 production of *No Fear*, a play devised by and for the Turkish community, and specially for Turkish workers in the motor car industry. It was performed by two Turkish actors and one Anglo/Celt. Lines were delivered here and there in Turkish. English, however, dominated. The actors participated in the research stages from which, two months later, grew the production.

My survey did not ask spectators the questions I have raised above. It would have been quite impossible to do so for numerous reasons, including the little time left after the show—especially in the workplace—for spectators to fill in the questionnaire. These questions, then, are part of my reflections on the subject. Ideas for some of them may be gleaned from replies to four open, qualitative questions in my questionnaire: 'What did you like about *No Fear*? What did you not like, and why? What would you change? What do you think is the main purpose of theatre?' There were 22 questions in all of a socio-demographic or sociocultural kind. (Take, for an example of the sociocultural kind of question: 'Is this the first play you have seen in Australia?') All were in Turkish or English.

The script of *No Fear* was inspired by the hunger strike of a Turkish worker in the Ford car plant in Melbourne. Ford's management was demanding the use of a new method for speeding up production in a tradeoff for wage rises. A Turkish shop steward who claimed that the new method was not efficient and would only increase workloads was sacked. Some 200 workers on his shift stopped work immediately. All but about 20 were persuaded by the Vehicle Builders' Union, which supported management, to go back. Those who did not were sacked. The shop steward continued his hunger strike for a month. He was joined towards the end of his campaign by two or three more hunger strikers who were also Turks. None was re-employed. These events provoked hot debates on the rights and obligations of individuals vis-à-vis their unions and on what a unionist's position should be as regards individual extreme actions.

The real-life incident is changed in *No Fear* where two Turkish workers, a man and a woman, are sacked for refusing to trial a new speed line. They occupy the factory manager's office spontaneously, not by design, which action sparks off an animated discussion between them as to the meaning of what they have done. Along comes the union organiser who continues the debate with them while she is locked out of the office. They eventually let her in and give in to the union's arguments without, however, leaving the impression that their show of force had been useless. The fact that their colleagues go out on strike against the new speed line, thereby showing their solidarity with the two renegades, suggests that collective action negotiated through unions and with their support for the interests of workers is the true way to act. This conclusion is, in fact, the *opposite* of what happened at the Ford plant; and the solution given by the stage production was received unfavourably by the Vehicle Builders' Union as a criticism of its actions.

The gestures and movements of the performers are eloquent, vivacious. Black wire-metal boxes serving as tables, chairs, windows and doors give a minimalist set. Music written for the show and songs in Turkish give the production a 'folk' dimension.

It is essential to note, first of all, that my sample of 224 respondents is small in respect of the several thousand who are presumed to have seen the production. It is impossible, moreover, to say what percentage this 224 represents of the (unknown) total. Be this as it may, 53% of the respondents are skilled as well as unskilled workers. Among the remaining occupational categories, as listed by the Australian Bureau of Statistics, are 15% of professionals (union leaders, project officers, writers, arts workers and bureaucrats responsible for government grants who came to see how their money had been spent!). Nurses are well represented. Since the show was also performed in a male prison, my sample includes inmates. They usually sabotaged the question on employment, stating that they were car thieves, bank robbers, drug dealers, and the like, which descriptions could well explain why they were in jail! When replies were straight, prison inmates usually had a trade (plasterer or motor mechanic, for instance) or a menial job (kitchen hand, car cleaner).

The ethnic composition of these respondents gives us 53 people of Turkish background (24% of the total, including those who say that they are Turkish-Australian). Forty-seven of these respondents were born in Turkey, while 37 replied in Turkish. Another 14% were of non-English-speaking background (notably Indian, Greek and Maltese). The majority at 53% is Anglo/Celtic Australian, a tiny few saying that they are English or Anglo-Scottish, but not using the adjective 'Australian'. Those remaining either did not reply or gave such answers as 'citizen of the world', 'socialist', 'democrat' and 'human being'. Most of the respondents in this remaining group were born in Turkey (which could make 28% of those of Turkish background in the sample).

By force of circumstance, all Turks and Turkish-Australians in the sample attended the public, community-hall performances given by the MWT. The great majority of them, men and women, are skilled blue-collar workers. According to the actors in the show, there were many workers from the Ford plant at these performances. A number of high-school students, children of these immigrants, appear in the sample.

Since my focus is on the Turkish community—essential to the present discussion on multiculturalism/multicultural theatre—I shall concentrate on the observations of Turks in reply to the four qualitative questions posed in my questionnaire. References to other ethnic groups will be made in order to highlight a particular point or draw a significant comparison or contrast between different groups.

Turkish respondents who declined ethnic definition of any kind (thus they were 'socialist', 'democrat', 'internationalist', and so on) were the only ones of the whole total for whom the strike at the Ford plant was an *interpretative* rather than merely informational point of reference. Thus a motor mechanic remarks in English: '[the play's] issues are based on the current crisis in the industry'. Another representative statement comes from an electrical welder who replied in Turkish. He liked the production because 'the topic was real and current; it was about an event that occurred only a short time ago'.

When not referring to the incident that had inspired the production, Turkish respondents, and notably those writing in Turkish, point out how the production deals with 'the story of the working class'. Or else they draw conclusions from what they have just seen. This statement from a machine operator, who describes himself as a democrat, centres more explicitly than anyone else on the labour issues explored. He writes in Turkish: 'The working class cannot achieve state power as long as it is intimidated; especially if it is divided'.

Observations as close to the bone as these were made by a few Anglo/Celts who describe themselves as political organisers or are tied up with leadership in some way. Only one rank-and-file worker, a fitter's assistant, belongs to this group of ideas. He states that 'management did not have the right to push people beyond their capacity and that by the unions and employers uniting anyone can achieve their aim in life; sackings are not the answer'. These respondents generally point out that what, on the other hand, they did not like about the production was its 'dubious' presupposition that 'the union organiser could be won to the workers' side so easily'. This point of view, as well as variations on it, is rarely to be found among Turks. Its scarcity makes the criticism of a Turkish factory worker all the more noticeable. He explains how he did not like the way the play 'made the workers seem stupid', especially as management 'doesn't always agree to it easily like they made it show'.

Turkish respondents, when critical, did not like the style of the play (in their view not real enough). Nor did they like the too few props, 'too much lighting', or the venue where the play was performed (reference to bad acoustics). These reflections of an essentially aesthetic kind are continued through, by the same respondents, in their commentary on what they would change. Thus they would have staged the play in a 'proper theatre venue' (rather than in a community hall), and would have used more performers and created more scenes (so as to 'broaden the topic', and similar remarks). They would also have used more or 'better props and decor'. The socialist motor mechanic cited earlier suggests that the production 'needed to create a factory appearance [and the] feeling [and] sounds of [a] real working factory'.

Otherwise, critical comments from Turks focus on their language difficulties. In the words of one of them: 'I do not understand English. As far as I can tell, the company is not concerned with targeting us.' In the words of another: 'I would have liked a Turkish play. The Turks did not understand the English and others did not understand the Turkish. Totally multicultural.' It seems that for this worker, who describes himself as Turkish-Arabic-Greek, being 'totally multicultural' is tantamount to being nonsensical: it is the *incapacity* for communication between different ethnic-linguistic groups. Apart from this terrible indictment of multiculturalism—the only allusion to the phenomenon among respondents from a Turkish background—what springs from respondents' hearts, now fairly consistently, is their feeling that they are *disempowered* by language. 'I did not understand it' or 'did not fully understand it' is a recurring theme. The fact that these respondents answer in Turkish indicates that they do not yet have an adequate command of English.

As far as our Turkish respondents are concerned, then, the bilingual nature of the production either does not warrant attention or deserves a negative assessment. Which either casts some doubt on the bilingualism of the enterprise, or suggests that bilingual theatre is viable most—or only?—when immigrants have a grasp of the host tongue. A third hypothesis is worth entertaining, namely, that, in order to succeed, bilingual theatre must develop very strong non-linguistic means of communication, as perfected by mime and dance. (The MWT, it must be said, strives to do this.)

And, of course, another cluster of issues raise their heads. Is bilingualism necessary for multicultural theatre? Can monolingual theatre which is in the majority language, as English is in Australia, be multicultural? What, though, of monolingual theatre which is in a minority language? It is proof of a multicultural society. But if it stays within the boundaries of its own linguistic community, how different is this situation from the community-bounded, even ghettoised cultures that existed before 'multiculturalism' was invented?

Perhaps it is significant that the spectators who praise the production's bilingualism, its 'real life drama of different ethnic backgrounds' and its portrayal of 'NESB [non-English-speaking-background] workers and the involvement in unions' are, with only one exception, Anglo/Celts. The same is true of spectators who say that the production 'made me feel strong' or that 'it was empowering'. Can we conclude from this that Anglo/Celts, who, in relation to the Turkish community, are outsiders looking in, are more sensitive than insiders to the issues that are presumed to be of concern to them before anyone else? Or are we here dealing with a problem of vocabulary and, therefore, with a corresponding way of conceptualising? The terms 'NESB' and 'empowering', for example, are used by Anglo/Celtic professional people who, as the rest of their commentary on my questionnaire also suggests, speak from a position of knowing what the debates on ethnicity and multiculturalism are about. This vocabulary is shared by professional artists—theatrical, visual or musical—who work in the 'multicultural' field. It is, ipso facto, the vocabulary of the directors, writers and performers of the MWT, Doppio Teatro, Filiki Players and similar theatre groups. Just as significantly, many of their members are of non-English-speaking background, the cause of multiculturalism thereby being propelled from within, from the standpoint of insiders. Nevertheless, it is *not* the language of the blue-collar workers in the sample, nor, more importantly, of our Turkish workers.

The fact that the Turkish respondents do not speak of empowerment as such does not mean that they have a poor self-image. Nor do they project a picture of themselves as a dispossessed group. We have already mentioned the spectators who feel disempowered by their lack of English; and impotence-exclusion through language, in whichever society it occurs has, as we all know, enormous consequences for immigrants with which the discomforts of mere tourists cannot begin to compare. We have also noticed how Turkish spectators refer to bilingualism only when offering a critique of the show. Bilingualism, in other words, is not uppermost in the minds of those who praise the show with little or no reservation. What comes first to their mind (by contrast with Anglo/Celtic professionals, though not Anglo/Celtic workers) is the production's 'encouraging workers to fight and struggle'. These words come from a toolmaker and sum up accurately the general point of view of his group.

The data suggests that, when empowerment is at issue, our Turkish respondents feel empowered by their sense of class unity and class struggle. Put differently, what this means is that empowerment for them is not a matter of identity politics, of what might be termed ethnicity as such, but well and truly a matter of mastering their role in the productive processes of society. This control over their own labour power is, in the view of Turks, the strength of *No Fear*. It must be noted that no other ethnic group within the same occupational category, shows such strong cohesion and conviction. Nor does it, therefore, dovetail so closely with the MWT's goals.

Once this has been said, however, it must also be pointed out that our Turkish respondents are certainly not the norm—and not even necessarily typical—of non-Anglo/Celtic spectators of comparable class and educational backgrounds. My research on Italian and Italo-Australian spectators shows that they are more receptive than the Turks here discussed to the idea of bilingual theatre.[7] By the same token, they are more caught up in identity politics and are, correspondingly, less concerned with class politics. In addition, they are less articulate, whether in Italian or English. The Turkish respondents, whatever language they reply in, have a flow of words to express their thoughts which no ethnic group of a comparable educational level, least of all Anglo/Celtic, can match, as far as my findings to date have shown.

The question of verbal facility—or at least as it appears on paper in answers to my questionnaire—is tied up with a generational factor. Most of the Turkish respondents are in their thirties and forties. (Schoolchildren, by the way, generally echo the positions and evaluations of their elders.) Most of the Italian respondents concerned are in their sixties or older. This is to say that they belong to an earlier immigration which, although not necessarily less well educated when education is measured by the number of years at school, appear nevertheless to be less well educated. They have also been in Australia much longer, which may suggest that the fire of opinion has grown smaller in them. A small pocket of them who are more articulate than the rest do not accentuate identity politics. Like their Turkish counterparts in expressivity, they foreground class politics. Like their Turkish counterparts, they tend to have had some involvement in oppositional politics. It is important, in the framework of this discussion, to note that a number of the Turks emigrating to Australia in recent years are political refugees.

These examples cannot be taken to be conclusive. Yet I would like to posit a hypothesis for debate and discussion. The Turkish workers at issue usually have not gone beyond the second year of high school—much like their Anglo or non-Anglo/Celtic equivalents. In the usual scheme of things, they would be considered to be poorly educated. Nevertheless, they grasp issues clearly, and are bold and articulate in ways that suggest a higher education than their formal level of education would allow. My hypothesis is that their politicisation has made this possible. It has provided them with tools not provided by their formal schooling. Furthermore, the verbal and conceptual skills acquired through their political education supersede the skills fostered at school. Much the same could be said of the politicised pockets among the Italians that I have studied elsewhere.[8]

If my hypothesis is tenable, we can argue that politicisation in class politics fills in the gaps, or even achieves more in the acquisition of basic skills, than school education. If this is so, then what are the consequences for literacy, understanding and critical thinking of the *depoliticisation* that we are witnessing across the whole world in the name of a political centre or the 'end of history', as a writer, who has been made too famous by the apocalyptic title of his book to be named, has called it? My question is of consequence to the multiple multiculturalisms burgeoning in the four corners of the world in the wake of renewed, late-twentieth-century nationalisms, all of which are heavily marked by identity politics.[9] And what culture can multiculturalism produce if identity politics, on the one hand, and depoliticisation, on the other, erode the literacy, acculturation and socialisation which, it seems, are already being eroded within schools across the whole world?

These questions, of course, are tough, and imply a pessimistic prognosis for modern times. Let us, consequently, leave them for happier days and return to our Turkish respondents for whom there can be no doubt that theatre culture goes hand in glove with political-economic struggle. When noting their views on the purposes of the theatre, Turkish respondents *invariably* stress education, explaining time and again that the theatre should 'provide people with political and cultural knowledge', 'provide messages' or 'communicate clear messages', 'help the working class with social and cultural issues', 'help the masses' or 'take up the issues and problems of the people and educate them'. The lexical and ideational combinations and collocations of our Turkish respondents show that they use 'working class', 'masses' and 'people' more or less synonymously.

The general pattern that can be observed is detailed in such replies as this from an electrical welder: [the theatre's purpose] is 'to form a relationship with the masses; to question and take up their problems; to make them think'. The commentary was written in Turkish, as was this: 'to unite people; to demonstrate the oppression of the people; to show social reality to the oppressed people'. When these replies are compared with answers from other groups, notably, by virtue of their majority, with those from Anglo/Celts, two points spring to mind: first, that our Turks never refer to entertainment, whereas everyone else places it second, after education, on their list; second, that our Turkish respondents consistently give the theatre the power of awakening political consciousness, whereas such a vocation is rarely ascribed to it by the remaining groups.

My question asked spectators to talk about the purposes of the theatre in general and not about multicultural theatre in particular. How Turkish respondents view the theatre, and the responsibilities they attribute to it, is not without consequence for multicultural theatre. For them, the theatre is principally a theatre of liberation—liberation from ignorance and economic and cultural inequality. As such, it is an empowering force. Their viewpoint can perhaps guide us in untying the knot of problems that obfuscate our thoughts on the reasons for, and the roles played by, the cultures of multiculturalism. The task is urgent for we cannot slumber in the complacencies of tokenism, which leave minorities in poverty and, often invisible, oppression. Nor can we become lost in the labyrinths of identity where, as if in mythic time, dwell the monster-minotaurs of racism and ethnic hatred. We need to live in *social* time and make of multiculturalism, whether in the theatre or in the streets, which are both places of culture, a social and not a totemistic force.[10]

Notes

1 The information presented above has been culled from *Multicultural Australia, Catalogue Number 25050,* Australian Bureau of Statistics, 1991.

2 *Estimated Resident Population by Country of Birth, Age and Sex: Preliminary 1991,* Catalogue Number 3221.0, Australian Bureau of Statistics, 1991.

3 For an argued case concerning this statement, see my 'Histoire/Identité: Le Contexte sociologique du théâtre australien', *Théâtre/Public* 91 (1990): 10–18.

4 Apart from my 'Histoire/Identité' above, see also Richard Fotheringham, ed., *Community Theatre in Australia*, North Ryde, 1987.

5 On the theme of the multiple forms of exclusion that plague immigrant populations, see the profoundly moving published research, essentially by interview, of Pierre Bourdieu's team of sociologists whose findings, although focused on France, are extremely relevant to the points raised in these pages. Thus, see *La Misère du monde*, Paris, 1993. For some theoretical reflections on how exclusion is generated in societies today through the hurdles set up by the triple alliance between nationalism, populism and ethnicity, see Michel

Wieviorka, *La Démocratie à l'épreuve: Nationalisme, populisme, éthnicité*, Paris, 1993.

6 An appropriate contrast would be, say, the factory theatre groups known as the Blue Blouses in the Soviet Union in the early twenties. These groups were composed of working men and women whose theatrical performances were so to speak built into the factory structure insofar as they took place—in or outside working hours—in the workplace and with the full approval of the managers and commissars in whichever industrial complex was involved. These groups were usually thought of as amateur groups, notwithstanding their reputed artistic competence. They were also touring groups, playing at factories and in geographic locations where no equivalent groups were available.

7 As yet largely unpublished data, although information supporting this contention can be found in my 'Audiences for Filef Theatre Group's *L'Albero delle rose/The Tree of Roses* and *Storie in cantiere/Stories in Construction*', *Australasian Drama Studies* 20 (1992): 93–118.

8 See 'Audiences for Filef' above.

9 A useful discussion on world-wide contemporary nationalisms as regressive movements and on their linkage with regressive identity politics as expressed, for example, in concepts of 'ethnic purity' and similar ethnic absolutes, see Michel Wieviorka, *La Démocratie à l'épreuve*, above.

10 Acknowledgement is due, for its support of the research referred to in the present article, to the Australian Research Council (ARC) Large Grants Scheme.

Feudalism Revisited: a Tribute to S. N. Mukherjee

John O. Ward

In this tribute to the stimulus of Soumyen Mukherjee as a teaching colleague, I am going to beg the reader's indulgence. Although I propose to make some comments on the continuing utility of the concept of 'feudalism' for the teacher of history, by way of comments on the reception and 'after-life' of the volume Soumyen, I and Edmund Leach edited together in 1984–85[1], and on the teaching venture in our department that accompanied it, I intend to be fuller and plainer in my references to an esteemed colleague than is, perhaps, usual in a Festschrift. I think all who know Soumyen will realise that this is the only appropriate way to go on this occasion.

In all my teaching career at the University of Sydney, I have had, by Australian standards, an excellent team of colleagues in the area of my expertise, medieval European history. I have also had fine colleagues in adjoining areas—ancient history and 'early modern' history. These latter are the natural areas from which it would seem appropriate to derive colleagues in joint 'inter-area' teaching ventures. And, indeed, I have from time to time, participated in such ventures. Why then would I choose to cooperate with an 'Asian area' colleague, someone of vastly different background from my own, in a teaching venture—*Feudalism, Comparative Studies*—that would seem fraught with obstacles, a teaching venture which, in fact, took an extraordinary amount of effort actually to launch, and which was, in some senses, ill-starred from the beginning? The answer to this question, I suppose, is part of my tribute to Soumyen Mukherjee. Somehow I found in him that spark of the heroic, that element of quest, the feeling that, for Soumyen, historical questions were always part of a life-long personal mission, the answers to which were difficult and even unpalatable. Somehow I sensed a personal commitment to the basic issues and lessons of historical experience that I did not readily find elsewhere, an unwillingness or an inability to let the smooth polish of middle-class western manners brush away the ragged edges of concern for the unsolved problems of the past, and their implications for the present and future. I do not recall now exactly what drew Soumyen and me together—though I will go into this a little in what follows—but in all our joint ventures, I have been continually reminded of the epic struggles of humanity, and of the importance of an informed knowledge of these struggles for any responsible attitude towards present and future problems. The very titles of our joint ventures—'Peasant Societies in Revolution: the Role of Millenarian Cults', 'Revolutions',[2] 'Feudalism in History', 'Marxism in History'[3]—contrast interestingly with the titles of my normal teaching assignments: 'Medieval History I', 'Heresy and Inquisition', 'Florence and the Age of Dante', 'The Rise and Fall of the First Reich: Germany and its Neighbours 919–1272 A.D.', 'Meaning in History-writing', 'Medieval Thought and Learning in the Twelfth-Century Renaissance', and the like. For the fact that he kept those epic currents before me, and for his eternally persuasive manner, and for his persistence in breaching the protective barrier that, over the years, I came to erect around my activities in the department, I will remain forever in debt to Soumyen. This paper is not an attempt to repay that debt (one can never repay debts of this sort). I will be content if I have at least outlined the debt.

First, however, a diversion. Perhaps the high point of the exotic world that Soumyen's pressures introduced me to was the lecture which he arranged with his friend Barun De for me to give to the Calcutta Centre for Studies in Social Science (of which Barun De was then Director and Professor of History), 4 February 1986. My competition was severe as it was the very day and hour at which the Pope was to address the crowds, not far off. The lecture itself was no high point (I present some of it below), and I have to record that the Pope got the lion's share of the potential audience on the day, but the experience of getting and being there was an absolute high point in my life, and possibly too no mean moment in the lives of the four ladies who formed my party for the month-long rail voyage around northern India.

Friends and students had long been urging me, a confirmed Europeanist, to make the acquaintance of India, where they argued, moments of medieval splendour could be experienced that would far outrun anything to be had among the carefully manicured and lifeless medieval monuments of Europe. Among these was someone to whom I will always owe a special debt among the many students whose reading, thinking and attitudes towards life have much influenced my own: Chris Kenna. The arrangement was that I, my wife Gail, my two teenage daughters Tara and Katie, and a lifelong colleague and friend Sharon Davidson, would rendezvous with a mutual special friend of us all, Devleena Ghosh (Berwick) amidst the spectacular ruins of the Black Pagoda in Konarak,[4] and then proceed to Calcutta, where I would vie with the Pope for an audience. Habituated to travel in Europe, I amassed a collection of rail time-tables and began to plan with the usual attention to split-second timing and unmissable connections that has long characterised my approach to European touring. The result was as spectacular a piece of work in its own way as were the ruins at Konarak. In one month we were to deplane at Bombay and visit in quick succession Aurangabad (and nearby monuments), Hyderabad (and nearby monuments), Bhubaneswar, Puri and Konarak, Calcutta, Darjeeling, Agra, Jaipur, Jaisalmer, Udaipur, and Ahmedabad. Such an itinerary did not permit loitering, and we deplaned at Bombay 4.31 a.m. local time, to board almost immediately the Nagpur Express train No.39, which departed Dadar Central Terminus at 12.35 p.m. My notes record that the Nagpur Express 'feels like a Queensland Mail train, hot, dry, ancient, but much more crowded!' We passed through the stench, squalor and dereliction of outer Bombay, the mountainous terrain around Kasara, splendid vistas above dry river beds and some fine agricultural scenes, with gaily coloured sari-clad women, neat mud-brick houses and tidy, varied crops, arriving at Manmad, a straggling town of mud streets and hovels, sprawling away from a large station complex full of food stalls, Hindi signs and people, at sunset. An impressive metre-gauge steam-locomotive hauled the Ajanta Express into the station and we got a space to ourselves in the single first-class car, with the usual two upper and two lower berths which acted as seats for six or eight people by day. Arrival at Aurangabad, for the Daulatabad fort, Ellora and Ajanta caves and sundry related monuments, completed probably the most extraordinary day of touring that I had so far encountered in my life. True, Hong Kong, Venice and Mont St Michel were experiences impossible to shelve, but for sheer ragged colour and seething sparkle, 26 January 1986 and the days that followed it were unbeatable.

I had, true to form, made a careful collection of tiny xeroxed articles and book chapters which I was attempting to digest for my Calcutta lecture. Never was tranquil contemplation of the past via the fossilised memoranda of scholarly print carried out in such a competitive environment. My travelling companions, bemused as they were by the day's encounters, accepted my preoccupations and attended competently to the logistics of getting us around the railway network and the string of unrelenting medieval sights that we passed through in Hyderabad, the Golconda fort, Bhubaneswar and Puri. The latter point we reached via the 4 p.m. WP class steam-locomotive-hauled Puri passenger, a massively crowded train (packed with non-paying passengers and all manner of merchandise, dead and alive), that trundled through paddy fields, jungle villages, teeming markets and palm trees, all etched against the setting sun. Due (if that is the word for occasions so replete with the never-before-seen and the unexpected) inspections of the Black and White Pagodas at Puri and Konarak mingled with experiences of religious pilgrimage that evoked the middle ages in a spectacular manner, before a night train brought us punctually to that sight of sights, Howrah railway station Calcutta and the nearby towering bridge of that name over the Hooghly River, with its unending procession of human rickshaws, human freight wagons and carriers, three-wheeler trucks, jam-packed buses, beaten-up scare-crow trams clanking over the worst track I have ever seen, and soldiers duly policing the bridge against tourists such as myself determined to try and capture some of the impressions they encountered on film. Confronted by one such soldier, I ended up dropping a lens, a camera and a selection of film onto the roadway in a series of manoeuvres that, although initially fraught with imagined potential disaster, in fact proved an essential diversionary tactic that enabled me to get away without surrendering the offending film. The idea that my efforts might endanger the security of the Indian nation was an odd addition to the unimaginable array of stalls, tables, shops, cottage industries, crumbling lacy Victorian apartment blocks, earthen footpaths, sewer outflows and repair teams, street barbers, human rickshaw depots, clunking trams, bulging buses, and jogging human freighters that formed my first taste of Calcutta.

The days that followed brought us all by indescribable struggling narrow-gauge steam railway to Tibetan order and soul-stopping Himalayan splendour at Darjeeling (where I recall a heated argument about the hiring of a blanket for a hotel room that cost, I think, each of us $1 for the night). After a day or two taking in the Tibetan New Year, we made our descent through stupendous vistas of terraced slopes, tea plantations and hillside towns and the tremendous touchable clutter of the numerous villages through which the train passed, to arrive at New Jalpaiguri late in the day. There we were to await the arrival of No.155 Tinsukia Mail, departing N. J. a little after 10.30 p.m. and arriving at Tundla, the junction station for Agra Fort Station, at 4.02 a.m. two days later.

This epic trip was to break our team. We had so far had spectacular good luck with the Indian Railways' Byzantine booking systems and had made timings that our friends back in Sydney assured us we would not be able to keep to. Our aim was to see Agra, Jaipur, Jaisalmer, Udaipur and Ahmedabad, before taking a plane on to Italy on 21 February 1986. The twenty-eight- or nine-hour trip on the Tinsukia Mail, sparing us the long ordeal of going again via Calcutta was a crucial time-saving cross-country effort actually to make up time on our already advanced schedule. I outlined to my companions what I had heard at the Darjeeling booking station, that Bihar State was full of well-organised bandits who did deals with the train drivers and diverted trains onto sidings during the night, from which vantage points they raped the women, cut the throats of all resisters and stole everything that was portable.[5] I reasoned that these stories were probably exaggerated and the risk of encountering them was not worth the additional time that the rail trip via Calcutta would require. In other words, the requirements of an advanced schedule was worth more than the possible risk to our property, our throats and the modesty of the female contingent. My wife and daughters, inured to this approach, made little protest, but Sharon, with a more sophisticated knowledge of the country, began to distribute her not inconsiderable volume of banknotes in various European currencies, around the pages of the books she was carrying, on the grounds, she said, that bandits would not bother to take books away, especially not 'Teach-Yourself-German' books and the like. The threat to her morals was something, I suppose, she could not prepare against, but something could at least be done about the banknotes.

Thus prepared, we duly boarded the Mail at N. J. in a compartment we were told we could occupy only until Patna (1300 hours the next day) when a top-level Indian parliamentary delegation would board and throw us onto the platform. We took this option because the only alternative was not to take the Mail at all at that point. Thoughts of banditry could not have been too compelling because we all fell asleep and awoke in the heart of hot and polluted Bihar State at Sahibganj station, a veritable cacophony and paradise of food wallahs and their wares. The extraordinary variety and availability of food at this station contrasted oddly with the solemn warning I had received at the Darjeeling tourist booking office, that Bihar State 'lacked food for travellers'.

Neither food, nor banditry, it turned out, nor even parliamentary delegations (ours never showed) were the problem on this trip. Physical stamina, however, was. As we awaited our connecting train for Agra in the confused cold of the early morning at Tundla, both Sharon and Gail began to manifest considerable signs of illness. Sharon ended up vomiting out the doors of the crowded third class carriage in which we eventually rode on to Agra, and Gail became pained and glassy-eyed, having obvious difficulty in breathing. The itinerary ground relentlessly on. Location of a $1-per-night-per-person hotel near Agra Fort station was followed by a punishing schedule of visits to all major sights, culminating in a sunset inspection of Shah Jahan's fabulous Taj Mahal. By this time Sharon was beginning to improve, but Gail became so distressed that we returned her to the hotel, finishing our itinerary without her, and making some compulsory carpet and mosaic factory-viewings on our way back. It turned out that she had contracted pneumonia, which required a few days hospitalisation (the entire cost of which, with ambulances here and there, and a bed for Tara to stay with her, came to the at-the-time massive sum of $200). Our schedule was properly broken, and Jaisalmer had to go. The compensation was that Fatehpur Sikri received a series of very careful inspections indeed, by the non-hospitalised members of the party, travelling by unpredictably-scheduled and very crowded steam-hauled third-class passenger trains which were nevertheless infinitely superior to the impossibly rough buses that most tourists used, and which, in view of the location of our hotel, were not very handy. We simply asked the railway staff to notify us when the train arrived, since this could vary by up to six hours. My disappointment at the failure of my carefully nurtured railway schedule was thought, by my companions, to have been uncharitable, in view of the suffering the same schedule brought to Gail (and to a lesser extent to Sharon). They have a point, indeed, but to this day I have not had a chance to make up for that lost opportunity of taking a metre-gauge steam-hauled night express to the fabled city of Jaisalmer, and, with advancing age, failing health, the ongoing dieselisation of the Indian Railways and recent disasters to Jaisalmer itself, I doubt that I ever will....

The point of this diversion is simply my way of saying that never before or since have I encountered travel and sights on this scale, and I owe the experience to Soumyen Mukherjee (and his students), without whom it would never have occurred. It demonstrates, I suppose, in a graphic way, the kind of lift that Soumyen gave to one's historical studies. This lift, however, must be described in a more comprehensive way, and the rest of this paper will be devoted to that aim. I propose to describe the origins of my joint teaching ventures with Soumyen, then to look at the most elaborate of these ventures, and finally to consider the aftermath of the volume that was associated with this venture[6] and which was, for myself, a notable historiographical experience. In connection with this last, I would like to offer some further thoughts on the meaning of feudalism in a Western context.

In one of the many unsorted files that contain the relics of my almost thirty years of teaching medieval history at Sydney University, I find a copy of a 'proposal for a "cross-cultural" seminar in History IV' that bears the names of 'J. O. Ward and S. N. Mukherjee' and is dated 2 May 1973. It was apparently written in connection with page 5 of a 'Response from the Professors of History to the Recommendations from the Departmental Advisory Planning Committee of 12 March 1973'. It is nice, in retrospect, to remind oneself that the present mania for teaching-impeding bureaucratalia has its parallel in the remote past. The 'Proposal' goes on to state that the 'Professors of History' claim that they are 'sympathetically open' to proposals for a 'cross-cultural seminar (in Fourth Year), cutting across periods in pursuit of some common theme such as revolutions and which might form a relatively stable part of the furnishings of History IV'. The authors of the 'Proposal' (J. O. Ward and S. N. Mukherjee) ventured a course entitled PEASANT SOCIETIES IN REVOLUTION:

THE ROLE OF MILLENARIAN CULTS, which, they claimed, 'could arise out of the existing interests of a number of members of the Department ... and could help meet the needs of students who would like to pursue an historical/cultural topic of considerable contemporary relevance, into its proper full-length context in time'. The provisional description of the course was as follows:

> Term I: European peasant revolutions and millenial cults. An introductory seminar or seminars could establish the theoretical, thematic continuity of the course, and thereafter, topics could be selected in accordance with staff interest/availability and student preference, from the fourteenth, sixteenth, seventeenth and eighteenth-nineteenth centuries.
>
> Term II: India, the revolution of 1857, related context and problems.
>
> Term III: a selection of analysis points, widely spread, of relevance in the contemporary context. Perhaps: New Guinea and the Cargo Cults, the Mau-Mau, Latin America, South-East Asia. Here the enlistment of specialist help from outside the Department might be necessary, or at least advisable, although the emphasis would be on the student's own exploration of the area. A concluding seminar or seminars might draw together the course enquiry as a whole.

The remainder of the 'Proposal' indicated that 'Sybil Jack, who has interests in the English Civil War and Millenial cults, and Ian Jack, who has interests in agrarian life generally and English peasant revolts, have both offered to' assist with staffing the course. The 'Proposal' contained nothing particularly threatening, and nothing inappropriate to a senior historian with wide connections throughout the university, and a junior colleague keen to take part in what looked like a stimulating adventure. To explain the undercurrents which, in the end, engulfed this 'Proposal', however, it is necessary to allude to two of those historical truths that never find offical record.[7] The first, a series of personality clashes that divided the 'Asian Area', formed an ongoing thread in the life of the Sydney history department, and the second, the jealously guarded professorial right to mount or at least to sanction the mounting of the senior seminar courses in Fourth Year, can only be alluded to here. Suffice it to say, that History IV at the time was made up of 'Seminar Courses' (major options, later called 'List A options' and in the early stages mounted by the professors or their favoured sons according to their whims), 'Special Options' (later called 'List B options', smaller-scale courses that could be mounted by any member of staff and were often quite narrow in their stated aims), and a 15,000 word thesis. This system had replaced an earlier triumvirate, of 'Historical Method' seminars (usually organised by J. M. Ward), 'Seminars on Prescribed Subjects' (the precursors of the later 'Seminar Courses'), and a thesis. I forget now the exact course of the tortuous negotiations that inaugurated Soumyen's and my first attempt to work together, but there is in my possession a carbon copy of a letter dated 7 July 1973, addressed to 'Dr S. N. Mukherjee', with copies to Professor J. M. Ward and myself. It is unsigned, but was written by Marjorie Jacobs, Professor of History at the time. It runs:

> I feel the need to resolve a misunderstanding between us (and also involving John O. Ward) which was revealed at this morning's departmental meeting. When I conveyed to the meeting the list of options so far proposed by members of the department, there was no intention on my part to suppress mention of a special option proposed by yourself and John Ward. On the other hand it is my impression that you misquoted me when you suggested to the meeting that I had advised you and John to think no more of the proposed course on peasant revolts and millenarian movements as a possible special option. My memory of our discussion of these matters is that at every point I advised against pressing these proposals on the Department in the form of a seminar but that I equally encouraged you to propose a special option for 1974 along whatever lines you might think fit. I could not consider that the proposal remained before us without alteration in the light of this advice. I assumed that some adaptation of your proposals would be necessary, and that John Ward's continued association with the project could not be taken for granted. Since I had heard nothing more about the matter I could only assume that it had lapsed, or that it might still be looked for. In either case it was no more appropriate for me to mention this proposal to the meeting than other possibilities which I have heard of, but which have not yet reached me in writing, and which may or may not eventuate. I am sorry for the misunderstanding and should be seriously concerned if anything beyond simple misunderstanding were involved. I repeat what I said at the meeting: that I am sure that the Department will welcome any proposal which you may have to make of a special option to be offered in History IV in 1974.

Needless to say, perhaps, the course was not proceeded with, or was not allowed to proceed in the form in which it had been conceived. Similar courses were appropriate at other universities (for example, UNSW), but not at Sydney. The next record of joint proposals between myself and Soumyen in my possession is a memorandum from Professor Jacobs, to Soumyen, dated 23/7/1979, in which she stated that 'in the absence of information about "Feudalism in History" the [departmental] meeting decided to accept it as an option which may be available in 1980'. Soumyen provided the information requested in a memorandum, undated, as follows:

> History IV 1980. FEUDALISM IN HISTORY. This will be a seminar on the origin and development of the idea and institution of feudalism in Europe and India. I think we should have 24 seminars during the year. The first six seminars will be on the development of the idea of feudalism from the philosophers of the Enlightenment to the twentieth century Marxists. Then we shall turn our attention to India and historians like Kosambi, Sharma, L. Gopal, Habib, Moreland, Thapar and Athar Ali. I shall be responsible for the first half of the seminars. There should be one essay, one tutorial paper and one two-hour examination. I would like John O. Ward to be responsible for the second half of the year with European development, comparing and contrasting it with the development elsewhere.

Written below my copy of this memorandum is a note from Marjorie Jacobs, saying, in part, that Soumyen 'also expresses regret that the above was included in the B options and not in the seminars. I was under the impression from my brief discussion with you that you contemplated a B option'. Yet, attached to the same memorandum, is a note from John Pryor saying 'I think you should press for it ['Feudalism in History'] as a List A seminar.... Two of my students have already expressed disappointment that there is no List A seminar outside the field of 19th–20th century European and Anglo-Saxon history and the Method seminars ... are really in the same field'. In the official list of History IV seminars for 1980 to which these notes are attached, 'Feudalism in History' is, in fact, listed as a 'List B' seminar. At that time the 'List A' options were in the hands of Ken Cable, Tony Cahill, Neville Meaney, Alastair Maclachlan, and M. D. Stephen. They dealt with 'Church, State and Society', 'Nationalism in Europe, America and

Australia', 'History Method' and 'History and Circumstance: the Role of Social and Individual Attitudes in the Writing of History'. A fairly safe bill of fare for tomorrow's statespersons....

In my records is a letter from myself to Marjorie Jacobs, dated 25/7/1979. In it I stated that, having had some experience of other 'List A' thematic courses ('Power Structures', 'Law and Society')

> I am happy to cooperate in 'Feudalism in History' in 1980, either as a List A or B, in accordance with the preferences of the Department, the students and Soumyen, with whom the idea originated.... I feel that in scope it is a valid 'List A' seminar (at least in comparison with such chestnuts as 'nationalism' or–worse–topics 'to be announced'!!).... I am not yet convinced that pursuit of the wraith of 'feudalism' cannot perform a useful didactic service, and am encouraged by the fact that at the 14th congress of Medievalists at Kalamazoo, Michigan, which I attended this last May (along with some 1399 other medievalists!), the largest audience and the best speakers were drawn to a 'forum' on 'whether feudalism' was a relevant conceptual tool for the study of medieval history'.... My portion of the year would concentrate on three approaches:
>
> (A) an examination of what leading modern historians and theorists take 'feudalism' to imply in a medieval context (E. A. Bloch, and R. A. Brown, Fourquin, Duby, Lyon, Strayer, D. H. Green, Perry Anderson, perhaps Marx).
>
> (B) an examination of what contemporaries understood by feudal relations and values, with particular reference to the structure of power in selected localities AND an examination of what detailed modern research into land-holding patterns, power and family relations, in particular areas reveals regarding the relevance of continued concentration on 'feudal institutions'. Areas to be selected from here would include: northern French / Flemish aristocratic society c.1000–1125 (Janet Martindale, Van Luyn, Duby, Guibert de Nogent, Galbert of Bruges); Germany (Leyser, Thompson, Hill, Gillingham and documents); Spain (Lourie, McKay); Southern France (Lewis, Bisson); Outremer; Norman England; France and England in the later middle ages ('Bastard Feudalism').
>
> (C) an examination of the place and role of 'feudal institutions' in Russia, Islam, Byzantium, Japan, China (Mark Elvin). Term III should leave space for concluding, comparative discussions.

In my outline I suggested that guest lecturers could be invited to enrich the envisaged coverage and half-day, day or even weekend symposia could be held in conjunction with the course, and that the ramifications of the subject extended into such areas as 'modern sociological research into the nature and functioning of elites, the development of rival (?) elites (bourgeosie, 'capitalism'), nineteenth-century Neo-feudalism (see S. J. Tonsor, 'Feudalism, Revolution and Neo-feudalism: a Review Article' *Comparative Studies in Society and History* 21 (1979): 131–38).

In her note of reply, of the same date, Marjorie wrote that 'I am under the impression that I did not yesterday consult you about the location of the unit 'Feudalism in History' in the History IV programme. I did that some time ago during Soumyen Mukherjee's absence from Sydney at the time of our early discussions of History IV 1980, and at that time had the impression that you favoured a B option'. Attached to Marjorie's note is a note in Soumyen's hand, dated 29/7 [?'8']/1979, asserting that 'whatever [Marjorie Jacobs[8]] might have said about feudalism, you will see the literature on it is extensive and important. Please read Kosambi chapters 9 and 10 [etc.].... I am extremely angry—not with you though'.

Somehow, nothing eventuated from these exchanges, and I have no record of any course being mounted by Soumyen and me before 1987, when, at long last, 'Feudalism: Comparative Studies' was put on, for about 15 students, with even an honours course (for two students, later one). It was mounted as a second-year 'Thematic Unit' ('T 15'). 'Thematic units' were, at the time, storm-in-a-teacup attempts by the department to display a certain up-market toney curriculum flexibility, but they usually degenerated into re-labelled conventional 'area' units, and, as such, were subject to periodical revivals. Ours was genuinely, indeed formidably, thematic, but I cannot say it attracted any very distinguished students. We arranged a nice 'Indian night' (at my place) and we invited a guest lecturer or two (for example, Jeremy Beckett on 'feudalism' in the Philippines, and Ken Macnab on Edmund Wilson's *To the Finland Station*).

Much the same course was advertised in the 1988 Departmental Handbook as Course 237.2, but I do not recall whether it went on or not. I recall wondering why such an apparently exciting course was so unattractive to students, and I had certainly not, in the past, had difficulty attracting enough numbers to keep courses going. In 1989, therefore, I decided to change the name to 'Marxism in History: the idea and reality of feudalism and the Asiatic mode of production'. I think this was the time the course attracted only 4 or 5 students and ran for a week or two before I closed it down, since mounting it involved at least that many staff. Soumyen was, I think, on leave at the time, and had suggested some replacement tutors. In 1992 I ran the course again, in its changed form (Soumyen was on sick-leave and provided a couple of guest lectures), and this time I got 30 or 40 students and some of these were the best I have ever had (Elisabeth Bos, Armin Wittfoth, Geraldine O'Hara), while others were equally memorable in their own way (Toby Eccles, Emma Rawling, James Mugambi, Emma-Kate Symons [whose father was at that time in adventure with Graham Richardson], and Michael Petersen [son of the former Director of the *Sydney University News*]). Battle-scarred students from this course still occasionally stop and say how much they got out of it. Because of Soumyen's suddenly announced sick leave, I called upon my colleagues to contribute lectures in their areas of expertise, in order to make up for the reduction of emphasis upon India, and their contributions were both willing and excellent. John Pryor came along to lecture on Marx's ideas about medieval feudalism, and becamed so involved that he scheduled for himself another appearance the week following; Iain Cameron lectured lucidly on 'Feudalism and the French Revolution', Ian Jack on 'Bastard Feudalism', and John Berwick on 'The Asiatic Mode of Production'. Mark Elvin came up from Canberra, lectured attractively on China, dined with the students and stayed with me for an interesting couple of days, and Rikki Kersten, in what in some ways was the 'pièce de resistance', delivered an inspiring talk on 'Feudalism' in modern Japanese political and historical thinking. It was a teaching experience I am glad to have had, even though one intelligent student (whom I was pleased to service somewhat later with my 'Heresy and Inquisition' course) abandoned the course because, as she claimed over the phone when I rang her up to find out why she had 'dropped', 'I wanted the facts of history, not theories about it'. I, however, enjoyed tackling head-on the notion that history was what you urgently or passionately needed it to be, and my only regret was that Soumyen could not have been more fully part of what was, in hindsight, the finest hour for his and my joint teaching ventures.

Soumyen and I decided to have one more go at jointly teaching this course, a kind of swan-song, as Soumyen's retirement was imminent. We therefore advertised it for second semester in 1994 (as 'T 15.2'), but in a strangely ironic manner, a secretarial slip on the part of the compiler of the Handbook for the year, killed it: the printed description attached to the title of our course, as it turned out when the Handbook appeared from the printer's hands, was not the one I had submitted, but the description of Iain Cameron's course 'Crime and Deviance: 1500 to the present' ('T 16.2'), even though that very description appeared, correctly, beneath the title for Iain's course and directly below the notice of our own course. Only 15 students were curious enough to enrol, and one wonders what they hoped to find. In the corridor one day late in semester one of that year, I encountered the departmental administrative assistant, who said 'Oh well, you'll have a light load next semester!' I, used to his bantering, said, 'Indeed! Why in particular?', to which he replied 'The Departmental Meeting has just decided to cancel your 'Feudalism' course because there weren't enough takers'. That was the way things were done then (and are still). So ended Soumyen and my joint teaching ventures. I do not think I will attempt to revive the course, because (a) students find the multiplicity of 'areas' too difficult, (b) Soumyen has retired, (c) who knows whether my colleagues would be so generous again with their fine contributions, and (d) I do not know how many more years I can count on in the department, and I have some unexpended energies for the courses which I am more professionally qualified to teach.

Behind our joint-teaching venture on Feudalism lay the volume in the Sydney Association for Studies in Society & Culture (SASSC) series that recorded the proceedings of a conference on the subject at St Andrew's College (University of Sydney) in March 1984,[9] and behind that lay the 'preliminary' workshop held in Terrey Hills some couple of years earlier. Soumyen was, of course, the animating spirit behind both, and I still have an amusing set of slides taken at the Terrey Hills site showing all of us in jolly and inebriated state, 'enjoying' feudalism, as it were. There was a camaraderie that was very much part of Soumyen himself (though he would not, in the end, accept our invitation to 'sleep with us' on some sort of vast communal mattress in the centre of the hall where the workshop was held!): it is hard to imagine our more straight-laced colleagues inspiring that sort of mayhem. The published volume evoked an interesting set of reactions, some of them unpublished,[10] and by no less a figure than R. W. Southern, who had been praised by Elizabeth R. A. Brown for not using the word 'feudalism' in his *Making of the Middle Ages* (1953)—'the purest'[11] book on the subject—and other publications.[12] Southern wrote, in reference to my chapter in the Sydney *Feudalism: Comparative Studies* volume:[13]

> As for your contribution to Feudalism, I thought it a very clearly articulated and well organised study of the various things 'it' has been taken by historians to be. And I agree with your conclusion that it is a valuable concept so long as historians both *are* clear and make clear to *others* what they mean by it. If these conditions are met (and they virtually never are), then you are quite right to call it stimulating and an incentive to organised study. Curiously enough, however, I don't remember that anyone before you has even tried so systematically to distinguish the types and sub-types of feudalism. And this may be because none of your foci has been (or perhaps ever can be) the exclusive focus of any prolonged study. Indeed, it is clear that one cannot have, say, focus V without I and II plus some elements of all the others. So, valuable though your analysis is as a retrospective study (as it might be [used] by a consultant examining the phases and symptoms of the disease), they [the foci] cannot in practice be kept separate, and it is not very clear in what ways later studies should or can be influenced by writers who may now be aware that they are slipping from Focus V to I or II and back again to V, perhaps in the space [?] of a single page, but can do nothing to stop it happening.
>
> In principle, as you mention, I have seldom (I should like to think never) used the word or concept,
>
> (a) because I don't know what I would mean by it, and
>
> (b) [because] whatever I meant by it would be alien to the thought and experience of the relevant period in the past.
>
> So I hope I shall never use the word in the future. Anyhow, I found your discussion interesting and enlightening.

This would have pleased Elizabeth Brown, who complained[14] in her review of our volume, that nowhere did the contributors define what they meant by the term 'feudalism'. She complained that fewer papers dealt with non-European societies than the title led her to expect, that most of the non-European authors said little to recommend the use of the term 'feudalism' as a tool of comparative analysis, while at least one (Jeffcott) actually questioned the whole procedure. Two essays were praised for providing 'important insights into the ways in which the term 'feudalism' has served political ends' (Kenna, Reynolds), and two others were singled out as 'particularly valuable' (Mukherjee's 'novel remarks on the genesis and development of the construct in the West', and my own 'comprehensive and penetrating analysis of the many meanings ... that have been associated with "feudalism"'). Brown was puzzled that, despite my analysis, I could still see some utility for the term and she concluded by repeating her view that she herself could not.

A wide-ranging and trenchantly critical discussion of our volume, together with that of T. J. Byres and Harbans Mukhia, *Feudalism and Non-European Societies*,[15] from the pen of Susan Reynolds, a noted opponent of the term 'feudalism', appeared in *Peasant Studies* for 1987.[16] Reynolds at least admitted that the issue discussed in the two volumes was 'intrinsically important', but that, aside from the problem of the link between feudalism and capitalism in non-European societies (contrasted with Europe), the debates about the meaning of the term 'feudalism' in European history were heuristically of little value: Reynolds claimed that I was afraid of my own conclusions and of Brown, whom (she wrote) Mukherjee did not fully understand. Marxist adherents of the heuristic value of the term 'feudalism', argued Reynolds, should not allow their views to be cluttered by petty debates about fiefs and vassals; she observed that it was difficult to see how the Norman Conquest, cropping up in both volumes, 'could have introduced feudalism to England in any Marxist sense'.[17] Like other critics, Reynolds noted how Leach in his introduction to our volume, rather torpedoed its own project,[18] but had an occasional good word for some of the contributions: my own chapter, though providing 'an acute and thought-provoking analysis', nevertheless, concluded timidly; Wright was 'interesting', Bennett drew some 'neatly described' contrasts between English and French historiographical traditions on feudalism, and Jeffcott's happy phrase 'the Cinderella slipper strategy' comes in (again) for notice.

In the rest of her valuable critique, Reynolds displays her (English) preoccupation with the need for an 'exact fit' between the labours of the historian and the past. 'The concept of the fief is post-medieval' (a theme to which Reynolds returns in her subsequent, sledge-hammer, book on the subject),[19] the aspect of personal freedom and unfreedom in 'feudal' societies, needs 'more rigorous study', the Marxist mode-of-production line of thought must be cleansed of fiefs and vassals, and possibly also of distinctions between labour-rent, money-rent, and rent in kind; if its emphasis upon structural change is to be adhered to, 'one must surely stick to some consistent hypothesis about what can or cannot bring about' this kind of change.

Reynolds concludes by suggesting that 'feudalism' as a tool of comparative social analysis is productive of more confusion than clarity, and that within Europe all aspects of the debate require harder confrontation with 'real empirical evidence, if not at first hand then at least as it is presented in serious and critical monographs'.[20] In the close-focus tradition of mature Anglo-American historiography, this is no doubt true. Building stones for the Master Builder, as Huizinga once argued,[21] must be properly hewn. Nevertheless, the notion of 'feudalism' does draw many things into debate that might otherwise moulder respectably on library shelves or here and there, in discrete and uncontroversial ways, in monograph/journal pages and conference sessions. History is more, perhaps, the well-arranged scholarly study in the English-speaking world, or the right sort of disourse in well-respected classes and symposia. Even if we closed the book on feudalism now, historians of thought and historiography would still have much to contend with.[22] Besides, as some remarks below are intended to suggest, many do not appear to be listening to Reynolds or 'Peggy Brown', to whom, in an irony of ironies, Reynolds declares 'homage and fidelity' on the dedication page of her *Fiefs and Vassals*.

It is difficult to predict at this stage the reaction of the scholarly world to Susan Reynolds' 500-page *Fiefs and Vassals*, but its brief seems a gloomy one: it is 'meaningless' to try and decide whether feudo-vassalic relations or institutions were less important than has up to now been thought, or to inquire into their origin,[23] or to say where they appeared, or to judge which part of Europe 'was most truly feudal'.[24] One wonders what Fulbert of Chartres[25] would have said in reply to Reynolds' assertion that the concept of vassalage is 'comparatively vacuous'.[26]

Perhaps, all in all, he might have agreed, but Duke William of Aquitaine wanted to know about it, so he had to make something up. Readers will be pleased to learn that Reynolds' 500 pages do not pretend to offer a 'comprehensive' survey of her topic—'the relation between the modern concepts of the fief and of vassalage on the one hand and the evidence of property law and of social and political relations that I find in medieval sources on the other'.[27] She has 'deliberately omitted ... the whole subject of feudalism in its Marxist sense ... [and] large areas of Europe'.[28] These latter include Spain and Jerusalem and 'a mass of local variations'. Hard confessions for a hardened empiricist, but there are already signs that the empiricist is at least in part fascinated by the discourse ('the different national traditions of writing about feudalism'). Reynolds' conclusion [29] suggests that she hasn't entirely given away an interest in feudal origins, but the respectful reference to 'modern knowledge' (about feudalism, and which sustains the mainly 'negative' conclusions of the book) is alarming in a postmodern age. Duby and Dockès,[30] it seems, were in error in supposing that their period was one in which unruly barons and knights made war upon each other and tyrannised over hapless peasants, because Reynolds tells us that no medieval historians now see 'the period' ('the whole middle ages') in that way. Are we banned from seeing a certain pattern in one part of the middle ages, because 'modern knowledge' bans it for 'the whole middle ages'? Let the reader judge.

It is also consoling to learn that when Reynolds comes to her 'more positive conclusions',[31] she fits comfortably enough into my focus Vb.[32] Nevertheless, the legacy of her book is the inutility of models, 'as a substitute for comparison of the evidence of actual phenomena'.[33] The historian must just bumble around, knocking into 'sources', 'evidence', bits and pieces and bric-a-brac left behind by past ages—'plodding through the uncertain evidence' is Reynolds' phrase[34]—in quest of limited enlightenment. That limited enlightenment at times runs the risk of bumping into another of our energising historiographical concepts—the so-called 'Twelfth-Century Renaissance',[35] and one is indeed led to wonder whether Reynolds would ever have been stimulated to write her massive *Fiefs and Vassals* had it not been for all those not-so-careful historians who bumbled around their sources with the additional impediment of a large travel-sack labelled 'Feudalism'.

It is possible that the concept 'feudalism' will survive Reynolds' armoured panzer attack.[36] Much recent literature, indeed, seems to have confirmed the emphasis, and the concepts 'feudalism'/'feudal relations' are strengthening their position in Western historical discourse, even if the utility of the feudal model is fading in the latest research into Japanese history.[37] A few comments on recent books may be permitted here, in approximate chronological order.

Georges Duby, himself, despite the praise awarded him by E. A. R. Brown for his (1953) work on the Mâconnais,[38] has been of late less than chaste. Abandoning his earlier close-focus 'research'-oriented inquiry, so obviously acceptable to the Anglo-American tradition represented by Brown and Reynolds, Duby has lately allowed his fancy to run free—at least as far as his English translators are concerned. Even these latter are not entirely to blame, as the original 1981 French of his *Le Chevalier, La Femme et la Prêtre* is quite happy to talk about 'the society we call feudal' and sets as the historian's task the comprehending of 'la féodalité'.[39] So too Duby entitled an article published in *La Pensée* for 1984[40] 'Les femmes et la révolution féodale', thoughts inspired by a course he had commenced on the condition of women in the 'society called feudal'. *The Early Growth of the European Economy: Warriors and Peasants from the Seventh to the Twelfth Century*[41] sins heavily in entitling an entire chapter 'The Age of Feudalism',[42] whilst the English edition of *The Three Orders*[43] has a chapter entitled 'The Feudal Revolution'[44] and amply indexes 'Feudalism' at the end of the book. The most recent of Duby's imports, as far as I have noted, is his *Love and Marriage in the Middle Ages*,[45] where we find 'Feudalism' nicely indexed (including the extraordinary 'feudalism—and attitudes to pain 168-71'!), and even defined (p.66: 'Feudalism is the parcelling out of power').[46] Just behind the latter is Duby's *France in the Middle Ages 987–1460* (English 1991, French 1987),[47] where, although not indexed, 'la féodalité' is alive and well,[48] and the important 'homage recital' of Galbert of Bruges[49] is taken to imply a moment when 'standard feudal practice crystallized in northern France'.[50]

It is time to wonder, indeed, whether the French and the English are parting company in regard to the continued usage of terms like 'feudalism' and 'feudal' (adherence to the latter always exposes one to the risk of slipping in the former). Robert Bartlett, in his *The Making of Europe: Conquest, Colonization and Cultural Change 950–1350*,[51] indexes 'feudalism, fiefs' amply, and is happy enough to announce that 'Along with fiefs came the language of feudalism' (p.54). Rodney Hilton published in 1990 a revision of his 1985 essays *Class Conflict and the Crisis of Feudalism: Essays in Medieval Social History*,[52] and in 1992 there appeared his *English and French Towns in Feudal Society* (Cambridge University Press). This was reprinted in 1995, and in the same year Michael Hicks' *Bastard Feudalism* was published by Longman. Malcolm Barber, however, in his recent textbook adopts a more chaste mode: 'For the "nominalist" historian, "feudalism" possesses no external reality whatsoever, and since it often misleads, its value as a "term of convenience" might also be regarded as highly doubtful'.[53] So too, Dominique Barthélemy's *L'Ordre Seigneurial, XIe–XIIe siècle*[54] sees 'feudalism' as the key word for 'l'ancienne histoire de France', a period which included the fifty years of French scholarship that followed the researches of Marc Bloch. It is now time, he argues, to replace the phrase 'feudal anarchy' for the period he is talking of, with the phrase 'seigneurial order'; in fact, the latest (French) orthodoxy seems to be that the word 'seigneurialism', though in some ways no more fortunate than the word 'feudalism', at least accords better with the facts: the seigneury becomes an essential stage in the history of European societies, reaching its apogee c.1050–75 and declining by 1250–75. In the 'seigneurial age', a warrior, ecclesiastic, family or community, has seized—or received by default—the powers which provide the authority from which to 'maintain the peace' within the little cell called 'the (private) domain'. Nevertheless, Jean-Pierre Poly and Eric Bournazel in their *The Feudal Transformation 900–1200*,[55] remark that

> Feudalism, in the strict sense of the word, can perhaps be seen as an essential stage in the development of an ideology of service, of an education in submission. Whatever the case, it is, whether we like it or not, the lasting foundation in Western Europe of a solid and complete political hierarchy. The state, which repudiates intermediary bodies the better to make use of them, can now despise or pretend to despise the submission of one man to another, a ritual fiction of an all-powerful paternity. But can one be so sure that even today it could survive without it[?] The state versus feudalism? Let us say, rather the state through feudalism.[56]

Consultation of the index ('Feudalism/Feudal hierarchy') will indicate how thoroughly permeated this discussion is by the notion of 'feudalism'. Indeed, 'Feudalism as an institution is the point of departure of this study'.[57] The French public, too, seem inured to the appearance of books, new or reprinted, with the theme 'feudal'.[58] Perhaps that is why, in a recent translation of *The Vézelay Chronicle*, my colleague and I felt bound to index 'Feudalism'![59]

As we move away from the notion that the past can be reconstructed in all its detailed objectivity by correct application of the principles of *quellenforschung* and philology, we are in the West becoming happier with the polemical or generalising terms of earlier ages, when truth had to be fought for and over. Indeed, there is every justification today for a new and improved edition of Soumyen's *Feudalism: Comparative Studies*, and, with luck, we may be able to coax this from him.

Since the completion of the volume, I have myself had occasion to think further on the past as opened up by the notion of 'feudalism'. At the time of my own contribution, I was conscious of omitting a number of specialised works on the subject,[60] but if I were to write my chapter again today, I suppose that I would stress further my tenth focus,[61] as I did—to end this paper where I began it—in my remarks to Barun De's seminar, on that fine but foully polluted day in February 1986. 'Feudalism' in this reading becomes a set of practices and attitudes characteristic of the transitional, personalised power-vacuums between—or beneath/beyond, in the case of mafioso structures—relatively stable, institutionalised, ideologically guaranteed state structures: oaths, gangs, retinues, loyalty to a man or leader, homage and a code of 'chivalry', pledges, gages, gifts, favours, fiefs and a variety of other informal mechanisms for building power come to the fore in these contexts (which is why, I imagine, Galbert of Bruges had occasion to decribe homage gestures, as if they were 'new'). One might speak of 'half-[centralised] power' situations, in which lords and sub-lords will contract with each other and with the strongmen upon whom each depends. The techniques and procedures of control and dominance in such situations will be personal and traditions of martial prowess (*chevalerie*) will develop to dignify the profession of those who hold the cards, the strongmen.

Admittedly, we are not to imagine a picture of uniform anarchy in the medieval West: even the rankest periods of anarchy no doubt left many groups and areas in relative peace. The point really is that 'feudalism' might well be seen as a kind of hegemonic political behaviour in certain definable circumstances, political behaviour that gradually evolved from and continued to conform in broadest detail to the vocabulary and apparatus of power bargaining in Europe prior to about the year 900 A.D. This 'discourse' of power, this set of ethical and ritual norms set the terms for political reality and political thinking until well into the era of the state (the thirteenth century perhaps). We may suppose that power in twelfth-century Flanders meant homage, enfeoffment, service (in broad terms) not because no other forms were economically or technically possible, but simply because people were habituated by the long, prior, struggles for power in the earlier middle ages, to thinking and acting that way. They would not cast off the habit of 'feudal' thinking until the power of the state showed them it was neither necessary nor feasible to retain such modes of thought and action. Even beyond that moment, of course, the long shadow of 'feudal' modes of power remained—and remain—dominant wherever people competed for hegemony.

'Feudalism', then, might best be viewed as a word for particular swings of the pendulum of power in any period, area or society: when the pendulum swings towards stable, structured 'formal' modes of controlling the resources and personnel of an area, we can less profitably use the term 'feudalism'; when the pendulum swings towards 'anarchy', then the informal, personalised modes of 'control' that are used by the most effective players in the game of survival, may well be termed 'feudalism'. This is why Nick Wright's paper in our volume was so interesting. It is also why Gurevich was right to look for the origins of feudalism in 'the contact of the barbarian peoples with the conquered populations of the Empire'.[62]

Two points, however, should be noted. First, the 'feudal' modes of power *do* provide initial ingredients for the construction of more lasting states than the 'pillage-areas' prevalent under 'feudalism', but these modes are transitional, and lead either to a new collapse or to the erection of permanent state structures. Even within the era of permanent state structures, unusual events can precipitate a relapse into 'feudal' conditions, as, for example, occurred in post World War II Germany.

Secondly, a perspective such as I have outlined, encourages us to look for the factors that enabled permanent state structures to be erected at all. Both bureaucratic statism (and its supportive, sustaining ideologies), *and* informal systems of clientage, dependence and bondage, exist in most societies and have their own histories. There are times when one is apparently dominant and the other is in comparative recess; it is useful to look at the mechanisms that determine this apparent dominance and recession, and to write history in terms of the oscillation, provided that we operate in a sensitive and not too schematic or jigsaw-like manner, and provided also that we recognise 'feudal' as the term historically appropriate only to the medieval West, and used outside that area solely as a sort of short-hand or tool for reasoning by analogy or model.

Essential to the construction/endurance of a successful, civilised, large-scale centralised bureaucratic state (once some exceptionally charismatic leader has set one up) are:

- a high social priority for letters and learning;
- a 'script' or literate culture of written documents;
- a powerful class whose access to social eminence is through mastery of script;
- an appropriate and rich administrative and ideological tradition accessible through script and through the script-conserving class;
- appropriate cultural institutions (schools) for replication and internalising of the values of script and its conserver class.

It was not for nothing that Charlemagne concerned himself so carefully with the provision of educational mechanisms by way of the cathedral schools of his day.[63] Through script mechanisms a hegemonic group can organise military, judicial and fiscal/extractive structures in such a way as to secure centralised predominance. In western Europe script governments rose and fell, until there came a time when they just went on rising, and are, of course, not only still with us, but are the dominant form of socio-political environment today. The 'Twelfth-Century Renaissance' marks—in western Europe—the great divide between the ephemeral script governments, and the permanent ones.

What has this to do with feudalism? Perhaps it may be as follows. 'Feudalism' is a name given for historical, rather than strictly etymological or functional reasons, to periods of history or types of society in which the five features I have just enumerated are marginally, minimally or not at all evident or present. Because all societies have passed through or experienced such phases in their history, feudalism is what Coulborn calls a 'uniformity' or a world evolutionary stage, but not a fixed or arbitrary one in its occurrence or its causation or termination. Nor, because of the relative absence of the five features just noted, can it be called a 'system'. 'System' is characteristic only of script culture and government. Societies in which one may speak of 'feudal law' in a written sense, are societies passing from feudal to a script phase; they are transitional rather than purely feudal.

However, because the absence or minimal presence of my five features does not necessarily indicate anarchy, we must further define feudalism as that phase, beyond anarchy, and different from tribalism, in which informal, oral customs and habits have grown up among diverse groups ensuring some measure of social cohesion and stability in a necessarily unstable and possibly always transitional phase in a society's history. Thus 'tribal' may imply fixed, long-term, and 'feudal' a period of transition between times of internally or externally induced disorder, or else between oscillations towards/from anarchy and script government.[64]

The links between these lines of thought and the Marxist 'feudal mode of production.' are not necessary ones. The village routines that produce the earth's goods are there to be 'managed', and Wickam has indicated the range of possible extractive modes here. The participants in the productive process must be distinguished from those who, by exercise of arms, and because they are not participants, end up as 'managers' or 'expropriators'[67] of the surplus fruits of the production structures (manors, villages, farms and the like).

These thoughts are presented more in deference to the spirit that produced the original SASSC *Feudalism: Comparative Studies* volume, than in any belief that they will satisfy those who wish their interpretive structures to lie much closer to the sources and the endless variety of past life as it must have been. My own research, on which a long string of applications for leave and grants has been based, does not relate to the issues raised in the present paper. Nor is it accurate to say that 'teaching feudalism' takes up any great portion of my teaching time. Nevertheless, if I were asked to name the one thread in my life at Sydney University that forced me more than any other to confront the reality of history-making and the nature of societies in the past, while at the same time forcing me to take into account the endlessly varied and intriguing world beyond the European West, I would have to point to the area of my teaching that one way or another had to do with Soumyen Mukherjee. That is why I am paying tribute to him in the present collection.

Notes

1 *Feudalism: Comparative Studies*, eds Edmund Leach, S. N. Mukherjee, John Ward, *Sydney Studies in Society and Culture* 2 (1985).

2 See *Revolution as History*, eds S. N. Mukherjee and J. O. Ward, *Sydney Studies in Society and Culture* 5 (1989).

3 I will comment further on these titles below.

4 I picked up a good guide to this in India: Debala Mitra's *Konarak*, Archaeological Survey of India, 1968.

5 That these stories were not entirely imagined is suggested by a fascinating few pages in John Westwood's *Railways of India*, Newton Abbot, 1974, pp.75–9. This book occupies an odd place in another episode which brought Soumyen and me together: the assessment of the doctoral thesis by Leighton Appleby 'Social Change and the Railways in North India c.1845–1914', 1990, but I must say nothing about that in the present context.

6 See above n.1.

7 Least of all in *History at Sydney, 1891–1991: Centenary Reflections*, ed. B. Caine and others, Sydney, 1992. Soumyen and I often contemplated a 'Secret History' of the department, on the Procopian model, to accompany the above 'official venture', but, alas, we never wrote it. This portion of my paper at least honours that one-time intention.

8 Soumyen's words here are unfortunately not printable.

9 'Feudalism: a Comparative Study in Social and Political Structures of Pre-industrial Societies', a conference held at St Andrew's College, 16–18 March, 1984. See above n.1.

10 Thomas Bisson said in a letter to me dated 2 August 1986 that our volume had made 'a stimulating contribution' to an NEH seminar for college teachers on the subject of 'Medieval European Feudalism', and David Nicholas, in a letter dated 29 October 1987, wrote that the volume contained 'a lot of material of considerable interest' and would have been better if 'your paper had been the first and ... other contributors had tried to place their articles within the various foci that you suggest'. He indicated that in the introductory analysis to a 'projected book of articles on feudalism' for which at the time he and Bryce Lyon were trying to find a publisher, 'the Sydney collection, and your article in particular, will find its place'.

11 E. A. R. Brown 'The Tyranny of a Construct: Feudalism and Historians of Medieval Europe' *American Historical Review* 79 (1974): 1080.

12 This is not strictly accurate: see Leach, Mukherjee, Ward, eds, *Feudalism:*

Comparative Studies, pp.50 and 65, n.80. In his revision of *St Anselm and His Biographer* (*Saint Anselm: a Portrait in a Landscape*, Cambridge, 1990), Southern has a section entitled 'Feudal Imagery and Universal Order' (Part III, Chapter 9, §vi). Here the word 'feudal' is commonplace, and even 'feudalism' secures a mention, if a guarded one (p.221).

13 In a letter to me dated 31 December 1985.

14 *Speculum* 62.4 (1987): 1030–2.

15 *Library of Peasant Studies*, No.8, London and New Jersey, 1985.

16 *Peasant Studies* 14.4 (1987): 250–9, 'More about Feudalism'.

17 'More about Feudalism', p.252.

18 This was also noted by Robert Stern in his review in *Asian Studies Association of Australia Review* 10.3 (1987): 163–4. Stern pointed out that our volume was 'a collection of separate essays in each of which 'feudalism' has its separate meaning or virtually none at all'. Nevertheless, he felt there was much to be 'mined' in the volume, that my paper was 'stunning', John Pryor's 'wonderfully succinct and readable, Pearson's 'lucid and succinct', and Michael Bennett's 'good ... however blunt'!

19 *Fiefs and Vassals: the Medieval Evidence Re-interpreted*, Oxford, 1994.

20 'More about Feudalism', p.258.

21 'The Task of Cultural History', in *Men and Ideas: History, the Middle Ages, the Renaissance: Essays by Johan Huizinga*, trans. J. S. Holmes and Hans van Marle, New York, 1970, p.20. Huizinga, of course, did not believe scholarship should even try and produce perfectly finished building stones for the ultimate 'master builder'. Indeed, he asks, 'is the labor expended by the machinery of scholarship not a hopeless waste of energy?' I hope Susan Reynolds has her answer to this question ready, should she ever meet Huizinga in 'another place' ... !

22 Compare Stern's conclusion, in his review of our volume, *Asian Studies Association of Australia Review* 10.3 (1987): 164: 'One of the lessons I take from the collection is that medievalists cannot, of course, banish the term 'feudalism' from the world's words but only from their own scholarly concerns. If they do that, they lose one of academia's most abused words, and abandon the field to our sloganeers and jargoneers'.

23 Am I thus to throw away my copy of Aron Gurevich's (Russian) 'Origins of Feudalism', carefully purchased in an Italian translation (*Le Origini del Feudalismo*, trans. Michele Sampaolo, Bari, 1990) from a Venetian bookshop and hassled through flight lounges and airport customs desks to the quiet of my lecture room?

24 *Fiefs and Vassals* p.14. Reynolds' adoption of the scientific mode of chapter subdivision underlines her apparent belief that 'history' is a scientific process, in which 'correct attention' will arrive at the 'right answer'.

25 His reply on the subject to Duke William of Aquitaine is translated in *The History of Feudalism*, ed. D. Herlihy, New Jersey and Sussex, 1979, pp.96–7. See also G. Duby *France in the Middle Ages 987–1460, from Hugh Capet to Joan of Arc*, trans. Julia Vale, Oxford, 1991, pp.78–9.

26 *Fiefs and Vassals*, p.15. . 27 *Ibid.*, p.14. 28 *Ibid.*, p.15.

29 *Ibid.*, Chapter 10, pp.475 ff.

30 G. Duby, *The Three Orders: Feudal Society Imagined*, trans. A. Goldhammer, Chicago, 1982 (esp. p.154 'The knights were oppression incarnate') and P. Dockès, *Medieval Slavery and Liberation*, trans. A. Goldhammer, Chicago, 1982.

31 *Fiefs and Vassals*, p.477 ff.

32 Leach, Mukherjee, Ward (eds) *Feudalism: Comparative Studies*, p.45; Reynolds *Fiefs and Vassals*, p.479. 33 *Ibid.*, p.480.

34 *Ibid.*, p.481. Note the 'limited enlightenment' projects mentioned on pp.480–81.

35 Cf. *Ibid.*, p.482 'a very long twelfth century.... Why did all these kinds of change happen some time around the twelfth century, and how were they connected?' I must stress to the reader that my remarks on *Fiefs and Vassals* are not meant to add up to a 'review' of it. The relationship between the arrival of the volume in our library and the deadline for the present contribution prevented anything like a 'review'. I simply ornament my points with some initial oblique references to the book. In his review in the *Times Literary Supplement* (10 March 1995, p.12), Patrick Wormald claims that 'Reynolds' central thesis, in sum, is that "feudalism" was conceived as an "ism" by the twelfth-century Italian lawyers who drafted the *libri feudorum*', thus further stressing the importance of that period in Western history.

36 Wormald's review, cited above n.35, suggests that the battle may be a short one. Historians, he suggests, will simply outflank Reynolds: rather than contesting her command of her own field, they will shift the focus to pre- or extra-legal zones (such as the pre-twelfth-century, 'pre-literate' period, or the world of the *chansons de geste*, with their rich evocation of a fief- and service-based 'feudal order') and point to the stimulus the 'wraith of "feudalism" ' has supplied for ongoing historical inquiry. For a German review see *Der Spiegel* 48 (1994): 188, 191. On the *chansons de geste*, 'the very high point of feudalism', see p.159 of H.-J. Martin, *The History and Power of Writing*, trans. L. G. Cochrane, Chicago and London, 1994.

37 See, however, Catharina Blomberg, *The Heart of the Warrior: Origins and Religious Background of the Samurai System in Feudal Japan*, Sandgate, 1994.

38 E. A. R. Brown, 'The Tyranny of a Construct: Feudalism and Historians of Medieval Europe' *American Historical Review* 79 (1974): 1081, and for the full title of Duby's book, p.1073 n.36.

39 Leach, Mukherjee, Ward, eds, *Feudalism: Comparative Studies*, pp.54–5, 66 n.97.

40 238 (March–April): 5–15.

41 French edition, Paris, 1973, English translation H. B. Clarke 1974.

42 English edition ch.6, pp.157–180.

43 1980, the original French being published in 1978.

44 Taken apart by Brian G. H. Ditcham in 'The Feudal Millenium? Social Change

in Rural France circa 1000 in Recent French Historiography', *Medieval History* 3 (1993): 86–99: 'It is at least arguable that "feudalism" in its purest form only existed in the pages of lawbooks and that patterns of power and domination were always much more complex and diverse than the pioneering work of a Marc Bloch would suggest.... It is perhaps time to look more closely at the practical realities of the exercise of local power in the period around 1000 without the blinkers imposed by presuppositions concerning a "feudal revolution", even if the result is to strip some of the remaining glamour and drama away from the millenium'. Ditcham, oddly, though much concerned with the 'Dubyan model' does not cite Duby's own *L'an Mil*, Paris, 1980.

45 Trans. Jane Dunnett, Cambridge, 1994, from the French of 1988.

46 We also have the two words *curtis* and *curia* combining to give a 'fairly accurate picture of feudalism, rooted in rural lordship and in the military system' (p.66), and 'feudal courts' and 'feudal states' pp.74, 76.

47 The English edition, sadly, lacks the magnificent presentation of the French: see my review forthcoming in *Parergon*.

48 French p.111, English p.79.

49 Herlihy, *History of Feudalism* I, p.98; Duby, *France*, English edn p.149, French p.184.

50 French: 'Un droit naissant. Féodal'. See also on Beaumanoir and 'the feudal ladder', the English edn, p.263.

51 Harmondsworth, 1993.

52 London, 1990. This volume joins Hilton's 'Feudalism in Europe: Problems for Historical Materialists' in the *New Left Review* 147 (1984, not represented in the collection) in dealing with 'the social and political crises of the late medieval feudal order'. Note also B. S. Bachrach's attempt to extend Chris Wickam's analysis, *Past and Present* 103 (1984): 3–36 in his paper 'The Angevin Economy, 960–1060: Ancient or Feudal?' reprinted in his *State-Building in Medieval France*, 1995. Wickam himself has commented on these matters recently in 'Systactic Structures: Social Theory for Historians' *Past and Present* 132 (1991): 188–203.

53 *The Two Cities: Medieval Europe 1050–1320*, London and New York, 1992, p.444.

54 *Nouvelle histoire de la France médiévale*, 1990, pp.7–8.

55 Trans. Caroline Higgitt (Europe Past and Present Series), New York andLondon, 1991, from the French of 1980.

56 *Transformation*, p. 357.

57 *Ibid.*, p.3. See too P. Bonnassie, *From Slavery to Feudalism in South West Europe*, trans. J. Birrell, Cambridge, 1991.

58 I cite, randomly: André Scobeltzine *L'Art féodale et son enjeu social*, Paris, 1973, 1988; J.-F. Lemarignier, *La France Médiévale: institutions et société*, Paris, 1970, reissued June 1994, with pp.109 ff 'Les Temps féodaux', III 'Féodalité et autorité publique' (9th/10th centuries onwards) and pp.231 ff 'De la féodalité aux institutions monarchiques (milieu XIIe–fin XVe siècles)'; Nguyen Khac Vien, *Vietnam: une longue histoire*, Hanoi, 1993, ch.III 'L'état

féodal centralisé—Les dynasties Ly et Tran (XIe–XIVe siècles)', ch.IV 'Une nouvelle étape de la monarchie féodale (La dynastie des Le, XVe–XVIe siècles)'; O. Guillot *et al.*, *Pouvoirs et Institutions dans la France Médiévale*, I *Des origines à l'epoque féodale*, II *Des temps féodaux aux temps de l'État*, Paris, 1994.

59 With John Scott: *Hugh of Poitiers, The Vézelay Chronicle and other documents from MS. Auxerre 227 and elsewhere, translated into English with notes, introduction, and accompanying material, and with supplementary essays and notes by Eugene Cox*, Binghamton, N.Y., 1992.

60 See, for example, the collection reviewed and the review itself by Paolo Cammarosano, 'Le strutture feudali nell'evoluzione dell'Occidente mediterraneo: note su un Colloquio internazionale', *Studi Medievali* s3, v22, 1 (1981): 837–69; G. Tabacco 'Fief et seigneurie dans l'Italie communale: L'évolution d'un thème historiographique', *Le Moyen Age*, 75, s4 v24 (1969]): 5–37 (with sequel; his recently translated (by Rosalind Brown Jensen) *The Struggle for Power in Medieval Italy: Structures of Political Rule*, Cambridge, 1989, amply indexes 'feudalism'); G. Bois *The Transformation of the Year 1000: the Village of Lourmand from Antiquity to Feudalism*, trans. J. Birrell, pref. G. Duby, Manchester, 1992; T. K. Keefe, *Feudal Assessments and the Political Community under Henry II and his Sons*, Berkeley, Los Angeles and London, 1983. Cf. also the sourcebook by Antonio Carile and Gina Fasoli, *Documenti di Storia Feudale*, Bologna, 1974. See now, too, Wally Seccombe, *A Millenium of Family Change: Feudalism to Capitalism in Northwestern Europe*, London and New York, 1992.

61 See *Feudalism: Comparative Studies*, pp.40–8 for my original ten 'foci'.

62 *Le Origini del Feudalismo*, p.202. The whole 'conclusione' pp.201 ff is fascinating.

63 See H.-J. Martin, *The History and Power of Writing*, p.127.

64 See Partha Chatterjee, 'More on Modes of Power and the Peasantry', *Subaltern Studies* 2 (1983): 311–49, ed. Ranajit Guha.

65 The distinction is clear in Akira Kurosawa's epic film *The Seven Samurai*.

Vietnam Protest

Michael Wilding

The war in Vietnam was the first television war, the media war, the media people said. Brought into the living room of the American people. Well, Graham didn't have a television and wasn't in America. Television programmed rubbish and offered no lures. Later it offered lures, though was no less rubbish. Later he adjusted to it, this the aim, the ambition, the pharmakon, the nepenthe, sitting in front of the beams hour after hour, wondering how to get in there, to be on the box. But that was after the war was over and there were no longer demonstrations and protests and readings and the alternative press to occupy the time. After the war was over television came into its own as the great domestic controller. And not only in the house, but in the pubs too, with its endless screening of horse racing and car racing and mud wrestling. And in the pubs where there wasn't television, and in some where there was, music was introduced so no one could talk protest and politics or anything else for that matter any more, the music was so loud.

But Vietnam: so easy to glide away from it, the topic too large, too violent, too present, too meaningful, how do you write about that, what has that got to do with literature, they would say in the university.

The Iliad?

But who reads *The Iliad* any more? Actually reads it? The *Odyssey*, yes: coming home from the war, sex and drugs and siren songs, adventure, movement, the voyage. And that was yet another sailing away from it.

There wasn't even an International Brigade. A literary death for communism. Too thirties. Was anybody actually volunteering to fight for communism?

You didn't need television to know about the war. The images spread. Images from news cameramen, moving or still. The Buddhist monk in flames, the gun to the head of the about to be shot, the women fleeing.

There was an aesthetic ranking of the verité image. Wow, what a picture, imagine.

He couldn't bear to. Who would want to imagine Vietnam? Who would want to imagine napalm, summary execution, severed limbs, death, maiming.

He wanted no images of this, these were images not to be preserved, images that needed no preservation, images that could never be expunged.

When he was ten or eleven Graham was conscripted to sell poppies for the blind. He remembered having to stand at the entrance of the cinema. The manager let them in to watch the feature for free, but he could remember neither who he was with nor what the movie was. Now here he was again, outside a cinema, handing out anti-Vietnam war leaflets, and again the name of the movie is forgotten. It was all so obviously so traumatic an experience that anything that could be was repressed. Presumably they were opposing the movie. He didn't enjoy this sanctimonious role, holier than thou, collector of coins for the blind and dispenser of propaganda for peace. And the unknown quantity of the public's reaction always gave it that edge of fear. It was an experience he could well have done without. And other than to say he must have experienced it he recalled nothing of it. Except the soldier. Young, eighteen or nineteen, hair short back and sides, he came up to Graham, in the street outside the cinema.

'Keep it up, mate,' he said. 'Good on you. It's fucking terrible there, mate, I can fucking tell you. Keep it up, mate, I reckon you guys are doing the right thing.'

In the Forest Lodge. Appropriate place for hunters' yarns, though not quite what the name might suggest, it was the pub closest to the university. He was there one afternoon in the beer garden and an American joined them, on R&R from Vietnam. The feeling was not very friendly towards Americans, the war was perceived as their aggression, Australia dragged into it, an unjust war whether they'd been dragged into it or not, a brutal destruction of a foreign people. But he weathered the vibes, this determined American, sat down, was he looking for congenial company around campus instead of the whores laid on by the CIA associated operation that controlled and catered for the R&R in Australia? Or was he another part of the CIA operation snooping around looking for dissidents. Operation Phoenix (Australia). Conversation was constrained. But he did concede, yes, there were chopper pilots who no doubt went out shooting villagers like they were deer, as off-duty recreation. It was a recent news story somewhere or other, and he conceded yes, he had heard of such things. Though it didn't seem to figure largely in his assessment of the situation, in the context of what was going on daily in Vietnam it was clearly hardly remarkable.

Readings against the war. Lunch-time readings on campus. He calculated it with an entrepreneurial eye: the potential audience for readings would be augmented by the political conscience audience, by those who wanted to register a protest against the war but wanted to do it relatively painlessly, and going to a reading offered an alternative to marching or rallying or shouting. It was capitalising on the mood of the moment and showing that fiction and poetry were part of that full world of the political, the contemporary, of life and death; not something contained in a syllabus or a gallery, not something quarantined off in a new critical nonsense of 'purely literary values'. They read in galleries, too. Anywhere. It was a way to build up an audience, to present what the syllabus controllers tried so hard to prevent. And you could have an audience with the lure of anti-war and a name that had some exposure. There were no big names. Big names were all foreign. Writers didn't get big names in Australia at this point.

When it came to doing an anthology of anti-war, that became the focus of battle. There was a scheme for a slim volume, elegant protest, chosen voices, the quivering few. Graham argued for something wider-reaching, getting as many writers as possible, as full a range as they could afford space for. This way some new names could be introduced and some elided and blacklisted ones restored. He heard someone had begun an anthology in Melbourne. That wasn't surprising. What was surprising was that it hadn't been done before. He went to Melbourne and found the project had fallen through; but he returned with what had been collected, a swag of avant-garde protest, another world of experiment and innovation and coteries. Together with the work already gathered it tipped the scales, swamped the élite selection. And the long search for a publisher began. So did the resentment of the élite, the names poised soon to be big names under the appropriate foreign aegis.

Why attempt to capture the tone and mood of that time when it was a mood and tone of innocence, ignorance, unauthenticity and delusion? Who were these figures who emerged as leaders of protest, foci of dissent, and how can they properly be represented without their later roles as media personalities, lawyers, computer specialists, economic advisers? Could they ever have been authentic, or were they all government men and women all along, on the first threshold of their careers with the great multinationals, putting in their three years undercover? Once you started to ask that, of course, everyone began to look unauthentic.

He walked down in one of the demonstrations with Iggy Noble. A couple of uniformed senior police policing the march raised a hand in acknowledgement at Iggy who smiled back, waving, saluting. Old activists known to the police. The image hung there, the smiling cop, flat hat, raised hand.

'That magazine Iggy ran,' Graham said to Joe.

'The one that folded with the first issue.'

'Well, after the first few. That could have been a total fraud. It could have been a CIA operation, just to get the names and addresses of subscribers. They really pushed for subscribers. They collected mailing lists off every left wing group they could. Maybe that's what he was doing those years he was overseas. Training at a secret CIA base.'

'You shouldn't go around saying these sort of things,' said Joe.

'Why not?'

'Because you don't know if they're true. You've got no evidence, it's all conjecture. You could harm someone's career.'

He supposed so. He could be maligning and defaming an innocent person. But he was still surprised at the vigour of Joe's attack, it made him uneasy, that he might have been defaming Iggy in the joy of creation, the excitement of the chase, following a narrative thread wherever it might lead, while Joe took the part of the censor, of responsibility, of care for the innocent. It hardly seemed a characteristic role. But there again Joe had had his own magazine that lasted only half a dozen issues and it was easy to forget that he might still be touchy about such forgotten moments.

Shelter a draft resister on the run. Show solidarity. Practical support, romantic gesture, complicity. Participation in the events of history. There weren't that many public draft resisters. A handful. The way to get out of the draft was to register and hope your number didn't come up. You had a good chance it wouldn't. If it did, you faked the medical. A code of convention emerged: bedwetting, asthma, anxiety. The army didn't want conscripts who didn't want to be there: not in a military situation: the Americans were losing too many officers to disaffected troops. If they figured you were trying to get out of it, you tended to get out of it. Pamphlets on how to fail your medical were readily available.

But there was also the campaign against registering for the draft in the first place. Here you recorded your heady defiance by not registering. In effect it was a loyalty oath for eighteen year old males and those who refused to register identified themselves immediately as subversives, unless they had the indemnity of provocateurs.

To have a leader of the Don't Register movement staying while the police had a warrant for his arrest was to endorse that ambiguous movement. Did Graham realise the ambiguities? Was this indeed the process through which he first began to recognise the advantages of passive evasion over head-on opposition? The resister and his wife stayed for a week, playing military marches on the record player. Occasionally they would phone up the Commonwealth Police to taunt them. Here we are, come and catch us.

'Get off the phone,' Graham would say, 'they'll trace it if you keep on talking.'

'Don't worry,' they waved, and brought the conversation to a leisurely end with all the civilised politenesses that ending a conversation required. They were well brought up law students. No unseemly curtailment.

Graham's publisher was down one time and encountered the draft resister, phoning away. He looked worried, the publisher, he was unhappy about all this involvement.

'You should stick to fiction,' he said. 'When's the novel coming along?'

But he was an American. Graham discounted the advice.

The worried look, though, hung there, a concern the full depths of which Graham never cared to plumb.

This was when he was living in what Joe used to refer to as the Gatsby house. If the police came the draft resister would have to escape by water, row out into the harbour. Romantic, dramatic, filmic.

The Commonwealth Police came round the University with photographs of wanted draft resisters. They came into the History Common Room, showed them to the staff, asking if anyone had seen them.

'Oh,' said Soumyen, 'all these white faces, they all look the same to me.'

'Of course they won't stop the war because a lot of kids and clergymen go around protesting. The only thing that will stop them is losing it.'

'So what's the point of the protest movement?'

'It annoys them. It gives them apoplexy and heart attacks and strokes and cancer.'

'Yes?'

'Permanent protest,' said Chris. 'What else is there to do?'

They sat with their feet on the table at the window and looked at the harbour. They had a flagon of wine between them and smoked some dope and looked out on the night.

'What are those flashing red lights in the water?' Chris asked.

'Ammunition barges.'

'I thought they were. Imagine if someone blew them up. Put a time fuse on them. Swam out there. What a blast! The gas tanks would all go up.'

On the water's edge were storage tanks for petroleum.

'Probably should wait till a tanker's in. Maximise the flammable materials. I wonder how much of the city it would take out. If all the barges detonated.... You'd only need to set off one or two, the others would set each other off. Though I guess it would be good to detonate the petrol storage places too. You'd have to plan it in detail.'

They sipped the wine and watched.

'You know, I should have gone in the army instead of dodging the draft.'

'Yes?'

'Yes. Should have gone and learned about explosives and weapons. The left was real dumb not to enlist. You know, I've been thinking about a scheme to paralyse the city. Remember when that tanker spilled oil on the harbour bridge; the traffic was piled up till midnight. The whole city was immobilised. Immobilised. Think of that.'

The still night, the black harbour.

'What you do is wait for a rainy night. You've got to have rain for the chaos, but not heavy rain that would wash the oil away. You could paralyse the place with strategic oil spills. Then you'd have to break into the control room of the television cameras that watch the traffic and demonstrations and everything. There's someone up there taping it all, you know that? Just get up there at rush hour and hold them up. Take over the controls. You could create total chaos from that control room. And you could watch when the police started to come or anything. You could put out all the traffic lights. Imagine that.'

'How would you get away with it?'

'You'd have to work on it but I reckon it's possible. Anyway, if it was a revolution you wouldn't want to get away, you'd be there to take control.'

'And what would you do then?'

'I don't know,' said Chris. 'It's crazy, it would be so easy to take control but no one ever thinks they can really do it so they don't even work out a scenario. They've got no real belief in revolution, any of them, any of those splinter groups. Three communist parties, four Trotskyite parties, all these workers' parties and revolutionary parties. Why don't they just seize control? Why don't they work out what they'd do when they got control? It would be easy in a city like this. It would be easy to do the whole country. All you've got to do is work out a plan for six cities. Maybe we should do a book on it. Scenarios of the revolution. A scenario for every major city. Maps, plans, diagrams. You could give alternative strategies. You could list all the people you'd need to round up and so on. Work address, home address. You could show all the crucial offices and civil defence places and bomb shelters and police radio shelters and emergency services. Just imagine if you knocked out the central police transmitter, they wouldn't be able to do anything. Or you could seize one of the FM stations and transmit on the police frequency and jam it. What do you reckon?'

'They gave me this ring in Hanoi,' Germaine said. 'They gave me two of them, actually. They're made from shot down American fighters. I want to give it to somebody. To somebody who would appreciate it.'

The demonstrations on the university front lawn, rallies before demonstrations. Graham went to them but he preferred not to speak at them and there was never any shortage of people wanting to speak, address the crowds through a microphone. It held no attractions for Graham. Or did it, and was he repressing them? Or was the sense of power and exhilaration that hung there as a temptation readily balanced by a knowledge of the potential for disaster, derision, the crowd turning. He was suspicious of demagoguery, performance. He neither wanted to be good at it nor bad at it. It wasn't something terribly difficult to do: a matter of morality and scruples as much as technique. But so was writing. He spoke at one or two meetings, introduced speakers. The last one ended in a mass onslaught on the lecture theatre where the attorney-general was speaking. Graham found himself with Chris against the doors. 'Shall we smash them in?' said Chris. It was a heady moment but it didn't seem like a good idea. They edged aside to talk while the crowd pushed and was pushed forward. Graham watched one of the anarchists pushing solidly from behind. He had the build of a football player and the manner of a coach and later became a high-profile exponent of anti-state, free enterprise monetarism beloved by the right through the eighties. Graham didn't enjoy being pushed from behind or from any other direction. He had never been fond of football players. And he didn't see that breaking down doors would stop the war. Once you damaged property the wrath of the bourgeois state knew no end. There was a heady derring-do direct action spirit promoted by the anarchists, and what was always noticeable was they pushed from behind and theirs were never the dirty hands. Writing, you had a better chance to consider who was doing the pushing. Once you moved to the theatre of action you were in a different arena, even more duplicitous and treacherous.

How could you write about Vietnam? If you were there, perhaps you could record something. But why would you be there? What would you be doing if you were there and whose side would you be on? Yet if you weren't there, how could you write about it? And to write about it, what did that achieve? The critique of war through the portrayal of war. The argument for peace through the presentation of napalm burns, dead villagers, tortured communists. It wasn't the sort of thing he ever wanted to see or hear. The utter ambiguity of the exposé froze there for him. The loving rendering of murder and violence under the guise of protest, the sheer aesthetic perfection, craft and technique enlisted in the service of art, verité killings. So you turn your back on the war and what do you write then, maybe you explore the roots of the war in your own society, but how do you do that? That would be a big project, to substantiate it. Though to guess, to stab in there intuitively, that wasn't so hard. The other approach offered was to say although you didn't write about the war, your style, your critical attitude, the texture of your prose was its own critique, it was all a matter of form, not content, of the sufficiently honed prose, the polished perceptions. The war itself was an intrusion into this rarer world of form. He didn't want to be in that rare world any more than in Vietnam.

Lunch time readings against the war, though a welcome variant on talks by political scientists, were very ordered, restrained, contained. There was a move for something larger, total theatre, rock bands, jugglers. One of the draft resisters had a birthday and said to his parents, 'Don't give me gifts, just pay-roll a couple of rock bands for an all-night be in.'

So they ran leads out of the downstairs rooms in the quadrangle and set up lights so it could be filmed and a sound stage for the rock bands and the people reading stories and poems had a difficult time holding the audience, while round the edges prowled pro-war college boys and engineers. The lawns that were not to be walked on were walked on and then the lawn walkers wanted further excitement. They had broken the taboo and waited for something to open up. The consciousness battles ensued. There were those who were happy to sit round in a semi-circle and listen to rock, and their only arguments were with people in front of them who stood up instead of sitting down; but there were others who wanted to break into the vice-chancellor's office and liberate the files, and there were others who climbed around on the roofs like mountaineers, fulfilling some long felt need to conquer those heights, and then in one corner a couple were dancing and the girl took off her top and this attracted a circle around them. This was a time when bare breasts were rare to public view, before topless beaches, before the introduction of colour television and the bare breasts that came to promote it. A ring of eager males stood around her cheering, more, more, they called, get it all off. But she didn't. It was after that that a fire was lit of all the underground papers brought along to give away, and the flames offered some phallic release for the frustrated watchers as burning pages of social analysis and anti-war propaganda and dope advocacy and comics and sexuality wafted upwards and danced around within the dark walls of the quadrangle and headed for the roof. Graham felt they'd unleashed forces he would rather not have unleashed. While down on the grass a sleeping bag totally zipped up and enclosed wriggled around like a jumping bean as a couple screwed inside it and the circle formed round about them.

Then they tried cleaning up the rubbish. The less lying around to set fire to the better. But Joe came by and kicked over the rubbish bins in the name of libertarianism. 'Don't be prefects,' he said prefectorially. 'Why should you clear up? Why recognise authorities? You wouldn't clear up after the vice-chancellor's tea-party, why should you clean up after this?' It was the sort of anarchism that appealed to the jeunesse dorée; leave it for the servants. Later it looked like deliberate provocation, at the time it was just annoying. But the place didn't burn down, they were greatly relieved nothing caught fire except the piles of newspapers, the half-naked girl illuminated in the flickering light.

In the midst of all this came the revelations about the CIA. How the Central Intelligence Agency had funded the Congress for Cultural Freedom and the magazines *Encounter, Partisan Review, Preuves, Quadrant.* Australia was part of the network. It was world encompassing. They had funded a similar network of international student organisations too. These were surprises and not surprises. Various editors expressed surprise and resigned their positions. Not in Australia. In Australia the editors said they didn't know, hadn't known, but weren't worried anyway, didn't feel uncomfortable, carried on as before.

The rumours had been around for years. To have them confirmed, to have the full specificity emerge, or something of it, was not something anyone needed to be surprised about. That was part of the horror of it, that it all fitted into place so predictably, at some level it must all have been known and repressed, preferred not to be known. But after the brief flurry of the revelation of what already had been suspected came the most interesting questions. What was the point? The global suborning of intellectual life. The conscription of literature to covert political ends. Was it as simple and as total as that? What about specifics? No doubt there were minor functions in the organisation or on the magazines that could have been used for cover; it let people have some ostensible work and income and put them in contact with all the visiting luminaries and all the resident luminaries they might ever want to meet or visit, making contact with people who might be useful contacts, arranging the invitations and funding for the spring seminars and summer schools. But what else? It was better to overestimate the intelligence of intelligence agencies than to accept the official media accounts of bumbling and incompetence. Stupidity was too uninteresting, anyway. Graham wanted a narrative of deeper complexity. He couldn't believe that the editors and advisory editors never knew the source of the funding. They knew the congress wasn't devoted to intellectual freedom except in a cold war, anti-communist, support American foreign policy and domestic policy way. They had to know that, everyone had to know that, otherwise the whole propaganda exercise was a disaster. The magazines might proclaim cultural freedom and run their token stories and poems but the real point was not the low high-culture pages but propagandising the American way. Of course it was possible that some of the editors had thought, here is a great source of finance, let us not inquire too closely but just get some of the funding, we will pretend our values are their values and we will run some of their token rubbish but our real purpose is something else. And who would ever know what their real purpose was or might have been? Finding a place for literature in the homes of diplomats and businessmen? Finding a source of patronage so they could invite their old friends to well paid seminars and publish their papers in well-produced journals, and get invited back in return? It was a nice theory that some of the editors were taking the CIA for a ride, but was it very likely that you could take an intelligence agency for a ride, unless they wanted you to.

Unless you had a CIA vision, unless you took the cold war seriously, unless you saw an imminent apocalyptic confrontation between capitalism and communism fought on every level including in the minds and hearts of the intelligentsia, it was impossible to comprehend. Apart from that there weren't any other stakes. So back in the files some section chief could record, seventeen major articles in support of US policy objectives and castigating Soviet policy placed in a premier English language intellectual journal, and his quota had been to place fifteen. And the editors of all the funded magazines could write reciprocally for each other, a poem here, a travel diary there, a book review or a review article always on hand. It looked like the magazines had their elegant articles and their prestigious names; and the prestigious names kept up their prestige by keeping their names in print, though without having to write anything too demanding; and the section chiefs could keep up their propaganda war quota of heavy stuff; and nobody had to struggle to place articles in resistant papers; and then various writers not involved in the whole deal would offer work or would be solicited for work and they were too involved in their own writing and ambitions to examine the structure of the magazines too closely and anyway they wanted publication and so they were drawn in; and gave this air of independence and prestige and respectability and openness to the ramshackle project that it was. It gave the mediocre who were ready to be suborned the chance of free trips, expensive seminars, prestigious publications; it gave the once distinguished the chance to keep their name alive, to potter along without ever having to write the book they were going to write. And in the end it became the only game in town.

And then there was the darker sense that there was a deeper plan beneath it all, which would alter the definition of what was being got out of it. Why suddenly now was the truth, if it was the truth, revealed, when suspicions had been around for years? Graham couldn't imagine that they couldn't have stopped the stories had they wanted to, paying somebody off here, running over somebody in a laundry van somewhere else. Which made it look like they'd wanted the revelations, as if they had even set them up. Maybe they knew secrets couldn't be kept for ever, maybe the life of an operation like this was limited like American motor vehicles, so the operation was designed to capitalise on the inevitable ultimate exposure. An operation is set up to fund magazines and draw into them all the social democrat, left liberal intellectuals. There was no need to draw in communists, they had their own organisation, the FBI funded seventy-five per cent of the American communist party's subscriptions, the only thing that kept the party solvent, and that ensured that the FBI knew what was going on, ensured that nothing was going on. The communists could be left to the FBI, and this operation could concentrate on the left liberals. All the beautiful people who believed in intellectuals. Before intellectual became a dirty word. And the whole point was to make intellectual a dirty word. The whole point was for the ultimate exposure of the CIA funding, to show how cheap intellectuals were, to show how easily you could suborn writers and film reviewers and men of letters and cultural commentators and professors of literature and angry young novelists. Who was ever going to trust those social democrat leftists again, now that the source of their secret funding was revealed? Who was ever going to believe in the concept of impartial, dispassionate, disinterested criticism from the universities when their academics had leapt into the seminars and junkets and magazines that the CIA had funded? Who would ever believe in the integrity of any organisation any longer now the CIA rules on how to handle organisations had been made public? 'Use legitimate, existing organisations; disguise the extent of American interest; protect the integrity of the organisation by not requiring it to support every aspect of official American policy.' Now everyone would suspect everything of having been suborned. Revealing the secret guidelines was the ultimate stage in the operation, the clinching manoeuvre, now there could never be trust again.

But to get too preoccupied with the historicity of the revelations and fail to realise that more of the same things were still going on and would continue to go on, was a mistake. A lure. Exploring the past betrayals, indicting the complicit figures, was marvellous for the youth rhetoric of the movement. It meant that everything of the past could be repudiated as suborned. Never trust anybody over thirty. It allowed the belief that this was a new order coming, that the activists were involved in a generational struggle, and the young were pure and clean and uncorrupted by all those cold war deadlinesses. It diverted attention away from the manipulation of the movement. Obviously the same sort of operation had to be continuing, phoney protest, phoney radicalism, phoney publications.

Again, did anyone want to look too closely when they were having such a good time? Having vowed not to publish in *Quadrant*, Graham had no wish to go round checking on the credentials of every other publication. What would be left? Increasingly they all began to look phoney, fronts and mind-control stations. But if the explicit revelations had never come, then this process of suspicion could never have developed. Suspicion was clearly part of the fail-safe design of the original operation; when the operation was ultimately revealed, it would continue to be effective in its very revelations, the paranoia generated could serve only to paralyse, evidence of manipulation leading to a mistrust of any co-operative activity for fear of the unauthenticity of the others.

The rhetoric of conspiracy, of course, had been unavailable for years; dismissed to the margins as sensational, silly, immature, fantastic, so that the range of expressible causality had become extraordinarily reduced. The revelations allowed the reintroduction of conspiracy to literature, the exploration of paranoia. Yet how did you write about it unless you were in it? How did you capture this narrative of bad faith, of the suborning and manipulation of a 'free' culture? Retrospectively you could see the signs of what had been done. It provided a stimulus to literary history; it provided some points for literary criticism, it gave a meaning and significance to that cultural stress on ambiguity and irony. 'Angleton boasted to me that he had recruited some of the best minds of the New Critics and poets into the OSS, where their facility at teasing out seven types of ambiguity from a text served them well in the interpretations of intelligence data.' (*Harpers*, October 1983) And if they were there in the OSS in the war, who could doubt that they were there in its successor organisation through the cold war, when Angleton was a deputy director of the CIA? Decoding the ambiguities of enemy intelligence soon led to the creation of ambiguity in their own literary production. Days spent in decoding and discovering what a targeted text meant were succeeded by nights of creating texts no-one should ever decode. And it was certainly safer to say nothing that could be decoded. American modernism.

It was a huge revelation, the CIA's intervention in cultural production. And from that you could assume that other agencies of other free world nations had similarly intervened. And conceive of other, infinite sorts of intervention. It brought into question the whole literary world. Well, that was a good thing. Over the years he tried to embody it in fictional form, tried to draw on the material for a novel, but he could never succeed. The material seemed recalcitrant, unrewarding. He could conceptualise it, intellectualise it, theorise it, and in the end he had to leave it at that. Why try to raise it to the status of art, why try to memorialise it in that way? It was an intrusion, an excrescence, a growth. It was a part of the picture, it should not be excluded, in any true picture it could not be excluded. But it remained the untransmutable dregs of anti-art, anti-life, anti-Christ.

Note

'Vietnam Protest' is an episode from a fictional memoir, or memorial fiction, with the working title *The Literary Pages*.

Approaches to the Ur-Mahabharata

Zdenko Zlatar

1 The problem of the Ur-*Mahabharata*

There is a sloka in *The Mahabharata* which can be translated like this: 'Whatever is found here can be found elsewhere; what is not found here cannot be found anywhere else'.[1] This illustrates very well the variety of approaches to, and interpretations of, the epic for over a hundred and fifty years. Yet, when all of them are taken into account, it can be seen that they fall into a combination of one or two of four categories:

1) *The Mahabharata* as a unitary epic;
2) *The Mahabharata* as a composite epic;
3) *The Mahabharata* as a *symbolic* representation;
4) *The Mahabharata* as a *real* event.

Of course, it is possible to combine (1) or (2) with (3) or (4), but it is not possible to hold (1) and (2) at the same time. Holding both (3) and (4) together is possible, but has not so far been put forward.

In the nineteenth century Max Müller stated that all the gods of the *Rig Veda* were aspects of the sun. If, as Mary Carroll Smith argues, the key to *The Mahabharata* lies in the *Rig Veda*, then this proposition must be looked at. It was Adolf Holtzmann, Sr, who first intimated it, and his nephew, Adolf Holtzmann, Jr, who argued in 1895 that *The Mahabharata* contained various layers and reworkings, and that the present version is both an expanded and a re-worked epic (an 'analytic' approach). This thesis was rejected by Joseph Dahlmann who in the same year 1895 defended *The Mahabharata* as a unitary epic (a 'synthetic' approach).

It was a brilliant American scholar, E. Washburn Hopkins, who, in

1901, in his great classic, *The Great Epic of India: Its Character and Origin*, and in other works,[2] demonstrated that

> the epic in its present form is swollen with many additions, but they are all cast into the shade by the enormous mass added bodily to the epic as didactic books, containing more than twenty thousand stanzas ... there can be no further question in regard to the correctness of the term pseudo-epic as applied to these parts of the present poem.[3]

Washburn Hopkins also, and in my opinion rightly so, dismissed the existence of earlier material in the pseudo-epic (i.e., *parvans* XIII–XVIII) as not proving that the latter was a part of the original or Ur-*Mahabharata*:

> No one has ever denied that there are early legends found in the late parts of the epic; but the fact that this or that legend repeated in the pseudo-epic is found in other literature, no matter how old, does nothing toward proving either the antiquity of the book as a whole, which is just what the 'synthetic' method contends for, or the antiquity of the epic form of the legend.[4]

Washburn Hopkins regarded the fourth book as an 'intrusion' in order to 'fill out an extra year, not recognised in the early epic, [for] the heroes [to] live at court in various disguises'.[5] And he went on to suggest that a huge volume of extraneous legends and didactic stuff now tagged on the epic.[6]

Better than anybody before him Washburn Hopkins realised that the Ur-*Mahabharata* had been 'hijacked' by the brahmins and reshaped to suit their *Weltanschauung*:

> That the priests developed the epic for their own interests, goes without saying; hence the long chapters of priestly origin on the duty of charity—to priests.... But besides didactic and legendary masses, it was necessary, in order to popularise the poem, to keep some sort of proportion. Hence the fighting episodes were increased, enlarged, rewritten, and inserted doubly, the same scene and description occurring in two different places.[7]

His observation that 'while there is an appreciable difference in the metre of the different episodes which were inserted whole, the fighting scenes are chiefly of one sloka-type,—a type later than that of some of the episodes, but on a par with that of the later didactic and narrative insertions'[8] was to prove of greatest importance when applied to the epic as a whole. And thus Washburn Hopkins concluded that 'its metres preclude the probability of its having been written by one poet or even several poets of the same era.... It appears to be a heterogeneous collection of strings wound about a nucleus almost lost sight of. *The nucleus, however, is a story*'.[9]

Following Washburn Hopkins' lead, Moritz Winternitz tried to extract the 'kernel' of the story: 'It is comparatively easy to extract a *kernel* from the enormous mass of songs of the Kauravas and the Pandavas, which in any case formed the subject of the actual epic.'[10] As Mary Carroll Smith points out,

> Winternitz tried to summarise the 'actual epic' by tracing the story *kernel*, but he failed to make any distinctions among the metrical, syntactic and/or formulaic constructions of the stories he summarised. When we analyse the narrative elements in the excised *tristubh* verses, the intense focuses on the dynastic quarrel of the Kauravas and the Pandavas makes Winternitz seem somewhat of a prophet.[11]

Before proposing my own approach to this problem of extracting the *kernel* or the *core* of *The Mahabharata*, let us review some recent attempts to do so.

2. Recent Approaches to *The Mahabharata*

S. B. Roy makes a distinction between a *purana*, i.e., ancient history, and *itihasa*, from *iti-ha-asa* or *itiha-asa*, which means current history. He points out that *The Mahabharata* alone was called an *itihasa*, because in c. 1400 B.C. *The Mahabharata* constituted current or recent history. Roy's *Date of the Mahabharata Battle* places it in 1424 B.C.

> Vyasa himself recorded contemporary history, from his own birth down to the Bharata battle (c. 1424 B.C.). Vyasa dictated the kernel of this history (=*Jaya*), immediately (said to be within *three* years) after the Bharata battle 1424 B.C. It was given a proper shape and recited by Vaisampayana (=*Bharata samhita*) in the victory celebration of the Pandavas over the Takshaka Nagas. The text was further elaborated and given the shape of a unitary comprehensive law book (Book of human

> conduct—as it is *and* as it ought to be) Ugrashrava. Mahabharata was recited by Ugrashrava also in the Naimisharanya conference of the sages (1316 B.C.) along with the Puranas.[12]

In Chapter 10 of his book S. B. Roy posits the existence of three layers of *The Mahabharata*, apart from the interpolations: 1. the original Mahabharata—the *Jaya* or the tale of the BATTLE AND VICTORY—was composed by Vyasa himself; 2. the main text was recited by Vaisampayana at the instance and in the presence of Vyasa himself; this text—the *Vaisampayana* recension—will be called the *Bharata samhita* or the Ur-*Mahabharata*; 3. the text recited by Ugrashrava Sauti ... 'say within 100 years of the battle at the latest'. This third recension is said to be made up of 100,000 slokas, whereas the *Vaisampayana* text was made up of about 24,000 slokas, without the *Upa-akhyanas,* i.e., the subsidiary tales and legends.

Roy divided *The Mahabharata* into two parts: the so-called *Purva-Bharata* which deals with the great war and ends with Yudhisthira's triumphal entry into the city of Hastinapur and the beginning of his reign, i.e., up to *Santi Parva* XII–40; and the so-called *Uttara Bharata* which contains the rest.[13] He concluded that A) 28,125 slokas belonged undoubtedly to the Ur-*Mahabharata*; B) 6,720 were doubtful; and C) 38,940 plus an unspecified number of unnumbered slokas is made up of the didactic material, and did not belong to the original version.[14] He justified such a classification by quoting R. C. Majumdar thus: 'The proper meaning of the word Mahabharata is the great battle. For, according to Panini, Bharata means the battle of the Bharatas (*Bharatas sngrama*) and in the Mahabharata itself we find *Mahabharatayuddha* (XIV.18.8) "the great Bharata battle", the title Mahabharata being an abbreviation of the latter.'[15] Roy's conclusion is that 'the Ur-Mahabharata is therefore likely to be the text "A" proposed above. The text "A" when recovered and purified of interpolations will give the history of India at the time of the battle, i.e. a few centuries before the Buddha. Its evidence will be reliable *prima facie*, i.e. it will be accepted unless controverted by any written evidence of an earlier inscription'.[16]

John D. Smith, on the other hand, is justifiably sceptical of Roy's and other scholars' supposition that the Ur-*Mahabharata*, once extracted, could serve as a *prima facie* history of India:

> As far as the question of historicity is concerned, there is little that *can*

> be said–and this is itself the chief thing that *must* be said ... The *Mahabharata* ... contains a great deal that was probably regarded as historical fact by the early bards and their literate successors; which is not to say that it bears any discoverable relationship to what *we* might regard as historical fact.... At an indeterminate point in the remote past, in the North-West of India, there may have been a dynastic struggle between people calling themselves Kauravas and Pandavas; or there may not. We have no way of knowing.[17]

Most important of the several recent approaches for this study has been Mary Carroll Smith's computer analysis of the irregular verses of the *tristubh* type in the epic. Her study, 'The Core of India's Great Epic', though undertaken as a Ph.D. thesis at Harvard in 1972, was published only in 1992 as a book entitled *The Warrior Code of India's Sacred Song*.[18] In it she outlined her approach thus:

> First, the metrical differences between the perfectly regular and non-regular *tristubh* verses are paralleled by significant narrative variations in the epic story and setting. Second, there are discernible connections of narrative line and detail occurring between passages in similar metre, even when the passages are widely separated over the presently constituted text. I have found that the metrical irregularities may be clues to complete kernels of a very old warrior story that has been expanded and amplified by *sloka* text, but never entirely lost within the gigantic whole. The inter-relatedness of groups of *tristubh* verses from one book of the epic to the other appears much more dramatic once the *tristubh* verses are excised and read as a text on their own.[19]

Carroll Smith proceeded to isolate and take out ('excise') from the bulk of the present epic the various kinds of *tristubh* verses. She concluded that 94 per cent of the Poona text of the epic was composed in *anustubh sloka* (four lines of eight syllables each) and the remaining verses were in *tristubh sloka* (four lines of eleven syllables).[20]

Using her new approach Carroll Smith was able to gain an overview of the whole *Mahabharata*: 'The *tristubh* verses constellate the Pandava/Dhartarastra struggle into five major groupings: Marriage Alliance; the Gambling Match; the Pandava Exile, the Embassies for Peace, and the Final Battles.'[21] She then passed this judgment on the epic as a whole:

> I discovered a discrete text of 2000 non-regular, 'Vedic-type', *tristubh* verses. Within these non-regular verses is the long-suspected warrior 'kernel' of the epic.... At the heart of the *Mahabharata* is a warrior text devoted to ethical concerns.... The presence of ritual in the *tristubh* epic identifies the text as belonging to the 'archaic' level of epic history.... Excising the *tristubh* verses creates ... the chance to view the warrior class without the intervening filter of a brahmanic commentary.... My position ... is that the excised *tristubh* verses present us with an heretofore unknown example of the Aryan warrior code.... The community of Aryan peoples is characterised by a polar opposition of 'us' and 'them'.[22]

Proceeding to apply her method to the first book, Carroll Smith found out that 'the *tristubh* verses create an actual epitome of the text in Book One.... The *tristubh* verses of *Adi Parvan* cluster into five discrete areas for metrical and narrative analysis: Table of Contents; Hymn to the Asvins; Snake Sacrifice; Yayati Episodes; Courtship and Marriage of Draupadi. Sections of the Table of Contents, and the Courtship and Marriage of Draupadi contain essential elements of the Kaurava-Pandava conflict in *tristubh* metre'.[23] This has already been noticed by J. A. B. van Buitenen, a translator of the University of Chicago edition of *The Mahabharata* who calls the Framework section an 'independent text which gives a story summary through Book Eleven, The Book of the Women'.[24]This leads Carroll Smith to argue that 'what is beyond question is the focus of the Framework verses on the Pandava-Kaurava conflict, which makes it difficult not to seize on the Frame as adequate proof of the warrior "kernel" that eluded Winternitz'.[25]

The second book, 'The Book of the Assembly Hall', is central to the epic as it exists, and to the Ur-Epic as well. It is dominated by the 'Gambling Match'.[26] Its meaning and importance will be analysed in the next section. According to Carroll Smith, 'from a narrative perspective, the "Gambling Match" serves as an excuse for the sons of Dhrtarastra to wrest the Kuru kingdom from their Pandava cousins'.[27] Applying her method to the game of dice, Carroll Smith came up with an astounding result:

> If we consider *tristubh* verses alone, we have a complete scene in which Duryodhana persuades his father, Dhrtarastra, to build a gambling hall so that he can invite Yudhisthira and his brothers to play. Dhrtarastra

> warns Duryodhana that there will be a disaster leading to a war (2.51.11), since it is clear that Duryodhana intends to win the right to rule all the Kuru lands. Duryodhana replies that the rules of the game had been handed down from ancient times without evil, or combat.... The one verse response made by Dhratarastra sets the epic theme of Fate into play. He says that the quarrel would not concern him for otherwise Fate would run counter to dicing. Without the need for any *sloka* verses, the basic disaster of the Bharata war is set in forward motion. The motive of greed and jealousy is all too clear when Duryodhana says (2.51.13) 'We will stand on an equal footing'.[28]

Another important recent approach to *The Mahabharata* has been by a Russian scholar, Grintser. His book, *The Ancient Indian Epic*,[29] has solidly established both *The Mahabharata* and *The Ramayana* as *oral epics*, and this has been widely accepted by Indian scholars. Applying Albert B. Lord's oral-formulaic approach to the Indian epics, Grintser posited several layers in *The Mahabharata*: 'Grintser had made three classifications of epic: archaic, classical heroic, and late. He had placed the *Mahabharata* in the "classical heroic" and "late" categories. "Archaic" is the classification for epic "in which the mythological way of thinking predominates"; "classical heroic" describes epic in which "myth is viewed not as prototype, but as artistic background"; and "late" is the classification for epic "in which the religious didactic element predominates". The "classical heroic" epic also shows a strong reliance on Fate.'[30] Carroll Smith found that this emphasis on Fate is present in the *tristubh* verses of the Gambling Match.[31]

It is specifically the metrical analysis of the 'Gambling Match' that convinced Carroll Smith that there probably was an earlier version of it in the *tristubh* verses alone.[32]

Book IV, 'The Book of Virata', is, according to both Washburn Hopkins and van Buitenen, a later appendix to the third book, 'The Book of the Forest'. The latter contains many additions as well, but as its recent translator pointed out, 'though one can hardly imagine that in a more original form *The Book of the Forest* had the same size as in the present, it can also not be doubted that it always formed an important part of it'.[33] It should be emphasised that the Pandavas were to spend twelve years in the forest, and the thirteenth travelling unrecognised (*incognito*) around the country. The significance of the number 12 is pointed out by van Buitenen: 'At the final game of dice it was stipulated that the loser would spend twelve years in a forest and a thirteenth year unrecognised in the open.'[34] We shall return to the significance of number twelve as far as the gambling match is concerned. It is the fifth book, however, which Carroll Smith concentrated on next:

> Book Five of The *Mahabharata*, *Udyoga Parvan*, has a preponderance of irregular type *tristubh* verses. That the material of the 'Peace Effort' was central to the most ancient versions of the epic is suggested by the large clusters of *tristubh* verses in Book Five. One sub-parvan, the *Samjayayana Parvan,* is a straight run of irregular *tristubh* verses from chapters 22 through 32 of the Poona text.... Even though the *tristubh* verses are split apart by long sections of *slokas*, it is possible to establish a continuous narrative when the excised *tristubhs* are rejoined for analysis.[35]

The sixth book contains the famous *Bhagavadgita*. It has been suspected by some scholars that it was a later interpolation, but, following Grintser, Carroll Smith argues that it 'is an essential part of an epic story devoted to warfare, its causes and results. The song itself is an expansion of advice that the warrior chieftain Krishna gives to the hero, Arjuna Pandava, as he is about to engage in battle with his cousins and their designated champion, his grandfather Bhisma.... The core reality of the *Bhagavadgita* is to be found in military violence.' Out of the 700 verses, 67 are composed in eleven-syllable *tristubh* metre. The rest of the verses are composed in eight-syllable *sloka* metre. 'The *tristubh* text gives us the long-suspected key to the warrior code in India's "Sacred Song".'[36] Carroll Smith has advanced the most persuasive arguments yet for regarding the *Bhagavadgita* as a part of the Ur-*Mahabharata*.

Already in Book IV, *The Book of Virata*, the importance of Time is spelled out by Bhisma in connection with the Pandavas' exile for twelve (or to be more precise, as Bhisma points out himself, thirteen, years): 'The instants are joined together, and so are the hours, days, fortnights, months, lunar houses, planets, seasons, and years: thus the wheel of time revolves with the divisions of time.'[37] Now Krishna reveals himself as Time incarnate; I am Kala, he says.

> The Sanskrit *kala* also means 'death' as well as 'time', but the most significant meaning, by way of making connections with other Indo-

European epics, is the translation of *kala* as 'Fate'. Krishna's message to Arjuna is that he is merely an instrument of the divine plan that numbers the enemy as already dead.[38]

According to Alf Hiltebeitel, who adopted Madeleine Biardeau's theory at the opening of his chapter 'Two Theophanies, Three Steps' in his book, *The Ritual of Battle*, 'the very idea of the dissolution or destruction of all things at the end of the world is rooted in Indo-European hero mythology. At some archetypal level, the heroic task of saving the world from all of the evils that threatened their heroic claims, became the essential religious vision of the Aryan peoples'.[39] Thus Mary Carroll Smith finds herself in complete agreement with Rudolf Otto who claimed half a century ago that 'the *Original Gita* then ... is no doctrinal *Text*, no doctrinal writ of *Bhakti* religion, but rather Krishna's own voice and deed, referring directly to the situation in which Arjuna finds himself; intended, however, not to proclaim to him any transcendent dogma of salvation, but to render him willing to undertake special service of the Almighty Will of the God.... This portion of the narrative, then, is the very climax of the whole Epic....'[40]

The vision of universal destruction presented to Arjuna by Krishna is related to the warrior's fury, similar to that that is the central motif of *The Iliad:* 'Menin aeide, thea, Peleiadeo Achilleos....' ['Sing to me, o Goddess, of Achilles' wrath...]. Mircea Eliade explains how this 'warrior's fury' is an aspect of 'Fire':

> In modern India, the (Muslims) believe that a man in communication with God becomes 'burning hot'. Anyone who performs miracles is called 'burning'. By extension, all kinds of people or acts involving any magico-religious power are regarded as burning. This sacred power, which causes both the shaman's heat and the heating of the warrior, can be transformed, differentiated, given various colorings, by subsequent efforts.... The 'wrath' and the heat induced by a violent and excessive access of sacred power are feared by the majority of mankind.[41]

The *Bhagavadgita* is the last extensive 'portion' of the original 'core' of *The Mahabharata*, though I think that the present version contains many subsequent interpolations and modifications to suit the Brahmin taste and vision. Carroll Smith regards the Ur-*Mahabharata* as including one fragment of later *parvans*: 'With the exception of a passage of four verses in Book Nine, and one of ten verses in Book Fifteen, there are no other irregular *tristubh* verses in the present text which need be considered part of the narrative core of the Bharata war epic.'[42] Thus she argues that the entire Book Twelve, *Santi Parvan*, is 'one of the greatest expansions known to world literature' while originally Bhisma's death-bed advice was put into four lines:

> Four non-regular *tristubh* verses (6.116.47–51) give the death-bed advice of Bhisma to the Pandavas and the Kauravas:
>
> Let half the kingdom be given to the Pandavas!
> Let the Dharmaraj rule Indrasprastha!
> Avoid violating your contract by deceit: It is the meanest thing among chieftains.
> You will have a soiled fame, O Indra of the Kurus!
>
> With Vedic conciseness, four non-regular *tristubh* contain Bhisma's dying advice to the ancient warriors.[43]

Carroll Smith regards Book VIII, *Karna Parvan*, as 'the last book of the *Mahabharata* to give sustained evidence of one having had a narrative core of irregular *tristubh* verse at its center'.[44] Her analysis of *The Bhagavadgita* leads her to question Wikander's and Dumézil's theory of tripartite functions of the Indo-Europeans:

> For reasons that often seem more related to later stratifications of Indo-European cultures in India and in Rome, Dumézil and Wikander place the King in the functional category of priests.[45]

Carroll Smith argues that 'the flaw in the tripartite function theory … is that by limiting the warrior function to "the exercise of physical prowess" it loses sight of the most creative aspects of the ancient *ksatriya* order which finds political activity, whether in fighting or negotiation, a simultaneous religious and political activity. The Dharma code of the warriors governs all'.[46]

I propose to examine briefly Georges Dumézil's theory of the Indo-European tri-function theory transposed from the realm of the myth into that of the epic. The three basic functions according to Dumézil are:

1. The first function embraces sovereignty and is marked by a priestly

stratum of society which maintains both magico-religious and legal order. The gods assigned the sovereign function are often presented as a pair, each of which reflects a specific aspect: religious such as the Indic Varuna, and legal such as Mitra.

2. A second military function assigned to the warrior stratum and concerned with the execution of both aggressive and defensive force, for example, Indra.

3. A third estate conceptualising fertility or sustenance and embracing the herder-cultivators. Here the mythic personages normally take the form of divine twins, for example, the Indic Asvins (horsemen).[47]

Following the pioneering research of Stig Wikander in 1947, Dumézil showed that the group of five heroes of *The Mahabharata*, the Pandava brothers, 'were duplications as to their characters, their actions, and their relationships (beginning with the very order of their birth) of the hierarchised group constituted in the earliest Vedic mythology by the gods of the three functions: the just king Yudhisthira is modelled on Mitra (simply rejuvenated as Dharma), the two kinds of warrior, Bhima and Arjuna, on Vayu and Indra, and the two twins Nakula and Sahadeva on the Nasatya twins'.

It has also been well known for quite some time what happened to the original *Mahabharata*. John D. Smith summarises the whole question admirably:

> The reason for the very marked dichotomy between the *Mahabharata* and what preceded it is not difficult to ascertain. As the Vedas and their supporting literature were the 'property' of the Brahmans, so the epic was the 'property' of the Ksatriyas, the caste of warriors and princes. The Epic dealt with 'their' legendary heroes, and put forward 'their' code of conduct: it was the statement of 'their' mythology. The two leading castes were not merely concerned with different events, personages, and conventions of behaviour; they were often, it would appear, specifically antagonistic towards one another.[48]

Smith goes on to say that the present *Mahabharata* bears little resemblance to this Ur-*Mahabharata* of the Ksatriyas, for the latter was taken over by the Brahmans who radically altered its structure as well as its tenor. Not only were numerous insertions and accretions added to the core, but the whole tenor of the whole was completely changed which accounts for many inconsistencies and contradictions. Smith concludes that 'by the end of the process, the text had, so to speak, changed hands: it was now the "property" of the Brahmans, and came even to be dignified as "the fifth Veda" '.[49]

3. The meaning of the Ur-*Mahabharata*

Thus, John D. Smith is indubitably correct when he argues that 'the "core" of the *Mahabharata*, whether by that we mean the narrative told in "irregular" *tristubhs* as excerpted by Mary Carrol Smith, or any other imaginable nucleus, is certainly a heroic story'.[50] If we take this approach to the Ur-*Mahabharata*, then we are in a position to try to tackle the big question: can we extract its mythopoeic essence—in other words, what does the Ur-*Mahabharata* mean, stand for, represent? Taking into account Carrol Smith's strictures that the four battle-books contain an increasing number of later insertions, I propose to deal only with the second book of the great epic, *The Book of the Assembly Hall*, that is, according to its modern translator, van Buitenen, 'the pivotal one of the eighteen Major Books of *The Mahabharata*'.[51] It is in turn dominated by the game of dice. The game of dice has a much deeper significance, but, according to one of the greatest modern Indian scholars, A. L. Basham, 'its import is not wholly clear'.[52] Van Buitenen argues that the game of dice was a part of the Vedic ritual of the *rajasuya*, called also *digvyavasthapana,* the 'separate establishment of the quarters', which, according to him, 'takes place when the king-to-be sets foot in each of the "five" quarters, i.e, the regular four and the one above. Accordingly, the manuals prescribe that the king take a step in each of the five directions, *so that he can be king on a cosmic scale. The five quarters sum up the entire universe: each one is associated with components of the Veda, the pantheon, the year—old symbol of the cycle of all natural life—and people.*'[53] [*my emphasis*]

In his book, *The Destiny of a King*, Georges Dumézil has investigated this concept of the division of the world as a part of his explanation of Yayati's parceling of his inheritance among his five sons, which is one of the cardinal points in the beginning book of *The Mahabharata*. This is how he explains this concept:

> These words surely have to do with five human groups. The expression

> is sometimes equivalent to the totality of the arya ... sometimes, in a comprehensive way, to the whole of humanity living on the earth.... This double interpretation is not contradictory: it was the arya who primarily interested the poets, and in many cases the arya constituted the only 'humanity' which concerned them.
>
> The division into five probably corresponded to an ancient conception, purely terrestrial, of the five *dísah,* or *pradísah*, the directions of the world, that is, the four cardinal points and the center ... When the expression was taken in its most comprehensive sense, the center might refer to the arya, surrounded on all sides by the barbarians (cf. the Chinese expression 'Empire of the Middle')....
>
> It is likely that this conception of the world and its occupation was even part of the Indo-Iranian tradition. To be sure, the Zoroastrian texts divide the world into seven parts ... ; but beneath these, in the very names and the distribution of the 'sevenths', one perceives a division into five with the four cardinal points and the center. Put simply, it is a question of a conception that is not purely terrestrial, *but which has been enlarged, cosmicized.*[54] [*my emphasis*]

Dumézil argues that the original five-part system has been changed into a seven-part system 'perhaps under the influence of Babylonian thought in which the number seven played such an important role'.[55] Taking Dumézil's suggestion that the division of the world has been cosmicized as our lead, we can argue that, like all such cosmic myths, it goes back to cosmogony. In Indian cosmogony 'five' is the constituent number, according to E. W. Hopkins:

> According to the old belief, the universe comes from a cosmic egg. The philosophical schemes, of course, discard this egg, but we hear of it in the popular accounts often enough and meet it in the first verses of the epic [*The Mahabharata*, I, 27]. 'Then he produced Brahman, born in a golden egg. Brahman lived in the egg a year. Then he came out and put together the four forms of all beings, and earth and heaven above—and then the middle space. After this he created egoism, a being, *bhuta*, and four sons besides, who are the fathers' fathers.'[56]

We can also apply this system to the totality of the arya, in which case it would refer to the Vedic 'five tribes'. But if we concentrate on the four quarters of the world and leave out the centre, then we can apply the four sides to the four castes of the *arya* and un-*arya*, as E. W. Hopkins explains:

> There were ... three Aryan castes in the Epic period. The ruling caste, comprising the king, his great lords and vassals, together with the knightly part of the army; the priestly caste, elevated by religious knowledge, often individually powerful as guiders of the king's will ... ; lastly the third caste called collectively the people, exalted only through their Aryan blood and their fully allowed claim to all Aryan privileges in the matter of legal rights and religious rites.... There was, too, another and un-Aryan caste.... These had, barring pretense, no spiritual or legal privileges. They possessed no property. Their wives were so in name. Their lives depended on their owner's pleasure. They were 'born to servitude', for they 'came from the foot of God'.* [57]

In the footnote to the last quotation [marked *] Hopkins states that 'it is an old myth that the people-caste came from the loins or thighs of God (Brahma or Manu), while the warrior-caste came from his arms, the priestly, from his head (mouth), and the slave-caste from his foot'.[58] But what is especially important is his next observation: 'The colour-distinction between the castes—the slave being black; the people, yellow; the warrior, red; the priest, white—may possibly indicate a real difference of hue.'[59] The four castes are, of course, *brahmana* ('priest'), *ksatriya* ('warrior', 'man of the ruling order'), *vaisya* ('Inhabitant', 'man of the people'), *sudra* ('slave').[60] Hopkins then concludes with this rider: 'Out of these elements was made the theoretical state of the Hindus. Yet earlier only the three upper castes were recognised as *tout le monde*.'[61]

We are now in a position to go back to the game of dice in the second book of *The Mahabharata*, and try to find out its inner, cosmic meaning. It is extremely important for this study that Hopkins claims that 'the Epic' [i.e., *The Mahabharata*] 'confines "playing" ' [of dice] 'to two things, *in hyperbole to war,* and in matter of fact to gambling'.[62] [*my emphasis*]. The game of dice is, moreover, the pivot of the *Ur-Epic,* of the original core of the epic: 'The whole plot of the Epic turns on a game of dice.'[63] The result is that 'the king plays away all he has, wealth, crown, brothers, and self; then his wife'.[64] After he himself became a courtier at another king's court he continued to 'fling out the charming *beryl, gold, and ivory dice, dotted black and red*'.[65] [*my emphasis*] In a footnote Hopkins says that 'the comm[entary] would make the words for materials refer to colour, blue, yellow, red, and white',[66] though he claims he cannot follow it. It seems to me that Hopkins did not pay attention to the *identity of colours* of dice with those of *the four elements of the state, the three Aryan and a non-Aryan caste.* Van Buitenen has argued that the entire second book, *The Book of the Assembly Hall,* is modelled on the ceremony of the Royal Consecration or *rajasuya,* and that the game of dice is an integral part of this ceremony.[67] In footnote 1 on page 71 van Buitenen cites J. C. Heesterman, *The Ancient Indian Royal Consecration* (Thesis Utrecht, The Hague, 1955), ch. XVII. He then proceeds to state that 'Apastamba and Hiranyakesin have the king play with a brahmin, *ksatriya, visya* and *sudra,* for parts of a cow (= earth ?)....'[68] He then argues that 'as the mode is clearly a yes-or-no game, with no scores being kept from play to play, every one throw decides the play; terms like *krta, treta, dvapara* and *kali, which require score-keeping*'.[69] Be that as it may, this only strengthens my argument that the individual games were regarded as a part of the Royal Ceremony *symbolising the Conquest of the World.* Van Buitenen sensed that himself: 'The game presented shows an interesting structure. It goes on in two sessions, each of ten throws. This parallism [*sic*] between the two sessions cannot be accidental; and I take it that, actually, or in the intention of the composer, it was to last for twenty throws exactly. This number is easily seen as the multiple of four and five; but, while we may point to the fact that both these numbers are important in early Indian dicing and that both represent totality, the typical obsession with number combinations in gaming anywhere, inclines me to discount any specific significance.'[70] The last sentence makes no sense: why bring up all these elements if they do not amount to anything?

In my opinion the twenty throws represent the *loss* over the four castes, *brahmin, ksatriya, vaisya* and *sudra* in the five quarters (the four quarters plus the fifth *dis,* the zenith, the centre). The throws are summarised by Van Buitenen thus:

During the first half the stakes are increasing; Yudhisthira gambles away (1) the initial stake; (2) multiples of one thousand *niskas*; (3) his chariot; (4) a hundred thousand serving wenches; (5) a thousand male servants; (6) a thousand bull elephants; (7) a thousand chariots; (8) his horses; (9) ten thousand bullock carts with their teams; (10) four hundred *nidhis* .... In the second half, Yudhisthira stakes and lose untold millions, in fact all his riches in chattels; (2) all his cattle; (3) all his land; (4) his pages; (5) Nakula; (6) Sahadeva; (7) Bhima; (8) Arjuna; (9) himself. At the tenth throw of this phase he stakes his wife Draupadi.[71]

My explanation of the throws is as follows: in the first half, the loss of: (1) the initial stake (2) *vaisya*; (3) *ksatriya;* (4) *sudra*; (5) *sudra*; (6) *ksatriya*; (7) *vaisya;* (8) *ksatriya*; (9) *vaisya*; (10) *vaisya.* In the second half, (1) the initial stake, (2) *sudra* (3) *vaisya* (4) *sudra*; (5) *brahmana;* (6) *Brahmana*; (7) *Brahmana*; (8) *Brahmana*; (9) *Brahmana*; (10) *incomplete.* An explanation is in order: (2) represent the wealth of the land garnered by the 'people', i.e., *vaisya*; (3) though the chariot stands for the *ksatriya*; for it is the instrument *par excellence* of the Aryan warriors, in this case it may stand for the brahmins, as explained by the Vedas (*Ratha*);[72] (4) and (5) expressly designate *female* and *male slaves*; (6) bull elephants are said to be 'death to any noise on the battlefield': they are another instrument of the *khsatriya*; as are the chariots (7) and horses (8); (9) stands for the 'people', 'sixty thousand broad-chesten men, who drink milk and feed on rice and grain' and (10) is again the riches ('400 coffers encased in copper and iron, each holding five buckets of beaten gold').

It should be pointed out that the order given by van Buitenen in his article is not the same as in his translation of Book II of *The Mahabharata*: (6) is (4) in the latter, and vice versa, which, if adopted, would give the following scheme: (1) X (2) V (3) B ? (4) K (5) Ç (6) Ç (7) V (8) K (9) K (10) V. I am inclined to regard (3) as pertaining to the brahmins since there is an analogy between the two sets of 10 throws (though not perfect), and the loss of brahmins in the first set calls for another in the second set. The second half should read as follows: (2) 'cattle ... milch cows ... etc.' stands for the *brahmins* ('our color of people east of the Indus'); (3) 'my city, my country, the wealth of all my people, *excepting* brahmins, all my people themselves, *excepting brahmins*' will represent *vaisya* (having already *staked and lost* the brahmins Yudhisthira makes that clear: 'excepting brahmins'); (4) the pages represent *sudra*; (5) through (9) will be explained below; and (10) there is a question of whether Yudhisthira was a slave (*sudra*) when he gambled Draupadi away; in that case it would be impossible for him to give away Draupadi. If he was still free, then she could be regarded as his slave, *sudra.* Thus the scheme looks like this: (1) X (2) B (3) V (4) Ç (10) Ç? Following Dumézil,[73] it is possible to break down (5) through (9) differently: either as: (5) V (6) V (7) K (8) K (9) B; or as: (5) K (6) B (7) K (8) K (9) B.[74] I would opt for the former, for in that case there would be a totality of the Arya in the fifth or royal quarter, i.e., the representatives of the three Aryan castes rather than associating the five brothers with only the first two privileged Aryan castes. This is precisely how Dumézil chose to interpret it in *The Destiny of the Warrior*: Arjuna represents Brahminic spiritual power, whereas Bhima represents the *ksatriyas*.[75] The result would then be: (5) V (6) V (7) K (8) B (9) B.

This five-region or five-quarter formula is also found in the very gaming table which is similar in design to the traditional Indian pachisi board: it consists of four sides and a centre.[76] As a part of the Vedic rite of the *rajasuya* the king held five dice in his hand which symbolised the five regions: 'He is become king of the regions.'[77] According to one version, the king played four games with a brahmin, *ksatriya, vaisya* and *sudra*; but according to another, he played games with a brahmin, *suta, gramani, ksattar*, and *samgrahitar*.[78] Thus, there is a difference between four and five which stems from the fact that sometimes four and sometimes five castes are mentioned in the Vedas, e.g., at Bharata's *rajasuya* there is this remark: 'This great achievement of Bharata, neither former nor later persons [have equalled]; the five classes of men have not attained his feats, any more than a mortal [can reach] heaven with his hands.'[79] But 'The Hymn of Man' [*Purusa Sukta*] knows only of four classes: 'His mouth became the Brahmin; his arms were made into the Warrior, his thighs the People, and from his feet the Servants were born.'[80]

In his well-known *Dictionary of Symbols* Cirlot makes the connection between time and the game of dice:

> The division into four parts—quite apart from the importance of its relationship with the four phases of the moon—coincides with the solar process and the annual cycle of the season as well as with the spatial arrangement of the four points of the compass on the conceptual plane. The cosmic ages have been applied to eras of human existence, and also to the life of a race or an empire. In Hindu tradition, the *Manvantara,* also called *Maha-Yuga* (or the Great Cycle), comprises four *yuga* or secondary periods, which were said to be the same as the four ages in Greco-Roman antiquity. In India, these same ages are called after four

throws in the game of dice: *krita, treta, dvapara* and *kali.*[81]

A. L. Basham in his classic, *The Wonder that was India*, comments that 'oblong dice [*aksa*] with four scoring sides were used; like the European gamester the Indian employed a special terminology for the throws at dice: *krta* (cater, four), *treta* (trey), *dvapara* (deuce), and *kali* (ace). So important was gambling in the Indian scheme of things that these four terms were applied to the four periods (*yuga*) of the aeon'.[82]

The four throws in the game of dice, namely, *krta, treta, dvapara,* and *kali* represent attempts to establish control over the four castes making up the (Aryan) world: *sudra, vaisya, ksatriya, brahmana.* But from a cosmic point of view the four throws of dice symbolise the conquest of Time, by trying to establish control over the four periods of the cosmic cycle, symbolised by the colours blue, yellow, red, and white. Basham comments that 'their lengths are respectively 4,800, 3,600, 2,400, and 1,200 "years of the gods", each of which equals 360 human years. Each yuga represents a progressive decline in piety, morality, strength, stature, longevity and happiness. We are at present in the Kali-yuga, which began according to tradition, in 3102 B.C., believed to be the year of the Mahabharata War.'[83]

The four periods of the cosmic cycle or *Maha-Yuga* are the descending ages following the mythical Golden Age. This Golden Age is symbolised by the Centre: 'The Golden Age stands ... for the "Centre" which precedes time....'[84] This 'Centre', according to Cirlot, 'is always reserved for the Creator, so that he appears as if surrounded by ... concentric circles spreading outwards, and by the wheel of the Zodiac, the twelve-monthly cycle of labour upon the land, and a four-part division corresponding both to the seasons and to the tetramorph.'[85] It should be pointed out that 'Hindu doctrine declares that God resides in the centre, at that point where the radii of a wheel meet at its axis'.[86]

At this point let us introduce the Russian folk-tale of the type 301 in which the hero visits three kingdoms—golden, silver and copper—in the underworld, fights the three Dragons, and rescues the three princesses. On his way back to the surface of the earth he puts each of the three kingdoms into an egg.[87] The egg, as we know from Vedic Indian mythology, represents chaos. As Toporov points out, 'the motif of the egg out of which the kingdom emerges (usually there are three eggs and three kingdoms hypostatising three cosmic zones); [the egg]

is obtained in the underground kingdom in the final analysis as the reconstruction shows, from the Dragon.'[88] In the *Rig Veda* the unknown creator of the universe is identified as the Golden Embryo or Egg. The latter figures in the cosmogonic myth of the golden egg separating into two shells that become sky and earth, and the yolk becomes the sun: 'In the beginning the Golden Embryo arose. Once he was born, he was the one lord of creation. He held in place the earth and this sky.'[89] Agni is the son of these two parents, the earth and the sky ('the two world halves'), and it swallows his parents, 'a graphic image which points to the change that takes place with the emergence of the third factor. Spirit and substance, in their ultimate, original essence, disappear as such, but to reappear under a different garb.'[90]

Jeannine Miller explains that to the Sun the task is given of propping up Heaven and Earth;[91] but the Sun is also intimately related to poets (which in this context can mean primarily epic poetry): thus in the *Rig Veda* VIII.6.10 the birth of the poet as a sun is described.

In this context it should be pointed out that there is an intimate link between Indra, the slayer of the primordial monster (the Dragon) *Vrtra*, and Agni:

> A link between Agni in his lightning aspect and Indra's bolt is found in III.34.3: 'he who fiercely burns (*usadhag v anesu*) amidst the forests killed Vyamsa', the demon of draught. In I.103.2 Indra 'strikes the serpent' and 'slays Vyamsa'. Whether the two are identical and whether both refer to Vrtra, the idea is the same. As Agni—as well as being 'Vrtra's slayer' (VI.16.14 & 48: *vrtrahan*) —is also the breaker of strongholds which is really Indra's prerogative, the question comes up whether the Indra-Vrtra myth was not grafted upon an earlier tale of the fire which gives release by disintegrating that which constricts and thereby grants liberation.[92]

The end result of the slaying of the Dragon is the coming out of the Sun: 'Indra ... also found the sun hidden away in darkness (*Rgv. III.39.5 suryam viveda tamasi ksiyantam*) ... and after slaying Vrtra raised it on high.'[93] And though it is not stated how and when gods [*devas*] gained immortality themselves, Miller comments that they 'were once bound by a curse as one may gather from *Rgv.* VII.13.2. Since they originally were not immortal, this curse may be the same as that which binds men: birth, growth, decay. Agni set them free, as he does men.'[94]

Accordingly, Agni must be seen as the most important of the trinity (Savitr, Agni, Soma) which is found as a principle active in all gods:

> Agni is the quickening flame, the dynamic power at the core of all beings moving all forward, the ruler of thought who grants illumination and ecstasy, for 'mightiest of all is his rapture and utterly inspired his wisdom' (Rgv. I.127.9). Of all the gods he is perhaps the most precious one both for deities and for men. So the gods having established the boon-bestowing (*dravinodam*) Agni protect him as their own immortal state (Rgv. I.96.6.).[95]

Agni is the link between Earth and Heaven which raises the mortal to highest immortality (*amrtatve uttame martam, Rgv.* VII.5.7). In Heaven he dwells in the third sphere, but he pervades all seven of them, and on earth he sits 'within the house, king immortal of mortals' (*Rgv.* III.1.18).[96]

Thus in Vedic mythology Agni as the Sun is seen as the centre of the universe. In a hymn entitled appropriately 'Guard Us from the Monstrous Abyss' Agni in the form of the Sun is called the embryo and seen as symbolic of all creatures ('teeming').[97]

The significance of Agni was pointed out almost a century ago by A. A. MacDonell:

> Born on earth, in air, in heaven, Agni is frequently regarded as having a triple character ...: 'From heaven first Agni was born, the second time from us (i.e. men), thirdly in the waters.' This earliest Indian trinity is important as the basis of much of the mystical speculation of the Vedic age. It was probably the prototype not only of the later Rigvedic triad, Sun, Wind, Fire, spoken of as distributed in the three worlds, but also of the triad Sun, Indra, Fire, which, though not Rigvedic, is still ancient. It is most likely also the historical progenitor of the later Hindu trinity of Brahma, Vishnu, Civa [*sic*].[98]

In the *Purusa-Sukta* (The Hymn of Man) the dismemberment of the primeval cosmic giant Purusa leads to the creation of the four classic classes or *varnas* (according to O'Flaherty, the first time this concept appears in Indian civilisation): '12. His mouth became the Brahmin; his arms were made into the Warrior, his thighs the People, and from his feet the Servants were born. 13. The moon was born from his mind; from his eye the sun was born. Indra and Agni came from his mouth, and from his vital breath the Wind was born.'[99] In *The Golden Embryo* hymn the four quarters of space are parted by the cosmic giant Purusa's arms.[100]

When applied concretely to *The Mahabharata* Agni's position is pivotal: in Book I, 'The Book of the Beginning', there is an episode on 'The Burning of the Khandava Forest', where Agni as Fire God enjoins Krisna and Arjuna to help him burn the forest that belongs to his enemy and superior, Indra/Varuna. In return Agni demands of Indra a gift of invincible weapons to the warriors, giving to Krisna a disc (a symbol of himself as the Sun) and to Arjuna the bows, quivers, and a chariot: 'Hand over at once that bow that King Soma once gave, and the two quivers, and also the chariot with the sign of the monkey. For the Partha shall accomplish a very great task with the bow Gandiva. And let the discus be presented to Vasudeva [Krisna] on my behalf.'[101] It is thus Agni who arms the two foremost warriors.

I already pointed out that Indra raised the sun, hidden in darkness, and raised it on high following the slaying of Vrtra. It must be emphasised that the 'second' creation of the world followed Indra's victory, for the unreleased waters symbolise chaos. The release of waters and the dismemberment of Vrtra's body leads to the restoration of the world.

There is no question that behind this cosmogony/cosmology lies the calendar-based progression of the sun within the Zodiac. At this point it must be emphasised that the Vedic year consists of *five*, not *four seasons*, and this is brought out beautifully by Mircea Eliade in his *The Myth of the Eternal Return*:

> The Vedic altar, to employ Paul Mus' apt formula, is time materialised. 'That fire-altar also is the Year,—the nights are its enclosing stones, and there are three hundred and sixty of these, because there are three hundred and sixty nights in the year; and the days are its yagushmati bricks, for there are three hundred and sixty of these, and three hundred and sixty days in the year' (X, 5, 4, 10). At a certain moment in the construction of the altar, two bricks called 'of the seasons' (*rtavya*) are laid, and the text comments: 'And as to why he lays down these two in this (layer):—this Agni (fire-altar) is the year.... Again, ... this fire-altar is Prajapati, and Prajapati is the year' (VIII, 2, 1, 17–18). To reconstruct Prajapati by means of a Vedic altar is also to reconstruct

> cosmic time. 'Of five layers consists the fire-altar (each layer is a season), five seasons are a year, and the year is Agni (the altar).... And that Prajapati who became relaxed is the year; and those five bodily parts of his which became relaxed are the seasons; for there are five seasons, and five are those layers: when he builds up the five layers, he thereby builds him up with the seasons.... And those five bodily parts of his, the seasons, which became relaxed, are the regions (or quarters; i.e. the four cardinal points of the compass and the upper region); for five in number are the regions, and five those layers: when he builds up the five layers, he builds him up with the regions' (VI, 8, 1. 15; 1. 2, 18ff). Thus, with the construction of each new Vedic altar, not only is the cosmogony repeated and Prajapati revived, but the year is constructed; that is, time is regenerated, by being 'created' anew.[102]

Moreover, as Eliade, points out, 'a territorial conquest does not become real until after—more precisely, through—the ritual of taking possession, which is only a copy of the primordial act of the Creation of the World.

In Vedic India the erection of an altar dedicated to Agni constituted legal taking possession of a territory. 'One settles (*avasyati*) when he builds the *garhapatya*, and whoever are builders of fire-altars are settled (*avasitah*)', says the *Satapatha Brahmana* (VII, 1,1, 1–4). Thus, Eliade concludes, 'the erection of an altar dedicated to Agni is merely the microcosmic imitation of the Creation'.[103] The three hundred and sixty days correspond to twelve months, but since a year has slightly over 365 days an additional thirteenth month, an intercalary one, was added. That the twelve times thirty refer to the Sun and to Agni identified as the Sun is made explicit in the *Rg Veda*, par excellence in 'The Riddle of the Sacrifice' (*Asya Vamasya*). When broken into days and nights it gives a number of seven hundred and twenty: 'The twelve-spoked wheel of Order rolls around and around the sky and never ages. Seven hundred and twenty sons in pairs rest on it, O Agni.... All the worlds rest on this five-spoked wheel that rolls around and around. Though heavy-laden, its axle does not get hot, nor has it ever broken in its naves [1.164. 11;13].'[104] In her introduction to this hymn O'Flaherty explains that 'the three or six or five naves or spokes are seasons (variously enumerated in different sacrificial reckonings)....'[105] The hymn, as O'Flaherty points out, identifies Agni, the Sun, Indra, Varuna, Mitra and others as One, thus establishing the interchangeability of supreme gods and their conflation into One, of supreme importance for this study: 'They call it Indra, Mitra, Varuna, Agni, and it is the heavenly bird that flies. The wise speak of what is One in many ways; they call it Agni, Yama, Matarisvan [1.164.46].'[106]

The representation of the Sun in the form of a wheel is possibly of Indo-European origin since it is also found among the Celts and the Germans.[107] The connection between the sun-worship and the horse sacrifice (*Asvamedha*) is brought out by Prasad Pandey:

> The horse plays a considerable part in Vedic sacrifices. The Sun is compared to and described as a white horse. Therefore, a horse was used in these sacrifices to represent the Sun-god. At the 'Sodacin' form of the Soma sacrifice, when the chant at sun-set is performed, a horse, either white or black has to be present; white colour represents the rising sun and black represents the setting sun. In the piling of fire-altar the bricks are put in place in the presence of a horse which is made to breathe over them. In the white Yajurveda, the Sun again has been addressed as a horse, while praising Savitr in Agnicayana ceremony. A white horse with black ears is mentioned in the Atharvaveda as of special value. Again, the horse has been invoked in the white Yajurveda, and a long eulogy of the horse is given in many verses. At another place, in the same work, the horse has been identified with the sun.... In Asvamedha sacrifices, the 'Adhvaryu ties an ornament of gold, perhaps a chain round the neck of the sacrificer and addresses it as a symbol of the Sun and identifies it with light.[108]

Coomarswamy's comment is that 'the wheel which later on becomes the mark of a Cakravartin, the discus of Visnu and the Buddhist wheel of Law, originally represented the sun'.[109] Since, as we have seen, the *Dharma* code of the warriors governs all, according to Mary Carroll Smith, then a representation of the Wheel as *Dharma* in a form of *Dharmaçakra* brings the two together.[110] Thus the Wheel of Agni, of the Sun, of *Dharma*, governs all.

4. The morphology of the epic: the Ur-*Mahabharata* as an example

Citing Hopkins's classic study as 'a tour de force of scholarship which remains as daunting now as it must have seemed at the turn of the century',[111] Smith summarises Mary Carroll Smith's computer analysis which tried to apply Hopkins's crucial insight stated in 1901 that *The Mahabharata* 'appears to be a heterogeneous collection of strings wound about a nucleus almost lost sight of. The nucleus, however, is a story.'[112] Carroll Smith pointed out that 'Hopkins seemed not to have associated the story nucleus with a metrical nucleus which could be detected by scansion.'[113] This is precisely what Mary Carroll Smith proceeded to do: she used a computer to find a correlation between narrative and metrical patterns, and found one not in the sloka verses, the most numerous in the 'C' Mahabharata, but in the *tristubhs*, to be more precise in the 'irregular', pre-classical *tristubhs*. Her conclusion was that 'the Indian tradition has preserved a nucleus of old Vedic-type ['irregular'] verses. The nucleus contains the basic story of the Gambling Match, the embassies for peace, and the final battle. Encrusted over the nucleus are successive layers of stories which can be identified by increasing occurrences of the upajati ['classical'] pattern of tristubh metre. The 'Great Epic' has evolved from a nucleus which is still extant.'[114]

Taking Hopkins' and Carroll Smith's findings we can now proceed to apply to the Ur-*Mahabharata* a *morphological analysis of the tale*, for, regardless of whether or not the 'core' is *historical* or *mythical* (and my opinion is that *it is both*), its epic presentation must follow the rules of the *genre*, in this case (if Hopkins and Carroll Smith are right) that of the folktale. We are now in a position to apply to the Ur-*mahabharata* the morphological rules advanced by Vladimir Propp in his seminal work, *Morphology of the Folktale.*[115] Now, the objection can be lodged that the Ur-*Mahabharata* being *an epic* story cannot follow the same rules as a *folktale*: but I propose to demonstrate that the Ur-*Mahabharata* is an *epic* elaboration of the tale type #301 (a hero's fight with a dragon) in Aarne-Thompson's classification scheme.[116] At this point it is necessary to recall three fundamental laws posited by Propp:

1. Functions serve as stable, constant elements in folktales, independent of who performs them, and how they are fulfilled by the dramatis personae. They constitute the components of a folktale.
2. The number of functions known in the fairy tale is limited.
3. The sequence of functions is always identical.[117]

In Chapter III of his *Morphology of the Folktale* Propp enumerates the functions of the *dramatis personae*, and comes to the conclusion that 'the number of functions is highly limited. Some thirty-one functions in all may be noted'.[118] Now I shall take only those *essential* functions necessary for explicating the 'core' of the Ur-*Mahabharata* and briefly summarise them thus:

III. The interdiction is violated (Definition: violation, Designation: d). As Propp explains: 'Functions II (Interdiction, Designation: g) and III form a twin element. The second half can sometimes exist without the first.... A fulfilled injunction corresponds ... to a violated prohibition.'[119] Now a violated prohibition in the Ur-*Mahabharata* is Dhritarashtra's raising to the throne which he as a blind man, according to the law, was not entitled to, and his fathering of sons, the Kauravas, which presented the challenge, to the Pandavas.

IV. The villain makes an attempt at reconnaissance. (Definition: reconnaissance. Designation: e.) This corresponds to the archery contest.

VI. The villain attempts to deceive his victim in order to take possession of him or of his belongings. (Definition: fraud. Designation: h). This is Duryodhana's action in the Gambling Match through Shakuni's cheating.

VII. The victim submits to deception and thereby unwittingly helps his enemy. (Definition: complicity. Designation: q). This is Yudhisthira's agreement to play the gambling match. Propp goes on to list VII. 1: 'The hero agrees to all of the villain's persuasions ... One notes that ... deceitful proposals, conversely, are always accepted and fulfilled (q1) ... The deceitful agreement constitutes a special form of deceitful proposal and assent ... Assent in these instances is compelled, the villain taking advantage of some difficult situation in which his victim is caught ...'[120] In this case, this was Yudhisthira's *necessity* to have a Gambling Match *as an integral part of the rajasuya*.

VIII. The villain causes harm or injury to one member of a family. (Definition: villainy. Designation: A). This is a *multiple* function. In our case, this covers both the violation of Draupadi, and Yudhisthira's loss of everything and of his brothers and Draupadi. It thus includes: 1. The villain abducts a person (Draupadi) or, more precisely, 5. The villain performs abduction in other forms; and 16. The villain threatens forcible matrimony.

VIII.a. One member of a family lacks something, he desires to have something. (Definition: lack. Designation: a). This is Duryodhana's claim to Yudhisthira's inheritance.

XI. The hero leaves home. (Definition: departure. Designation: î). This is Yudhisthira's and other Pandava's departure for the exile. Propp explains that 'departure ... denotes something different from the temporary absence element.... The departures of seeker-heroes and victim-heroes are also various. The former have "the search" as their goal; the latter travel along a route in which a search is not involved, which, instead, prepares a series of adventures for them.'[121]

XVI. The hero and the villain join in direct combat. (Definition: struggle. Designation: H). This is the war between the Pandavas and the Kauravas. Propp adds the following: '1. They fight in an open field (H.1.). Fights ... with an enemy army ... etc.

XVIII. The villain is defeated. (Definition: victory. Designation: I). 1. The villain is beaten on an open field (I.1.).

XIX. The initial misfortune or lack is liquidated. (Designation: K). This function, together with villainy (A), constitutes a pair. The narrative reaches its peak in this function.

The functions XX–XXX in Propp's morphology have to do with the two different actions of a folktale, namely, the victory over the villain (HI), and the difficult task and its resolution (MN). Propp, however, makes it clear that 'it is necessary to choose a single element which is obligatory for all folktales and to make the division according to its varieties. A (villainy) or a (lack) is the only such obligatory element.... If we carefully examine those folktales which consist of two moves, we will come up with the following: if one move contains a fight and the other a difficult task, then the fight always occurs in the first move and the difficult task in the second.'[122] Since the Ur-*Mahabharata* does not have MN, but only HI, we can dispense with the functions XX–XXX.

XXXI. The hero is married and ascends the throne. (Definition: wedding. Designation. W). It should be pointed out that sub-function 3. allows that 'sometimes, to the contrary, only accession to the throne is taken into consideration (W*)'.[123] This is Yudhisthira's triumphant entry into the city of Hastinapura and the beginning of his reign, i.e. *Shanti-parvan* XII-40. To this should be added parts of *Ashavedhika-parvan*, i.e. the horse-sacrifice, in my opinion, in order to close the circle: the Ur-*Mahabharata* starts with the rajasuya and ends with the rajasuya.

Talking of the ways in which characters are introduced into the course of action Propp distinguishes two basic forms of initial situations: '1) the situation presenting the seeker together with his family ... and 2) the situation introducing the villain's victim, together with his family.... Some tales give both situations.... Certain situations of this type have been handled epically. In the beginning the seeker is not at hand. He is born, generally in some miraculous manner. The miraculous birth of the hero is a very important narrative element. It is one of the forms of the hero's appearance into the initial situation. The hero's birth is usually accompanied by a prophecy concerning his destiny.'[124]

All of this, of course, applies to the Ur-*Mahabharata* where the first book, *Adiparvan*, narrates the miraculous birth of both the heroes and the villains, of the Pandavas and of the Kauravas.

Propp also included three functions which deal with the role of the donor (XII–XIV):

XII. The hero is tested, interrogated, attacked, etc. in preparation for receiving either a magical agent or helper (Definition: the first function of the donor. Designation: D). 1. The donor tests the hero (D1). The Pandavas' donor was Krishna. At this point let me quote from Chapter X ('Krishna Vasudeva') of Iravati Karve's fine book, *Yuganta: The End of an Epoch*:

> Both sides started preparations. To secure allies they visited the neighbouring kings.... Duryodhana and Arjuna reached Krishna's house at the same time. Krishna was sleeping. Arjuna sat at the foot of the bed, Duryodhana at the head. As soon as Krishna woke, both requested for his help. Krishna agreed to help both sides. To one side he would give his famed soldiers, the Narayania. On the other side he himself would be present, but would not take up arms. Since on waking he had seen Arjuna first, he gave the choice to him. Arjuna chose Krishna, and Duryodhana, well-satisfied, went away with the army. Krishna, pleased at Arjuna's confidence and, at his request, agreed to be his charioteer. Arjuna had made the right choice. The Pandavas did not lack warriors, what they needed was a dispassionate, determined counsellor. That they found in Krishna.[125]

Under XII. 7 Propp listed 'Other requests' and proceeded to explain that 'the hero is presented, on these occasions, with the possibility of rendering assistance. Objectively, this amounts to a test, although subjectively the hero does not sense it per se (d7).' This will cover Krishna's reaction to Arjuna's unwillingness to fight his own kinsmen during the very first day of the war. This gave occasion to Krishna to offer his remonstrance, a core of the *Bhagavadgita*.

XIII. The hero reacts to the actions of the future donor. (Definition: the hero's reaction. Designation: E). 9. The hero vanquishes (or does not vanquish) his adversary (E9). This is clearly Arjuna's response to Krishna's remonstrance. According to Karve, 'Arjuna at last agreed to fight, but refused to stand against Bhisma. In exasperation Krishna leapt from his chariot, whip in hand, to kill Bhishma himself. Arjuna jumped down, embraced Krishna's feet, and begged him not to break his vow. The next day Arjuna wounded Bhishma, removing him from the battle.'[126]

XIV. A magical agent at the disposal of the hero. (Definition: the provision, receipt of a magical agent. Designation: F).

Propp explains that 'the following things are capable of serving as magical agents: 1) animals ...; 2) objects out of which helpers appear ...; 3) objects possessing a magical property ...; 4) qualities or capacities which are directly given, such as, the power of transformation into animal forms etc. All of these objects of transmission we shall conditionally term magical agents.'[127] He then explains XIV. 2 as 'the agent is made known (F2).' The agent made known in the Ur-*Mahabharata* is Krishna's form in Chapter XI of the *Bhagavadgita*. In this vision Krishna appears as Time/Fate' 'I am Fate' [*Kalo 'smi*]. As Carroll Smith explains, 'the Sanskrit *kala* also means 'death' as well as 'time', but the most significant meaning, by way of making connections with other Indo-European epics, is the translation of *kala* as 'Fate'.... In the *Bhagavadgita*, Arjuna is told by the God, Fate personified, to stand and fight since his enemies are all marked for destruction.... The decision to kill or be killed is a major part of the anguish in Arjuna's conundrum. Krishna's message to Arjuna is that he is merely an instrument of the divine plan that numbers the enemy as already dead.'[128]

Thus, the war that lasted for eighteen days is a logical outcome of Arjuna's 'conundrum' and Krishna's 'revelation'. As Propp makes clear, 'if all the tasks of the donor are registered under a heading, we see that these tasks are not accidental. From the point of view of the narrative per se they are nothing other than one of the devices of epic retardation: an obstacle placed before the hero is surmounted by a means he is given for the attainment of his goals.'[129]

At this point Propp made one of those far-reaching conclusions that have made his work a classic: 'From the historical point of view, ... the fairy tale, in its morphological bases, amounts to a myth.'[130] He explained that 'morphologically, a folktale may be termed any development out of villainy (A), or a lack (a) through intermediary functions to marriage (W*), or to other functions used in the capacity of the denouement. Terminal functions are, at times, a reward (F), a gain or the general liquidation of misfortune (K), a rescue from pursuit (Rs) etc. This type of development is termed by us as a move.'[131] He argued specifically that *'non-fairy tales may also be drawn up according to the scheme cited.'*[132] [*my emphasis*] He then went on to posit a far-reaching hypothesis: 'We are able to unfold the picture of transformations, it would be possible to satisfy ourselves that all of the folktales given can be morphologically deduced from the folktales about the kidnapping of a princess by a dragon—*from that aspect which we are inclined to consider as basic.*'[133] [*my emphasis*]

The conflict between the Pandavas and the Kauravas can thus be seen as a mythological representation of the epic cycle. Grintser has offered the following epic cycle outline:

1) a miraculous birth of the hero(s)
2) his/their enemies: chthonic beings, par excellence the Dragon
3) a breakdown of original harmony caused by:
   a) the envy or enmity of their enemies
   b) the ill-will of the goddess, e.g. in *The Iliad*
4) a temporary (near-) death of the hero or heroine by:
   a) the former's exile
   b) the latter's kidnapping or enslavement
5) a hero's quest:
   a) in the underground, infernal regions
   b) his fight with the Dragon (his enemy)
6) a hero's victory over the Dragon, symbolizing his victory over death
7) a hero's return and the restoration of original harmony.[134]

Using Joseph Campbell's diagram in his *Hero with a Thousand Faces*[135] we can apply Grintser's outline to it thus:

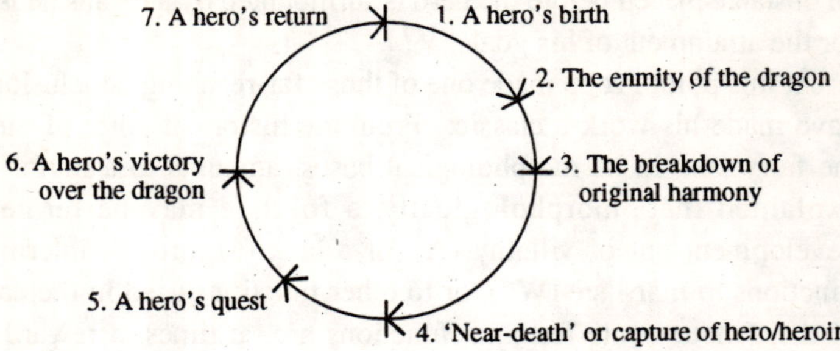

Applying the above diagram to what is indisputably the core of *The Mahabharata* (the so-called Ur-*Mahabharata*), we can summarise its outline thus:

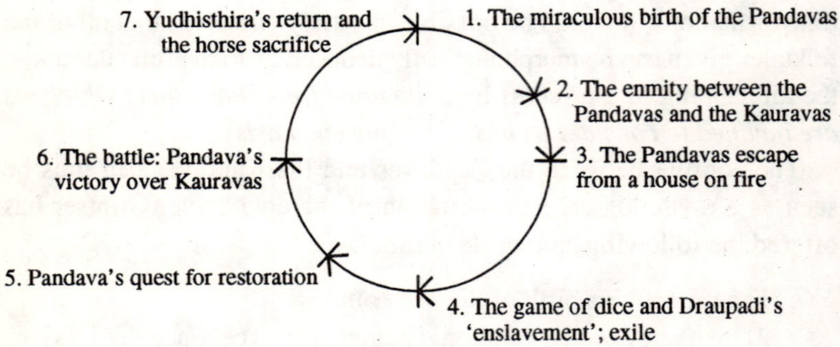

Grintser is right when he states that behind this scheme lies the calendar-based cosmological system. For this diagram can now be applied to the very act of cosmogony as well:

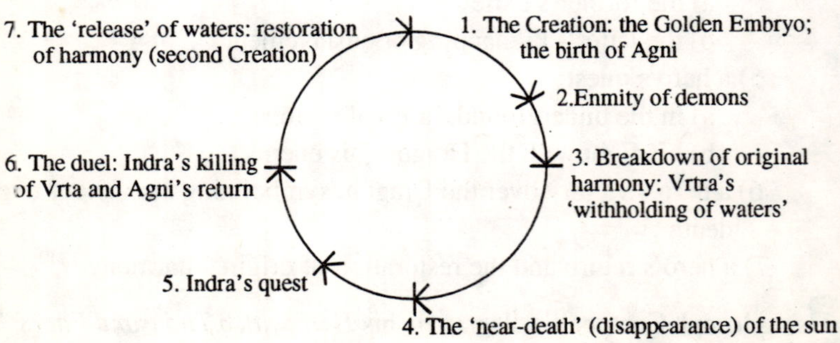

We are now in a position to offer a summary outline of the Ur-*Mahabharata*, based on Propp's morphology of the tale, and combining it with Mary Carroll Smith's and my own interpretation of the Gambling Match. In my opinion, the Ur-*Mahabharata, whether or not it was actually divided into parvans*, would entail portions of the following parvans:

I.	Adi parva
II.	Sabha parva
III.	Vana parva
IV.	Virata parva
V.	Udyoga parva
VI.	Bhisma parva
VII.	Drona parva
VIII.	Karna parva
IX.	Shalya parva
X.	Sauptika parva
XI.	Stri parva
XII.	Shanti parva (up to 40.)
+ XIV.	Ashvamedhika

With the exception of the last book, *Ashvamedhika*, this is also the view of S. B. Roy who divided the present *Mahabharata* into *Purva-Bharata* and *Uttara-Bharata*, and who claims that most if not all of the Books XII (after 40) through XVIII are later additions. So is the *Prolegomena* consisting of the first seven *sub-parvan of Adi-parva.* In Table I Roy offered an analysis of the sub-parvana of the critical edition (i.e. the Poona edition) of the present *Mahabharata.* He divided all verses into three categories: A = indisputably belonging to the Ur-*Mahabharata*; B = doubtful; C = definitely not belonging to the Ur-*Mahabharata.* He came up with the following results:[136]

Purva Bharata (I.7-XII.40)

A = 27,572 B = 5,676 C = 15,674 Total = 48,922

of which *Vana parva* alone

A = 1,079 B = 327 C = 8,941 Total = 10,347

Uttara Bharata (XII.40-XVIII.95)

A = 553 B = 1,044 C = 20,974 Total = 22, 571

of which *Ashwamedhika* alone

A = 0 B = 308 (?) C = 2,467 Total = 2,775

The Grand Total is thus:

Prolegomena			
A = 0	B = 0	C = 2,292 + X	2, 292
Purva-Bharata			
A = 27,572	B = 5,676	C = 15,674 + X	48,922
Uttara-Bharata			
A = 553	B = 1,044	C = 20,974 + X	22,571
Mahabharata			
A = 28,125	B = 6,720	C = 38,940 + X	73,785

It seems to me that the Ur-*Mahabharata* (=A) *must* include the horse-sacrifice, for 'Asvamedha sacrifice was related to Sun-worship in this period.... The presiding deity of the Asvamedha sacrifice was the Sun-god, and the sacrifice was just a way of worshipping the Sun-god for various objects, *such as victory over his enemies....*'[137] In order to complete the circle started with the *rajasuya,* this ceremony of final victory must be a part of the original epic cycle. Thus 308 verses marked (?) by Roy must be included. However, verses marked (?) by Roy under A in Book VII (*Drona Parva*), numbering 3,557, and 257 as *Aishika* sub-parvan in *Sauptika parva,* should perhaps be dropped. This would bring the total to 24,619. This number is pretty close to 24,000 couplets as stated in I.1.61. If we subtract another 616 verses from the *Bhagavadgita,* which are all later additions,[138] we come as close as possible, in a preliminary study, to 24,000 verses: actually to 24,003. Accordingly, we can conclude: 1) that Mary Carroll Smith has come as close as possible to the so-called *Jaya,* i.e. the 'core' of the Ur-*Mahabharata,* whose author was supposedly Vyasa; 2) that the actual Ur-*Mahabharata,* consisted of about 24,000 verses, as stated in I.1.61 and I.56.32 ; this text, also known as the Viasampayana recension, 'will be called the Bharata samhita or the Ur-Mahabharata' (S. B. Roy, 149–150); and 3) that the Ur-*Mahabharata* must have consisted of 12 books, *the same number as the months of the lunar year, with the additional 13th book of the Horse-Sacrifice* [*Ashvamedhika-parva*] *sybmolizing the return to the 'normalcy' established by the first rajasuya in Book Two, just as the Vedic year was divided into twelve months plus an additional thirteenth period.* The whole scheme then looks like this:

period. The whole scheme then looks like this:

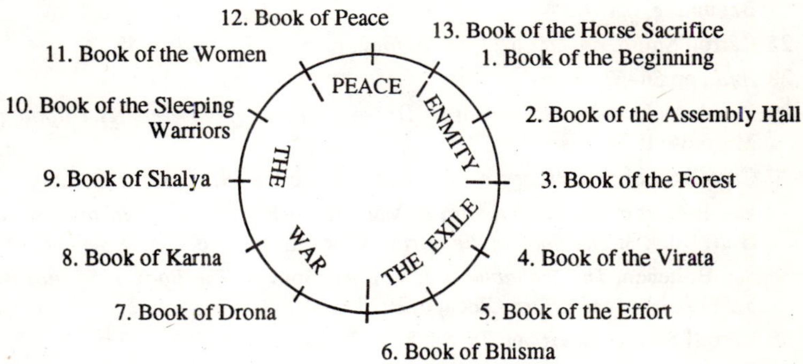

Notes

1 I.56.34, in J. A. B. van Buitenen, trans. and ed., *The Mahabharata*, Vol. I: *The Book of the Beginning*, The University of Chicago Press, 1973, p.130. All references, unless noted otherwise, are to this translation.

2 E. Washburn Hopkins, *The Great Epic of India: Its Character and Origin*, New York, 1901, and other of his works: *The Social and Military Position of the Ruling Caste in Ancient India*, New York, 1889; *Epic Mythology*, Strassburg, 1915; 'The Bharata and the Great Bharata', in *American Journal of Philology* 19 (1898): 1–24.

3 E. Washburn Hopkins, *The Great Epic of India*, 381.

4 *Loc. cit* 5 *Ibid.*, p.382 6 *Ibid.*, p.384. 7 *Ibid.*, p.385. 8 *Idem.*

9 E. Washburn Hopkins, *The Great Epic of India*, p.363.

10 Mary Carroll Smith, *The Warrior Code of India's Sacred Song*, New York and London, 1992, p.14. 11 *Ibid.*, p.14.

12 S. B. Roy, *Date of Mahabharata Battle*, Gurgaon, 1976, pp.43–44. For a further discussion on Iitihasa see S. N. Mukherjee, '*Mahabharata*: An Ideal *Itihasa* (History) of Ancient India', in L. S. Davidson, S. N. Mukherjee, and Z. Zlatar, eds, *The Epic in History*, Sydney Association for Studies in Society and Culture, Vol.II, Sydney, 1995, pp.10–11.

13 *Ibid.*, p.152. 14 *Ibid.*, p.158.

15 R. C. Majumdar, 'Myth and Reality', p.176 quoted by Roy, *op. cit.*, p.162.

16 Roy, *op. cit.*, pp.162–163.

17 John D. Smith, 'Old Indian: The Two Sanskrit Epics', in A. T. Hatto, ed., *Traditions of Heroic and Epic Poetry*, Vol. I: *The Traditions*, London, 1980, p.51.

18 Carroll Smith, *The Warrior Code of India's Sacred Song.*

19 Carrol Smith, *op. cit.*, p.15. 20 *Ibid.*, p.17. 21 *Ibid.*, p.7.

22 Carrol Smith, *op. cit.*, pp.116–117. 23 *Ibid.*, p.24.

24 J. A. B. van Buitenen, *The Mahabharata*, Vol. I, Book I: *The Book of the Beginning*, p.437.

25 Carroll Smith, *op. cit.*, p.27 26 *Ibid.*, p.55. 27 *Ibid.*, p.55.

28 *Ibid.*, pp.56–57.

29 Pavel Aleksandrovich Grintser, *Drevneindiiskii epos: Genezis i tipologiia*, Moscow, 1974.

30 Carroll Smith, *op. cit.*, pp.9–10. 31 *Ibid.*, p.58–59. 32 *bid.*, p.60.

33 van Buitenen, *The Mahabharata*, Vol. II, Book 2:*The Book of the Assembly Hall*; Book 3: *The Book of the Forest*, Chicago, 1975, p.177.

34 van Buitenen, *The Mahabharata*, Vol. III, Book 4: *The Book of Virata*; Book 5:*The book of the Effort*, Chicago, 1978, p.4.

35 Carroll Smith, *op. cit.*, pp.78, 88, 8. 36 *Ibid.*, pp.8, 101.

37 van Buitenen, *The Mahabharata*, Book III, Book 4: *The Book of Virata*; Book 5: *The Book of the Effort*, p.97.

38 Carroll Smith, *op. cit.*, pp.112–13.

39 *Ibid.*, pp.108–09, summarizing Alf Hiltebeitel, *The Ritual of Battle: Krishna in the Mahabharata*, Ithaca and London, 1976.

40 Rudolf Otto, *The Original Gita*, London, 1939, p.14.

41 Mircea Eliade, *Rites and Symbols of Initiation*, New York, 1958, p.86.

42 Carroll Smith, *op. cit.*, p.92. 43 *Ibid.*, p.94. 44 *Ibid.*, p.95.

45 *Ibid.*, p.109.

46 John D. Smith, *op. cit.*, p.110.

47 This is based on Georges Dumézil, *The Destiny of the Warrior*, Chicago, 1968, p.5. It is applied to *The Mahabharata* in his *Mythe et Épopée*, Vol. I: *L'ideologié des trois fonctions dans les épopées des peuples indo-européens* (Paris, 1968), Part I: 'La Terre Soulagée', pp.31–257.

48 *Ibid.*, p.49. 49 *Ibid.*, p.50 50 *Ibid.*, p.73.

51 van Buitenen, *The Mahabharata*, Vol. II, Book 2: *The Book of the Assembly Hall*; Book 3: *The Book of the Forest*, Chicago, 1975, p.3; on this book, see J. A. B. van Buitenen, 'On the Structure of Sabhaparvan of the Mahabharata' in J. Ensink and P. Gaeffke, eds, *India Maior: Congratulatory Volume Presented to J. Gonda*, Leiden, 1972, pp.68–84.

52 A. L. Basham, *The Wonder that was India: A Survey of the History and Culture of the Indian Sub-continent before the Coming of the Muslims*, London, 1954; 1963; 1967; 3rd rev. ed. in paperback, 1985, p.207.

53 van Buitenen, *Mahabharata*, Vol. II, p.18.

54 Georges Dumézil, *The Destiny of a King,* trans. Alf Hiltebeitel, Chicago, 1973, pp.9–10; this is the translation of *Mythe et épopée:* Vol. II: *Types épiques indo-européens: un héros, un sorcier, un roi*, Paris, 1972. 55 *Ibid.*, p.11.

56 E. W. Hopkins, *The Great Epic of India: Its Character and Origin*, Calcutta, 1961 (originally published in 1901), p.187.

57 E. W. Hopkins, *The Social and Military Position of the Ruling Caste in Ancient*

India, as Represented by the Sanskrit Epic, Varanasi, 1972 (originally published in 1889), pp.17–18. 58 *Ibid.*, p.18 n.*. 59 *Ibid.*, p.18 n.*.

60 *Ibid.*, pp.18–19. 61 *Ibid.*, p.19. 62 *Ibid.*, p.66.

63 *Ibid.*, p.66. 64 *Ibid.*, p.66. 65 *Ibid.*, p.67. 66 *Ibid.*, p.67, n.*.

67 van Buitenen, 'On the Structure of Sabhaparvan of the Mahabharata', pp.68–84. 68 *Ibid.*, p.71. 69 *Ibid.*, p.80. 70 *Ibid.*, p.80. 71 *Ibid.*, pp.80–81.

72 Jeanine Miller, *The Vedas: Harmony, Meditation and Fulfilment*, London, 1974, p.52: 'The chariot plays a considerable part in Vedic, as in all ancient, lore and various meanings may be attributed to it in different contexts. More often than not it is no physical vehicle at all.... This vehicle could be a way of describing that which helps to find, perform or frame the *brahman* for in the same order of thought we find the *rsis* themselves "fashion, even as chariots, those prayers (*brahmani*) that yield fuflfilment" (*vardhana*)(V.73.10: *ima brahmani vardhana ... ya taksama rathan iva*).... Similarly praise is magnified by means of thought as though a chariot (I.94.1: *Imam stoman ... ratham iva sam mahema manisaya* "this praise even like a chariot shall we magnify with our wise insight").'

73 Georges Dumézil, *Mythe et Épopée*, Vol. I, *Idéologie des trois fonctions dans les épopées des peuples indo-européens*, Paris, 1968: 'Dans le tableau des naissances, un seul parait: *ksatra* (I *123* 44769), avec son dérivé *ksatriya* (I *123* 4790), mais, bien que les cinq garçons soient uniformément des *ksatriya*, le mot n'est écrit qu'à propos du second et du troisième, de Phima et d'Arjuna, dont le valeur fonctionelle est en effet celle de guerriers ... le titre brahmana est hautement iterativement revendiqué par Yudhisthira (IV *123* 7226, etc.), tandis que l'un au moins des jumeaux, Sahadeva, le prétendu bouvier, se proclame *vaisya*' (IV *10 284*, 286), and the table on p.72.

74 *Ibid.*, pp.79–80: 'Les épithètes caractérisant le ballatre et le guerrier s'appliquent en partie exclusivement à Nakula (*darsaniya, atiratha, sarvayuddhavisarada*, etc.), en partie à Nakula et aux jumeaux (*yuddhadurmada, rabhasah yuddhe*), en partie aux jumeaux (*rupasampannau, yasasvinau*, etc.), mais jamais à Sahadeva seul.... Au contraire, les épithètes qui caractérisent Sahadeva à l'exclusion de Nakula semeuvent dans un domaine sémantique précis auquel Nakula n'a pas de part...les nombreaux adjectifs qui expreiment la sagesse, l'intelligence, la bonté et la pudeur de Sahadeva ne s'appliquent jamis, non plus que leurs synonymes, à Nakula.... Cette distinction de nature—qui, à la réflexion, s'accorde aisément à celle du palefrenier et du bouvier, les chevaux intéressant surtout la fonction guerrière, le ksantriya, et le bovins, par leurs produits laitiers essentiels au culte, intéressant plutot la fonction sacrée, le brahmane—explique dans la trame épique plusieurs comportements différents de Nakula et de Sahadeva, et aussi l'affinitié particulière que manifeste le premier pour ses frères guerriers, notamment pour Bhima, le second pour son frère le 'roi juste', Yudhisthira.'

75 G. Dumézil, *The Destiny of the Warrior*, p.5.

76 See the photo in Figure 13.4, 'The Game of Dice', in David Williams, ed., *Peter Brook and The Mahabharata*, London and New York, 1991, p.135, with the explanation: 'at the gaming table—similar in design to the traditional Indian

pachisi board'. Also see two color photos entitled 'The Game of Dice' (facing p.33) and 'Yudhishthira losing the game' in the Section 'The Game of Dice', in Garry O'Connor, *The Mahabharata: Peter Brook's Epic in the Making*, San Francisco, 1989. Photos are by Gilles Abegg.

77 J. C. Heesterman, *The Ancient Indian Royal Consecration* (Thesis, Utrecht), The Hague, 1955, Ch. XVII quoted and cited by van Buitenen, 'On the Structure of the Sabhaparvan of *The Mahabharata*', p.71 and fn.1. 78 *Ibid.*, fn.1.

79 H. T. Colebrooke, 'On the Vedas, or Sacred Writings of the Hindus', in his *Essays on History, Literature, and Religions of Ancient India: Miscellaneous Essays*, New Delhi, 1977, p.42, describing the 38th chapter (or third of the 8th book) of the *Rig Veda.*

80 O'Flaherty, ed., *The Rig Veda*, 31 [No. 10.90].

81 J. E. Cirlot, *A Dictionary of Symbols*, London, 1962, 2nd ed., 1971, p.5.

82 Basham, *The Wonder that was India*, p.207. 83 *Ibid.*, p.321.

84 Cirlot, *op.cit.*, p.5. 85 *Ibid.*, pp.40–41.

86 *Ibid.*, p.40, citing Marius Schneider, *La danza de espadas y la tarantela*, Barcelona, 1948.

87 V. N. Toporov, 'Parallels to Ancient Indo-Iranian Social and Mythological Concepts', in J. C. Heesterman, G. H. Schokker, V. I. Subramoniam, eds, *Pratidanam: Indian, Iranian and Indo-European Studdies Presented to Francisc us Bernardus Jacobus Kuiper on His Sixtieth Birthday*, The Hague-Paris, 1968, pp.113–114.

88 *Ibid.*, p.118.

89 *Rig Veda* 10.121, 1, in O'Flaherty, *op. cit.*, p.27.

90 Jeanine Miller, *The Vedas: Harmony, Meditation and Fulfilment* , London, 1974, pp.xxxi–xxxii. 91 *Ibid.*, p.xxxii. 92 *Ibid.*, p.30.

93 *Ibid.*, p.177. 94 *Ibid.*, p.200. 95 *Ibid.*, p.179. 96 *Ibid.*, p.189.

97 *Rig Veda* 1.185, 2, in O'Flaherty, *op. cit.*, pp.204, 205, n.4: 'The embryo or seed (*garbha*), is the sun or Agni, here symbolic of all creatures (hence teeming).'

98 MacDonnell, *op. cit.*, p.95.

99 O'Flaherty, *The Rig Veda*, 'Purusa-Sukta, or The Hymn of Man', p.38.

100 *Ibid.*, 'The Unknown God, the Golden Embryo', p.28 and n.7.

101 van Buitenen, *The Mahabharata*, Vol. I: *The Book of the Beginning*, p.416.

102 Mircea Eliade, *The Myth of the Eternal Return* (1954, 1989), pp.79–80, quoting *Satapatha Brahmana*, trans. Julius Eggeling in *The Sacred Books of the East*, Vol. XLIII, Oxford, 1897, pp.386, 29–30, and XLI, Oxford, 1894, pp.293, 152; and Paul Mus, *Barabudur* I, Hanoi, 1935, p.384ff; on 'construction time', *ibid.*, II, pp.733–89. Eliade's work was first published in French as *Le Mythe de l'éternel retour: arcétypes et répétition*, Paris, 1949.

103 *Ibid.*, pp.10–11 citing and quoting Ananda K. Coomaraswamy, *The Rg Veda as Land-nama-bok*, London, 1935, p.16ff.

104 O'Flaherty, *op. cit.*, p.77. 105 *Ibid.*, pp.75–76. 106 *Ibid.*, p.80.

A. B. Keith, *Religion and Philosophy of the Veda and the Upanisadas*, 2 vols., Oxford, 1925, I, p.67. 108 *Ibid.*, pp.33-35. 109 *Ibid.*, p.35, fn.3.

110 *Ibid.*, p.72, fn.1: 'Allan and Cunningham take wheel as "Dharmacakra". But this symbol was never the monopoly of one sect. And, it is more than certain that originally, the wheel represented only Sun.'

111 *Ibid.*, p.52 citing Washburn E. Hopkins, *The Great Epic of India*, New York, 1901, pp.191–362.

112 Hopkins, *op. cit.*, p.363.

113 John D. Smith, *op. cit.*, 52 quoting Carroll Smith, 'The Core of India's Great Epic', Unpublished Ph.D. Thesis, Harvard, 1972, p.2. 114 *Ibid.*, p.65.

115 V. Propp, *Morphology of the Folktale*, ed. with an introduction by Svatava Prikova-Jakobson, trans. by Laurence Scott [Bloomington, 1958].

116 Stith Thompson, *Motif-Index of Folk Literature: A Classification of Narrative Elements in Folktales, Ballads, Myths, Fables, Mediaeval Romances, Exempla, Fabliaux, Jest-Books and Local Legends,* 6 vols., Helsinki, 1932–1936; based on A. Aarne, *Verzeichnis der Märchentypes* in *Folklore Fellows Communications* #3, Helsinki, 1911.

117 V. Propp, *op. cit.*, p.20. 118 *Ibid.*, p.58. 119 *Ibid.*, p.26.

120 *Ibid.*, p.28. 121 *Ibid.*, p.36. 122 *Ibid.*, pp.92–93.

123 *Ibid.*, p.57. 124 *Ibid.*, p.77.

125 Iravati Karve, *Yuganta: The End of an Epoch*, Poona, 1967, p.202.

126 *Ibid.*, p.203.

127 Propp, *op. cit.*, p.40.

128 Carroll Smith, *op. cit.*, pp.112–13.

129 Propp, *op. cit.*, p.81. 130 *Ibid.*, p.82. 131 *Ibid.*, p.83.

132 *Ibid.*, p.90. 133 *Ibid.*, p.103.

134 Grintser, *op. cit.*, pp.287–88.

135 Joseph Campbell, *Hero With a Thousand Faces*, Princeton, 1968.

136 Roy, *op. cit.*, pp.153–58.

137 L. Prasad Pandey, *Sun-Worship in Ancient India*, p.36.

138 Phulgenda Sinha, *The Gita as It was: Rediscovering the Original Bhagavadgita*, La Salle, Illinois, 1987, esp. pp.130–9. Rudolf Otto, *The Original Gita*, London, 1939, put the number of original verses at 128. G. S. Khair, *Quest for the Original Gita*, Bombay, 1969, put the number at 121, spread through the first six chapters. N. G. Sardesai, 'The Bhagavadgita from the Island of Bali', *Modern Review* (Calcutta, July 1914): 32–8, has only 86; Shanti Prakash, *The Adi Bhagavad Gita* [*The Original Bhagavad Gita*], Fyzabad, 1936, has 84 verses.

Publications by S. N. Mukherjee

Books

Sir William Jones: A Study in Eighteenth-Century British Attitudes to India, Cambridge University Press, 1968.

Calcutta: Myths and History, Subarnarekha, Calcutta, 1977.

Sir William Jones: A Study in Eighteenth-Century British Attitudes to India, 2nd ed., Orient Longman, Bombay, 1987.

Calcutta: A City of Splendid Palaces and Dingy Streets, 1986 Basham Lecture, Australian National University Press, 1987.

Calcutta: Essays in Urban History, Subarnarekha, Calcutta, 1993.

The Citizen Historian: an Exploration in Historiography, Sydney Association for Studies in Society and Culture, Manohar, Delhi, 1995.

Edited Books

The Movement for National Freedom in India, St Antony's Papers No. 18; Clarendon Press, Oxford, 1966.

With Sir Edmund Leach, *Elites in South Asia,* Cambridge University Press, 1970.

Selected Works of Jawaharlal Nehru, Vols 1–3, Orient Longman, New Delhi, 1972–74. (S. N. Mukherjee edited these volumes but on his resignation from the project the editorship was taken over by Dr. S. Gopal and S. N. M.'s name does not appear in the publication.)

With Professor Michael Allen, *Women in India and Nepal,* Australian National University Press, 1982.

India, History and Thought: Essays in Honour of A. L. Basham, Subarnarekha, Calcutta, 1982.

With Professor Stephen Knight, *Words and Worlds: Studies in the Social Role of Verbal Culture,* Sydney Association for Studies in Society and Culture, Sydney, 1983.

With Professor Sir Edmund Leach and John O. Ward, *Feudalism: Comparative Studies,* Sydney Association for Studies in Society and Culture, Sydney, 1985.

Edited and translated with Marian Maddern, *Bankim Chandra Chatterjee, Sociological Essays: Utilitarianism and Positivism in Bengal,* Riddhi-India, Calcutta and Wild Peony, Sydney, 1986.

With J. O. Ward, *Revolution as History,* Sydney Association for Studies in Society and Culture, Sydney, 1989.

With Michael Allen, *Women in India and Nepal,* 2nd edn, Sterling Books India, New Delhi, 1990.

Editor of the Bengali translation of Michael Wilding, *Paraguay Experiment,* Papyrus, Calcutta, 1995.

With L. Sharon Davidson and Z. Zlatar, *Epics in History,* Sydney Association for Studies in Society and Culture, Sydney, 1995.

Books in Progress

Kalkatar Atmasamikhsha: Aitihasik Patabhumite. Edited by Professor Ashin Dasgupta, Ananda Publishers.

Calcutta, An Historical Biography, Penguin, India.

Chapters in Edited Books

Introduction to Manik Bandopadhayaya, *Padma River Boatman*, trans. Painter and Lovelock; University of Queensland Press, 1973.

'The Social Implications of the Political Thought of Raja Rammohun Roy', in R. S. Sharma, ed., *Indian Society: Historical Probings*, People's Publishing House, Delhi, 1974.

'*Bhadralok* and Their *Dals*: Politics of Social Factions in Calcutta, c. 1820–1850', in P. Sinha , ed., *Calcutta: an Urban Experience*, Riddhi-India, Calcutta, 1988.

'*Bhadraloks* of Bengal', in Dipankar Gupta , ed., *Social Stratification*, Oxford University Press, Delhi, 1991.

'Afterword', in Peter Hinton, ed., *Disasters: Image and Context*, Sydney Association for Studies in Society and Culture, Sydney, 1992.

'The Lion, His Son and the Jackal' and 'Rupamati and Baz Bahadur', in *Many Flowers*, Asia Education Foundation, Melbourne, 1994.

Articles

'The Tradition of Ramagupta and the Nationalist Historians', *East and West*, Rome, 1962.

'A Note on Sir William Jones and the Slave Trade in Bengal', *Bengal Past and Present*, Calcutta, 1963.

'Sir William Jones and the British Attitudes towards India', *Journal of the Royal Asiatic Society of Great Britain and Ireland*, London, 1964.

'Afro-Asian Studies in India', *Afro-Asian and World Affairs*, 1, Delhi, 1964.

'Introduction to the Movement for National Freedom in India', in S. N. Mukherjee, ed., *The Movement for National Freedom in India.*

'Origins of Indian Nationalism: Historiography of Modern India', *Afro-Asian and World Affairs*, 4, 1967.

'Class, Caste and Politics in Calcutta', in E. R. Leach and S. N. Mukherjee, eds, *Elites in South Asia.*

'The Idea of the Village Community and the British Administrators', *Enquiry*, III, 3, Delhi, Winter, 1971.

'Satinath Bhaduri's 'The Vigil': an Essay on the Novel and History', *Teaching History*, Sydney, October 1973.

'Rabindranath O Soviet Viplab', *Katha Sahitya*, Calcutta, December 1974.

'The Citizen Historian', *Arna*, 20, Sydney, December 1974.

'Daladali in Calcutta in the Nineteenth Century', *Modern Asian Studies*, 9, 1, Cambridge, February 1975.

'Old Calcutta: the Other Image', *Sunday*, Calcutta, May 1976.

'Kalkatar Atmasamikhsha', *Anandabazar Patrika*; special issue on Calcutta; Calcutta, November 1976.

'*Bhadralok* in Bengali Language and Literature: an Essay on the Language of Class and Status', *Bengal Past and Present*, XCV, Part II, July–December 1976.

'Raja Rammohun Roy and the Debate on the Status of Women in Bengal', in M. Allen and S. N. Mukherjee (eds), *Women in India and Nepal*.

'Gauriya Samaj: A Literary Society of the *Bhadralok* of Calcutta', in S. N. Mukherjee, ed., *India, History and Thought: Essays in Honour of A. L. Basham*.

'Women's Space and Women's Language in the Novels of Bankim Chandra Chatterjee', *Journal of the Oriental Society of Australia*, XVII, Sydney, 1985.

'The Idea of Feudalism: From the *Philosophes* to Karl Marx', in E. R. Leach, S. N. Mukherjee and John O. Ward, eds, *Feudalism: Comparative Studies*.

'Digbhranta Asiatic Society', *Ananda Bazar Patrika*, June 1987.

'Languages of Calcutta: Social Control of Verbal Culture', *Journal of the Oriental Society of Australia*, XVIII–XIX, 1986–87.

'Kathar Kathay Kalkata', *Ananda Bazar Patrika*, April 1989.

'Marxist Historians in Search of a Revolution in India', in S. N. Mukherjee and John O. Ward, eds, *Revolution as History*.

'Raja Rammohun Roy and the Debate on the Status of Women in Bengal', in Allen and Mukherjee (eds), *Women in India and Nepal*.

'Women's Space and Women's Language in the Novels of Bankim Chandra Chatterjee', in Allen and Mukherjee, eds, *Women in India and Nepal*.

'Polygamy and Genealogy in the Gupta Age: a Note on Feudalism from Above in Ancient India', *Journal of the Oriental Society of Australia*, XXII–XXIII, 1990–91.

'Daladalite Dosh Nei', *Ananda Bazar Patrika*, December 1992.

'Ramayana, Anya Deshe', *Ananda Bazar Patrika*, September 1993.

'Poetics and Politics: Sir William Jones and the Debate on Aesthetics in the Eighteenth Century, *Deccan College Bulletin*, April 1994.

'Sir William Jones and Poetics', *Bengal Past and Present*, 1993 Pratul Gupta Memorial Lecture, 1995.

Review Articles

S. Gopal, *British Policy in India*, Cambridge 1965, in *Cambridge Review*, Cambridge, 1966.

G. Cannon, *Oriental Jones*, London, 1964, in the *Bulletin of the School of Oriental and African Studies*, London, 1966.

A. Seal, *Emergence of Indian Nationalism*, Cambridge, 1968, in *Modern Asian Studies*, Cambridge, 1969.

C. H. Philips and M. D. Weinwright, eds, *Indian Society and the Beginnings of Modernisation c. 1830–1850*, London, 1976, in *Journal of Asian Studies*, U.S.A., 1978.

R. Inden and R. Nichols, *Kinship in Bengali Culture*, Chicago, 1977, in *South Asia*, Australia, 1979.

Bryan R. Wilson, *Magic and Millennium: A Sociological Study of Religious Movements by Tribal and Third-world Peoples*, London 1973, in *Journal of Religious History*, Australia, 1980.

A. Ostor, *The Play of the Gods*, Chicago, 1980, in *Oceania*, Australia, 1984.